THE KINGFISHER
ILLUSTRATED
NATURE
ENCYCLOPEDIA

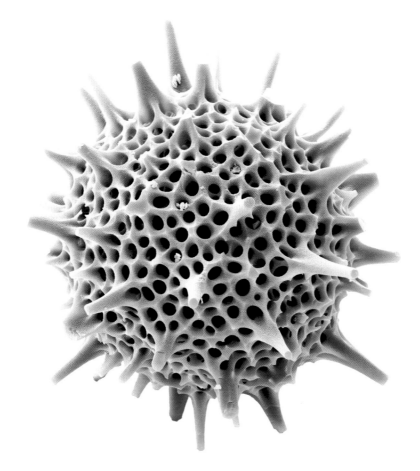

Editors: Miranda Smith, Russell Mclean, Paula Borton

Coordinating Editor: Sarah Snavely

Senior Designer: Malcolm Parchment

Designers: Peter Clayman, Carol Ann Davis, Sam Combes

Editorial Assistance: Jennifer Schofield, Carron Brown, Sheila Clewley

Picture Research Manager: Cee Weston-Baker

Senior Production Controller: Nancy Roberts

DTP Coordinator: Sarah Pfitzner

DTP Operator: Primrose Burton

Artwork Archivists: Wendy Allison, Jenny Lord

Illustrations: Julian and Janet Baker

Indexer: Sue Lightfoot

KINGFISHER
a Houghton Mifflin Company imprint
222 Berkeley Street
Boston, Massachusetts 02116
www.houghtonmifflinbooks.com

First published by Kingfisher in 2004
1 3 5 7 9 10 8 6 4 2
1TR/1103/TIM/GRS(GRS)/128MA(3.2GB)

Note to readers:
The web site addresses listed in this book are correct at the time of going to print.
However, due to the everchanging nature of the Internet, web site addresses and content can change.
Web sites can contain links that are unsuitable for children. The publisher cannot be held responsible
for changes in web site addresses or content or for information obtained through third-party
web sites. We strongly advise that Internet searches should be supervised by an adult.

LIBRARY OF CONGRESS CATALOGING-IN-PUBLICATION DATA
has been applied for.

ISBN 0-7534-5576-5

Printed in China

THE KINGFISHER
ILLUSTRATED
NATURE
ENCYCLOPEDIA

By David Burnie

KINGFISHER

BOSTON

Stages in the formation of Earth, around 4.7 billion years ago

CONTENTS

The fossilized skeleton of *Archaeopteryx*, an early type of bird

Campylodiscus diatoms—types of microplants that have a protective case built out of silica

A colony of African fruit bats
roosting in a cave

A wildcat hissing and baring its teeth
to scare off an enemy

Leaf-cutter ants carrying pieces of leaves
back to their nest in a South
American rain forest

On the lookout for prey, a puma peers over a cliff in Navajo Tribal Park in northeastern Arizona. Also known as the cougar or mountain lion, the puma hunts on its own, and deer are some of its favorite food.

INTRODUCTION

For almost four billion years life has flourished on Earth—as far as we know, the only life-supporting planet in a seemingly barren and inhospitable universe. From the simplest viruses to the largest land animals, the living things that inhabit Earth have always formed highly complex relationships between themselves, as well as with their environments. *The Kingfisher Illustrated Nature Encyclopedia* celebrates this incredible diversity, bringing to life the wonders of the living world and exploring every major plant and animal group on the planet.

The encyclopedia is divided into three parts. The first, "A Planet Apart," introduces Earth, exploring the formation of our planet and the first origins of life. Since then the unpredictable process of evolution has created a limitless variety of life-forms in every habitat—and also caused the extinction of 99 percent of the world's species along the way.

Part two, "The Living World," leads the reader through the five kingdoms of life—animals, plants, fungi, protists, and bacteria. No one knows exactly how many different types of living things exist on Earth, but scientists have identified more than 2.5 million species, a number that is increasing all the time.

The third part, "Wildlife Habitats," is a remarkable journey through the many different environments that support life on Earth. From the bitter cold of the highest mountains to the blackness and extreme pressure on the ocean floor, living things have adapted to survive in almost every habitat that our planet has to offer, however unpromising the conditions. Species profiles highlight animals and plants of special interest such as the gnarled welwitschia plant of the Namib Desert and the Arctic bumblebee— one of the northernmost insects in the world.

The Kingfisher Illustrated Nature Encyclopedia presents a fascinating picture of life on Earth, and at a time when the living world is increasingly threatened by human activity, no subject is more essential to understand.

Seen from space, Earth and the Moon look very different.
The Moon is dry and barren, but Earth is cloaked by swirls of
clouds, showing that it has an atmosphere. Sunshine glints from
the surface of the oceans, while a patchwork of green and brown
reveals some of the habitats found on land. No other planet in
the solar system looks anything like this, and none—as far as
we know—is home to living things.

PART 1
A PLANET APART

INTRODUCING EARTH

DESPITE YEARS OF SEARCHING, ASTRONOMERS HAVE
STILL NOT FOUND ANYWHERE IN THE UNIVERSE
THAT REMOTELY RESEMBLES EARTH. OUR PLANET
IS ONE OF NINE IN THE SOLAR SYSTEM, BUT AS
FAR AS WE KNOW IT IS THE ONLY ONE THAT
IS HOME TO LIVING THINGS.

△ *Earth's magnetic field protects us
from particles given off by the Sun. In the
Arctic and Antarctic these particles create
shimmering curtains of light called auroras.*

Compared to most of the outer planets, Earth is small. Jupiter is over 86,800 mi. (140,000km) across, and it could swallow Earth 1,300 times. Mercury, Venus, and Mars are much more like Earth in size, but they are either roasted by the Sun or steeped in bitter cold. Earth alone is somewhere in-between—a planet awash with water and brimming with life.

△ *Powered by warmth from the Sun,
Earth's water keeps moving. Rainwater
flows over land in rivers and also through it
in soil and porous rocks. Underground water
can take thousands of years to reach the sea.*

A WORLD OF WATER

Water is a substance that makes Earth unique. It exists in other parts of the solar system, but it is usually frozen. Most of Earth's water is liquid. It slowly circulates to spread out the Sun's heat, and it evaporates to form clouds and rain. Without water, Earth's surface would be as dusty and lifeless as the Moon's.

Around 97 percent of the world's water is in the oceans, while two percent is locked up

in glaciers and polar ice. Freshwater makes up almost all of the rest. Only a tiny amount—just 0.001 percent—consists of water vapor in the air.

THE ATMOSPHERE

On the Moon the sky looks black. Down on Earth the sky is blue. That is because Earth is surrounded by the atmosphere, which scatters light rays coming from the Sun. But the atmosphere does more than make the sky an attractive color. It protects living things from harmful radiation, and it helps keep the surface of the planet warm. It also contains gases that are essential for living things.

Nitrogen makes up almost four fifths of the atmosphere. All living things need this gas, but only microbes can collect it directly from the air. They build it into chemicals that plants and animals can use.

Oxygen is even more important, as living things use it to release energy. It makes up around one fifth of the atmosphere, and because it dissolves in water, oceans, lakes, and rivers contain plenty too. A third gas—carbon dioxide—is much rarer. It makes up only 0.033 percent of the atmosphere, but all plants and many microbes need it to grow.

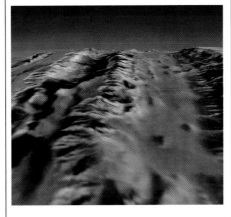

△ Some of the surface features on Mars look as if they may have been formed by flowing water. Today the surface of Mars is dry, although there are ice caps at the Martian poles.

△ Earth is the third planet from the Sun in the solar system. Our nearest neighbors are Venus and Mars. Venus has an acidic atmosphere and is very hot, while Mars has a thin atmosphere and is cold.

EARTH'S CHANGING SURFACE

The average temperature on Earth's surface is 57°F (14°C). But at Earth's core it is at least 8,132°F (4,500°C). Heat from the core flows up toward the surface, melting rock, triggering volcanic eruptions, and keeping continents on the move. Some of these changes make life dangerous for Earth's inhabitants, but they also create opportunities. Without them life on Earth would probably be much less varied today.

▽ Earth's atmosphere is over 250 mi. (400km) thick, with most water vapor in the bottom 7.5 mi. (12km) in a zone called the troposphere. Conditions here are always changing, as weather fronts shift.

HOW EARTH FORMED

COMPARED TO THE ENTIRE UNIVERSE, EARTH IS STILL YOUNG. IT FORMED AROUND 4.7 BILLION YEARS AGO WHEN A CLOUD OF GAS AND DUST SHRANK UNDER THE PULL OF GRAVITY, AND THE SOLAR SYSTEM WAS BORN.

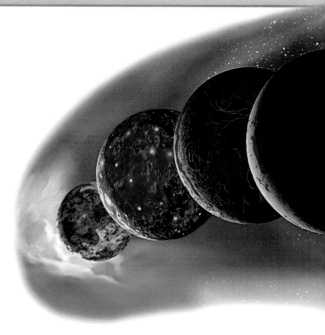

The newly formed Earth was completely different from the planet we know today. It had no atmosphere or water, and it was as lifeless as the Moon. But as Earth aged heat built up inside of it, and the planet began to change. Heavy elements, such as iron, sank down into Earth's core, while lighter ones drifted up toward the surface. As the surface cooled, minerals began to crystallize, producing Earth's first solid rocks. The heat also triggered violent volcanic eruptions—a development that paved the way for life.

△ After Earth formed its surface gradually cooled, allowing solid rock to develop. Earth's inner core stays hot from pressure and natural radioactivity. It will take hundreds of millions of years for this internal heat to fade away.

△ Unlike the Moon, Earth is studded with volcanoes. Around 600,000 years ago an eruption in North America produced 240 cu. mi. (1,000km³) of lava and ash. Bigger eruptions occurred in the distant past.

AIR AND WATER

Earth's rocky crust formed around 4.5 billion years ago. Volcanoes were much more active than they are now, and they produced vast beds of lava that poured out over the surface of the planet. At the same time volcanic eruptions released immense clouds of gas and water vapor. Light gases, such as hydrogen, drifted into space, but heavier ones were held in place by Earth's gravity. These formed a primitive atmosphere with a lot of nitrogen, carbon dioxide, and water vapor but not much oxygen.

By around four billion years ago the world had cooled enough to allow some water vapor to condense. At first the vapor formed tiny droplets, coating the world in clouds. But once the vapor had built up to a critical level, the first rains began to fall. Some downpours may have lasted for thousands of years, and so much water fell that seas and then oceans began to appear. These oceans were the birthplace of living things.

UNDER BOMBARDMENT

Young Earth was frequently hit by debris from space. Most of this material consisted of dust, but from time to time devastating

meteorites slammed into the surface. Shortly after the crust formed, another planet may even have crashed into Earth, increasing its weight by half and almost smashing it apart.

Some scientists believe that the Moon was produced in the aftermath of this impact. According to this theory, a huge amount of rock was flung into space and then recaptured by Earth's gravity. Another possibility is that the Moon was captured intact after approaching Earth from another part of space.

THE ROCK CYCLE

On the Moon, meteorite impacts leave permanent craters because there is nothing to wear them away.

Earth's surface, however, is constantly reshaped by wind, rain, and ice. Volcanic activity creates even bigger changes, as it builds up mountains and keeps continents moving.

These changes have been happening ever since the oceans and atmosphere first appeared. They break down rocks into tiny particles, which are then washed down rivers into the sea. Here the particles form sediment that builds up on the seabed. After thousands of years the sediment turns into solid rock. If this is forced up it can turn into dry land, and the rock cycle begins again.

In many parts of the world Earth's crust is like a giant sandwich made up of layers of sedimentary rock dating back millions of years. The layers act like a record of Earth's past, showing what conditions were like when the rock formed. The fossils trapped inside of them also show what was alive at the time.

THE OXYGEN REVOLUTION

No trace is left of Earth's first rocks because they were destroyed long ago. The oldest rocks ever found date back around 3.9 billion years.

Even though these rocks do not contain fossils, scientists still believe that it is likely that life was already underway when they were made. These primitive life-forms lived in a world where oxygen was very rare. But over the next two billion years the atmosphere's oxygen level began to rise until it reached around 21 percent—the level it stands at today. Amazingly this change was brought about entirely by living things.

The creatures responsible for this transformation were microscopic bacteria. Using light, water, and carbon dioxide, they developed a way of living called photosynthesis (see pages 84–85). The bacteria took carbon dioxide from the air and released oxygen as a by-product. Each bacterium released only a tiny amount, but over trillions of generations oxygen poured into the air. Without these early bacteria the atmosphere would be unbreathable, and animal life would not exist.

▽ *In the Grand Canyon river water has sliced its way down through 1 mi. (1.6km) of rock—the greatest depth visible in one place anywhere on Earth. The oldest rocks, at the bottom of the canyon, date back two billion years.*

How LIFE BEGAN

Nobody knows how life started on Earth or where this amazing event took place. But every year scientists come a little closer to finding out. Two things seem certain— life appeared a long time ago, and the first living things were much simpler than anything alive today.

Some people believe that living things were especially created and that life on Earth dates back only a few thousand years. But almost all of the world's scientists disagree. They think that life dates back almost four billion years to a time when our planet was still very young. They believe that life began through random chemical reactions that eventually built up living things. This process may not have happened only on Earth—in other parts of the universe, other planets may have living things too.

△ *Every year Earth is hit by hundreds of meteorites. In 1996 a team of NASA scientists investigated meteorite ALH84001, which is known to have come from Mars. They announced that they had discovered bacteria in the meteorite, but since then other scientists have questioned their find.*

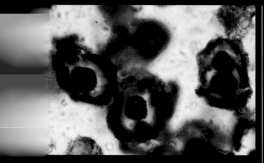

△ *These microscopic fossils from Canada are around two billion years old. They show the outlines of cell membranes—one of the key features of all known living things.*

ESSENTIAL EQUIPMENT

Living things are incredibly varied, but deep down they use the same working parts to stay alive. They all consist of cells, and each cell contains a complete set of chemical instructions, or genes. Cells are like microscopic bubbles, and they are surrounded by special membranes that protect them from the outside world. Cells can use energy from their surroundings, and they can also multiply and grow. Genes are even more important. They contain all the information needed to build cells and to make them work. They are able to copy themselves, and they are handed down when cells reproduce.

To understand how life began, scientists have tried to guess how cells and genes first developed. Both are very complicated, which makes it highly unlikely that they could have appeared, premade, by chance. They might have developed step by step, however, from much simpler beginnings. Over a long time random chemical reactions could have built up the equipment needed for life.

MYSTERIOUS WORLDS

Over 50 years ago an American chemist named Stanley Miller carried out an experiment to imitate conditions on young Earth. Through entirely random reactions, the test produced some of the carbon-based chemicals found in living things. Miller's results were sensational, but since then scientists have made even more remarkable discoveries.

Carbon-based chemicals have been detected in meteorites, comets, and even in "empty" space. These chemicals are much simpler than any gene, and they are not living. But they are the chemical nuts and bolts from which living things are made.

Recently some researchers have suggested that chemicals from space helped kick start life on Earth. A few have even proposed that living microbes could have arrived in this way. But most scientists favor the idea that life on Earth is "homegrown"— that it developed gradually in sheltered surroundings, as carbon-

▽ *A scientist adjusts equipment during a reproduction of Stanley Miller's famous experiment on the origin of life. The original test lasted many days.*

containing chemicals became more varied and complex.

On young Earth the continents were rocked by volcanic eruptions, so any complex chemicals on land would have quickly been destroyed. But the seas were much less hostile. Seawater is good at dissolving chemicals and allowing them to react. Over millions of years rain would have washed chemicals into the sea, and many carbon-based substances could have built up. The result was a promising brew that is often known as the "primeval soup."

THE CHEMICAL WORKSHOP

The open sea is good at mixing up chemicals, but it is not an ideal place for complex molecules to survive. Many scientists think that the

△ *Volcanic gases bubble up from a hydrothermal vent on the ocean floor. Vents like these may have been some of the places where the first living things appeared.*

chances would have been better on the seabed or in cavities inside of rocks. Rock crystals may have acted as chemical work surfaces, allowing big molecules to form. At the same time dissolved minerals could have supplied the energy needed to link their atoms together.

Hydrothermal vents are rich in these minerals, which is why some biologists believe they could have been the nursery of life.

Before life actually began, during a long "prelife era," random chemical

△ *Living stromatolites line the shore of Australia's Shark Bay. Fossil stromatolites are among the oldest signs of life on Earth.*

reactions produced many types of carbon-containing molecules. Some of these molecules may have acted as catalysts, speeding up reactions thousands or millions of times. But at some point a momentous event took place—a molecule appeared that could copy itself and that could survive long enough to breed. From this moment on life was under way.

SHARING THE PAST

So far all of this is guesswork, and none of it can be proven. But once life did appear, evidence shows that it soon spread throughout the seas. Fossilized bacterial mounds, called stromatolites, have been identified that date back 3.4 billion years. Although their heyday is long gone, living stromatolites still exist today.

During life's long history millions of different species have evolved. But all of them have the same type of cell membranes, and their genes work by using exactly the same chemical code. This makes it almost certain that today's living things share a single far-off ancestor, which began life in the sea long ago.

THE BIOSPHERE 1

OVER THE PAST 3.7 BILLION YEARS LIVING THINGS
HAVE MANAGED TO SPREAD ALL OVER EARTH.
THEIR HOME IS THE BIOSPHERE—A LAYER OF
LIFE THAT ENCIRCLES THE ENTIRE PLANET.

Earth measures over 7,440 mi. (12,000km) across, but the biosphere is never more than around 16 mi. (25km) from top to bottom. If Earth were the size of a basketball, the biosphere would be no thicker than a sheet of paper. But packed into this layer is every single thing that lives on our planet—from the tallest trees and heaviest animals down to the smallest microbes. Some parts of the biosphere are teeming with life, as living conditions there are almost ideal. Others have much fewer inhabitants, as extreme heat or cold makes it difficult to survive.

LIFE HIGH UP

If a space probe parachuted to Earth searching for living things, the first concrete signs of life would appear around 12 mi. (20km) up in the air. Nothing actually spends its entire life this high up, but microbes, spores, and pollen grains can all be carried here by the wind. Once they have reached these great heights, it can take them days or even weeks to drift back down to the ground.

At an altitude of around 0.6 mi. (1km) flying animals start to appear. This part of the biosphere is home to insects and birds, which use the air as a highway. Birds are the most powerful fliers, but insects outnumber them many times. A single swarm of locusts can contain more than 70,000 tons of insects fluttering on billions of filmy wings.

LIFE ON LAND

If the probe touched down on land, it would almost certainly find life right away. In fact some parts of the biosphere are so full of life that it might not reach the ground at all. Near the equator trees thrive in the bright sunshine, heavy rain, and year-round warmth. The result is dense tropical forests and one of the richest habitats on Earth.

Farther away from the equator the biosphere becomes less crowded, and habitats start to change. Earth's weather patterns mean that tropical forests gives way to scrublands, and scrublands give way to deserts. Here life is thinly spread out, especially in places with less than 2 in. (5cm) of rain each year. Farther north and south in the world's temperate regions the climate is much more moist. This part of the

biosphere is full of plants and animals, although there are fewer species than in warmer areas.

In polar regions and mountains strong winds and intense cold make life difficult. Drought can also add to the problem. In Antarctica's "dry valleys," for example, no rain or snow has fallen for over one million years. These desolate places are the most lifeless parts of the biosphere and Earth's closest equivalent to the surface of Mars.

UNDERGROUND EARTH

The biosphere does not stop at the ground—instead it continues under the surface. Fertile soil teems with animals, fungi, and microbes that recycle dead remains. Living things also flourish in caves, while some bacteria survive in water-filled cracks in rocks deep underground. Experimental drills have found these bacteria at depths of 1.2 mi. (2km), and some experts believe that life underground could stretch even deeper.

2

1

▽ *This view of Earth's surface shows a slice through the biosphere, along with living things from a variety of habitats on land. To find out about habitats in water, turn to the next page.*

1 *Earthworms live in soil, where they help recycle the dead remains of plants. Soil is an important part of the biosphere on land, as most plants need soil to grow.*

2 *In deserts some plants come to life only after it has rained. Others survive droughts by storing up water in their stems or roots.*

3 *In mountains the yellow-billed chough lives at altitudes of up to 19,680 ft. (6,000m). Birds are good at surviving high up because their plumage keeps them warm.*

4 *Pollen grains are produced by flowers. They are small and light, and some are specially shaped so that they drift for long distances through the air.*

5 *Temperate forests grow in parts of the world where it never gets very hot or very*

cold. *Most of the trees lose their leaves in the fall and grow a new set in the spring.*

6 *Grasslands are home to the largest herds of mammals that live on land. The biggest grasslands are in warm parts of the world.*

7 *In the soil amoebas eat other microbes, as well as the remains of larger living things.*

3

4

5

6

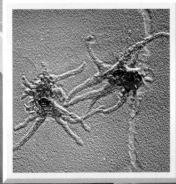

THE BIOSPHERE 2

IF YOU PICK A RANDOM POINT ANYWHERE ON EARTH'S SURFACE, IT IS TWICE AS LIKELY TO BE AT SEA THAN ON LAND. OCEANS MAKE UP AN ENORMOUS PART OF THE BIOSPHERE, AND LIVING THINGS ARE FOUND THROUGHOUT THEM—FROM THE SURFACE TO MORE THAN 6 MI. (10KM) DOWN.

Earth has five oceans and many smaller seas. Unlike land habitats they are all connected, and the water they share is constantly on the move. Near the surface, currents can flow as fast as rivers, while in the oceans' depths they usually inch along at a slow crawl. Because the oceans are linked, water life has been able to spread to every corner of the world. Regardless the oceans are divided into different habitats in the same way as the land.

SHELVES AND REEFS
Altogether the world's coasts are at least 310,000 mi. (500,000km) long. On some the seabed drops away very steeply, so the water quickly becomes thousands of feet deep. On others the seabed slopes much more gently— for example halfway between New Guinea and Australia the seabed is as little as 230 ft. (70m) deep. These shallow areas are formed by continental shelves—vast underwater ledges reaching out from the land.

Continental shelves cover only a small part of the oceans, but they are important habitats. Bottom-dwelling fish feed on animals that live on the seabed, making continental shelves some of the most fertile fishing grounds in the world. Tropical coral reefs have even more inhabitants. They are among the busiest parts of the entire biosphere.

LAYERS IN THE SEA
Although ocean water moves around, it has built-in boundaries such as the division between the sunlit surface water and the perpetual blackness below. Another boundary is called the thermocline—a zone where the water temperature rapidly drops as you go deeper down. These two boundaries are not far from the surface, and they often coincide. Together they split the oceans into two different layers.

The top layer contains only two percent of the world's saltwater, but it is home to all of the water life that needs daylight to survive. In this vital part of the biosphere microscopic algae collect light and use it to grow.

Deeper down the cavernous dark layer contains everything that can exist without light. Here animals live in a world of intense pressure and constant cold. The only warm places are hydrothermal vents, where volcanically heated water gushes up through the ocean floor.

DESCENT TO THE DEPTHS
The middle depths of the oceans are some of the emptiest parts of the biosphere. But even at the greatest depths there is a lot of life on the seabed. This is because the seabed collects all of the dead remains that drift down from high above. These remains form ocean sediment—a sticky substance that animals sift or burrow through, looking for food.

Seabed sediment builds up very slowly, but it can be up to 1,640 ft. (500m) thick. Even beneath the sediment, bacteria live in cracks in the ocean crust, surviving at depths of several miles. Where they fizzle out, life—and the biosphere—gradually comes to an end.

2

1

▽ *This view of the biosphere shows ocean habitats along with some of their inhabitants. The oceans are always changing because the ocean floor is created and destroyed by Earth's volcanic heat. Around 250 million years ago there was just one ocean, but it was as big as all of today's oceans put together.*

1 *Remote islands often have unique land plants and animals and distinctive wildlife in the surrounding sea.*

2 *The surface waters of the oceans teem with microscopic algae, as well as animals that feed on them. Together they* make up the plankton—a huge collection of living things that drifts with the current.

3 *Rocky coastlines are important breeding grounds for seabirds and marine mammals, especially where steep cliffs keep predators at bay.*

4 *Coral reefs grow in regions where the water is shallow, clear, and warm. They are home to a large portion of the world's fish.*

5 *Some parts of the seabed are carpeted with brittle stars. These animals catch particles of food with their slender arms.*

6 *Bacteria live around hydrothermal vents and also in water-filled cracks that reach deep beneath the ocean floor.*

3

4

5

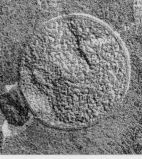

6

THE WORLD OF WATER

LIFE STARTED IN WATER, AND SINCE THEN LIVING THINGS HAVE SPREAD TO EVERY WATERY HABITAT ON EARTH. TODAY GIANT ANIMALS CRUISE THROUGH THE OCEANS, WHILE MICROSCOPIC CREATURES TEEM IN PONDS AND POOLS. HERE THE STRUGGLE FOR SURVIVAL CAN BE INTENSE.

All living things need water, but for many it serves as a habitat as well. Water life ranges from the smallest and simplest creatures to the world's longest and fastest-growing living things. So why does water make such a desirable home? One answer is that conditions in the water are much more stable than on dry land. Another is that there is so much of it. The world's oceans contain more than 0.34 million cu. mi. (1.4 billion km³) of water, making them by far the largest habitat on Earth.

△ Giant kelp is the world's longest and fastest-growing seaweed. It can shoot up from the seabed over 197 ft. (60m) before hitting the surface. Its leafy fronds have gas-filled floats to keep the plant upright.

▷ The biggest animals in the oceans all live by filtering food from the water. This is a basking shark—measuring up to 33 ft. (10m) long, it is the world's second-largest fish. It has small teeth and traps food by using its gills as a strainer.

This lifestyle works because water is packed full of drifting life. Some of the smallest drifters are single-celled algae that survive by soaking up the energy in sunshine. They are the key to life in the open water, as they make the food that animals can eat. But even in the clearest water sunlight only reaches a depth of around 820 ft. (250m). As a result algae live near the surface, so most animals live there too.

Freshwater is often shallow, so light can reach all the way to the bottom. In the summer it can be packed with microscopic life, which is why pond water often looks green.

FLOATING FOOD

For many water animals eating involves swimming through their food. Using different body parts—from trailing tentacles to gaping mouths—they scoop up food as they swim along. For a sea gooseberry the daily catch may weigh under 0.04 oz. (1g), but for whales it can be over one ton.

KEEPING AFLOAT

Land animals use a lot of energy working against the pull of gravity. But in water, life is much easier. Freshwater is over 750 times more dense than air, so it is very good at buoying up living things. Many soft-bodied animals simply float along with the current—a leisurely way of life that has no equivalent on land.

△ *Sea gooseberries, or ctenophores, are soft-bodied animals that catch food by trailing two slender tentacles lined with sticky cells. They swim by beating rows of "paddles" that reflect sunshine like tiny mirrors.*

whipped up by storms, most of the planet's water moves very slowly, creating a world that is always calm.

But water's density has some disadvantages as well. Compared to air it is very thick or viscous, so it takes a lot of effort to push through it. That explains why wading through water can be hard work. It also explains why nature's fastest swimmers are streamlined, as a smooth body shape helps the water slip past them as they move.

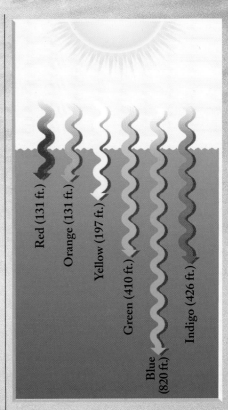

Red (131 ft.)
Orange (131 ft.)
Yellow (197 ft.)
Green (410 ft.)
Indigo (426 ft.)
Blue (820 ft.)

△ *When sunlight shines through water, it gradually fades away. The red and orange parts of sunlight are absorbed first, while blue travels the farthest of all. Below around 820 ft. (250m), the water in oceans and deep lakes is always dark.*

VITAL INGREDIENTS

Pure water is rare in nature because water is very good at dissolving things. It dissolves minerals when it flows through the ground and gases when it falls through the air. This is good news for water life because plants and animals need dissolved substances to survive.

One of the most important of these is oxygen, which gets into water from the air. Dissolved oxygen is invisible, but it is vital for almost all living things. The colder water is or the more stirred up it becomes, the more oxygen it dissolves. Another important ingredient is salt. Freshwater contains a small amount, but in every 2.2 lbs (1kg) of seawater there

▽ *Some water animals breathe air, but most get their oxygen from the water around them. This sea slug, or nudibranch, gets oxygen through a tuft of feathery gills on its back.*

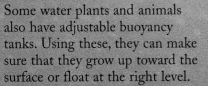

are around 1.2 oz. (35g) of salt. If all of this salt were spread across the seabed, it would make a layer 184 ft. (56m) thick. Some water animals can travel between freshwater and seawater, but most have adapted to a particular salt level and cannot survive if they are switched between the two.

Some water plants and animals also have adjustable buoyancy tanks. Using these, they can make sure that they grow up toward the surface or float at the right level.

Water has some other benefits too. Because it is dense, it takes a long time to heat up or cool down. This is good for water life, as it means that there are no sudden temperature changes, unlike on land. It also takes a lot of energy to get water moving. Although rivers rush down mountainsides, and the oceans are

LIVING ON LAND

LAND IS HOME TO ALMOST ALL OF THE WORLD'S FLOWERING PLANTS AND TO A LARGE SHARE OF ITS ANIMALS. MANY TYPES OF MICROSCOPIC LIFE EXIST HERE TOO. BUT COMPARED TO LIVING IN THE WATER, SURVIVING ON LAND IS A SURPRISINGLY DIFFICULT BUSINESS.

△ A tough body case enables beetles to crawl through narrow spaces without damaging their wings. The case is waterproof, so it stops beetles from drying out.

△ Conditions on land vary much more than in the water. This plant is growing in ground that has cracked open during a drought—unless it rains soon the plant will not survive.

Because we live on land, it is easy to imagine that it makes an ideal home for living things. But nothing could be further from the truth. Life on land is tough, and it takes special adaptations to survive. To make up for this Earth's land surface is amazingly varied, so land dwellers have been able to develop an incredible variety of different lifestyles.

▷ African elephants are the largest land animals alive today. For animals this heavy, lying down is a lengthy business, but wallowing in mud or bathing is often part of a herd's daily routine.

things. Animals support themselves with skeletons made of even harder substances, including shell and bone. An insect's skeleton works like a case, but a bony one holds up an animal's body from the inside. Some dinosaur skeletons supported animals weighing over 50 tons, which shows just how successful this system can be. But skeletons do not have to be big to be strong. The hero shrew, from Africa, has such a tough spine that it can survive having a person step on its back.

DRY TIMES

Gravity is not the only problem land dwellers have to deal with. Just as important is the threat of drying out. One way to get around this is to live in damp places, a tactic used by frogs and toads, as well as by animals that live in the soil. But damp habitats are not always easy to find, and they often dry out themselves. To be really successful on land, animals and plants need ways of holding onto the water that they contain.

In mammals, birds, and reptiles this job is done by skin. Skin works like a raincoat in reverse, as it keeps water from escaping to the outside air. Every day we need to drink to refresh our moisture levels, but

TAKING THE WEIGHT

When astronauts return from space, they have to get used to Earth's gravity. Something similar happened long ago when Earth's first land dwellers emerged from the sea. Gravity has very little effect on

water life, but on land it can make living things collapse.

Plants and animals avoid this fate by having special strengthening systems. In plants these include wood—a tough but springy material that supports the world's tallest

many desert animals can get all of the water they need from their food. Insects are even better at managing their "water budget" because their body cases also serve as a water barrier. Many of them eat dry food and never drink a single drop of water in their entire lives.

Because plants do not move, they can store up water when it is wet and use it when the weather turns dry. Cacti often store enough water to fill a bathtub, and the water in a baobab tree (see page 202) could fill a small swimming pool.

△ *Flying is a very efficient way of moving around—in a single day these carmine bee-eaters of central Africa can travel over 62 mi. (100km) to find food.*

BREEDING ON LAND
Lastly and most importantly, plants and animals have to produce young that can survive on land. Flowering plants do this by growing seeds— packages of cells that are designed

to survive heat, cold, and drought. Many land animals lay waterproof eggs, but most mammals have a very different way of reproducing. Their young develop in the watery surroundings of their mother's womb, hidden away from the outside world.

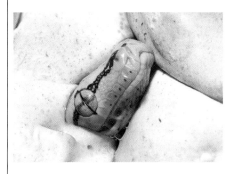

△ *Taking its first glimpse of the world, a young green tree python emerges from its egg. Reptiles were the first animals to develop waterproof eggs, helping them live in dry places.*

◁ *Arching its neck, a giraffe takes a drink. Unlike humans, giraffes get most of their water from their food, so they can go without water for several days.*

ENERGY FOR LIFE

EVERY DAY THE SUN BOMBARDS OUR PLANET
WITH ENOUGH ENERGY TO KEEP A CAR RUNNING
FOR OVER ONE TRILLION YEARS. THIS ENERGY
POWERS THE WEATHER AND WARMS UP EARTH, AND
MORE IMPRESSIVELY IT KEEPS LIVING THINGS ALIVE.

Just like machines, living things need energy to work. They use energy to power their cells, and once these are running they can do many different things, including growing and moving around. But this energy has to come from somewhere, and it has to be replaced whenever it is used up. Since life began living things have developed two different ways of getting their energy supplies. Some collect it directly, usually by gathering light. Others—including ourselves—get it secondhand by digesting food.

POWERING UP

Most people enjoy relaxing in the warm sunshine, but our bodies cannot do much with light energy. We use it to see and to produce vitamin D, but that is where the list comes to an end. But for many bacteria and almost all of the world's plants, light energy is vital to survival. The bacteria and plants soak it up like living solar panels and use it to make themselves function. This process is called photosynthesis—you can find out about it on pages 84–85.

△ *Almost all animals have specialized diets, but just about every species is food for something else. Here one spider has caught another and is turning its catch into a meal.*

◁ *Measuring up to 11 in. (28cm) long, millipedes are some of the largest creatures to feed on plant remains. Not only are millipedes slow movers, but they are also cold-blooded. This combination makes them very economical with energy.*

Plants collect around one percent of all the light energy that reaches Earth. That may not sound like a lot, but it is more than 300 times the energy generated by all of the power plants in the world. This energy creates billions of tons of plant matter—from roots and leaves to flowers and seeds. Some energy is used when plants grow, but a lot is built into the plants themselves. This built-in energy is passed on to animals whenever they eat plant food. Once the energy has made this jump, it is passed on whenever one animal eats another.

FEEDING TIME

To release energy from food, animals have to break it down. They do this by combining it with oxygen—the same chemical change that takes place when things catch on fire. Fire releases energy very quickly and in dangerous amounts. If animals used this way of getting energy, their bodies would be cooked from the inside out. Instead they release it in a series of carefully controlled steps so that not too much heat is produced. This way of releasing energy is called cellular respiration, as it uses oxygen and takes place inside of cells.

Animals are not the only living things that respire. Respiration is carried out by all living cells when

they break down food. Plant cells respire because they make food by photosynthesis and then break it down when energy supplies are low.

FAST AND SLOW

In the animal world each species uses up energy at a different rate. Shrews, for example, seem to live

▽ *This diagram shows how much energy different mammals use for each unit of body weight. The rate for humans is set at one. Small mammals use energy quickly because their bodies lose heat more rapidly.*

Elephant (0.3)
Horse (0.5)
Human (1)
Cat (3.25)
House mouse (7.8)
Shrew (35)

their lives in fast-forward. They are always on the move, always eating, and hardly ever rest. Snakes and crocodiles, however, are very different. They seem to spend their time lazing around, and they can rest for several weeks after a large meal.

These differences result from each animal's metabolism, which is the sum of all of its body chemistry. Shrews have a very fast metabolism, as they use up a lot of energy keeping their tiny bodies warm. Snakes and crocodiles, on the other hand, are cold-blooded. Their metabolism is slow because they need much less energy to stay alive. Humans, like most large mammals, are somewhere in between.

At any given moment an animal's metabolic rate depends on what it is doing. When animals are active their metabolic rate goes up, but when they are sleeping it goes down. When animals hibernate, their metabolic rate drops even more. A hibernating bat uses energy 40 times more slowly than an active one, so the food reserves in its body can last for many weeks.

BOTTOM OF THE PILE

Energy is not only passed on in living things, but it is also found in dead remains, such as the dead bodies of animals, rotting plants, and many types of natural waste—including animal droppings and fallen leaves. Many forms of life tap into this energy source. They include animals that scavenge for food (see pages 132–133), as well as fungi and bacteria. Together these living things are known as decomposers because they break down and dispose of waste.

Decomposing is a reliable way of obtaining energy, as sooner or later all living things die. It is also very thorough, as once it is finished every scrap of available energy is released. Decomposition comes to an end when there is no energy left to pass on.

CHEMICAL TRICKS

Without sunlight to make plants grow, humans would not survive for very long. The same is true for other animals and most fungi and bacteria.

△ *Without decomposers such as fungi, plants would still be able to collect energy from sunlight, but they would run out of the nutrients they need in order to grow.*

However in some of the world's remotest places—such as submerged rocks and deep-sea vents—bacteria live by collecting dissolved minerals and making them react. Unlike everything else in the living world, these tiny creatures do not need solar energy at all. These bacteria are known as lithotrophs, which literally means "rock eaters." Some of them survive on a diet of manganese or iron, while others process sulfur. Lithotrophs are of great interest to scientists, as it is possible that lithotrophs live on other planets as well as our own.

CHANGING CLIMATE

FOR THE PAST 50 YEARS OUR PLANET HAS BEEN WARMING UP, BUT CLIMATE CHANGE IS NOTHING NEW. THROUGHOUT EARTH'S HISTORY, LIVING THINGS HAVE HAD TO ADAPT TO THESE CHANGES.

△ *The world's climate is influenced by many different things. One of them is cloud cover. Clouds reflect sunshine back into space, but they also work like a blanket, holding in Earth's heat.*

Earth's climate is like an incredibly complex machine with billions of separate parts. Predicting what it will do next is very difficult. Looking back is easier, however, because of evidence that the climate leaves behind—such as the thickness of tree rings or the makeup of ancient air trapped deep in polar ice. They show that the world's climate is very variable and that major changes can happen much faster than scientists once believed.

ICE AGES

Twenty thousand years ago Earth was a very different place. Immense glaciers covered most of the Northern Hemisphere, reaching as far south as present-day New York City. Even in places such as New Guinea, glaciers flowed down from the highest mountains. So much water was locked up in ice that the sea level was over 328 ft. (100m) lower than now.

For plants and animals these cold conditions had far-reaching effects. On the positive side there was much more land because so much of the former seabed was high and dry. This made it easier for animals and plants to spread out, as they could travel between places that are now separated by the sea. But on the negative side life could be extremely cold and harsh. To keep warm, ice age mammals depended on deep layers of body fat and long, shaggy fur.

WHY THE CLIMATE CHANGES

This ice age was not the first that Earth has experienced, and it is unlikely to be the last. As far back as scientists can see, Earth's climate has swung between warm periods, called interglacials, and times when it has been much colder. Many experts believe that these climate swings are caused

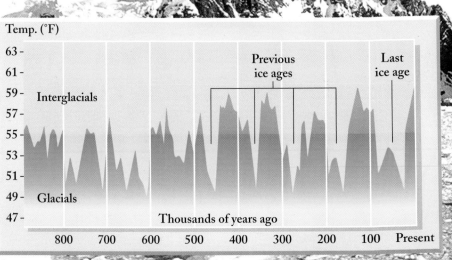

▷ *This chart shows how the world's average temperature has changed over the past million years. There have been several major warm periods, called interglacials— some brief, others more long lasting. We are currently living in an interglacial period.*

Temp. (°F)

| | | Previous ice ages | Last ice age |

63 –
61 –
59 – Interglacials
57 –
55 –
53 –
51 –
49 – Glacials
47 –

Thousands of years ago

800 700 600 500 400 300 200 100 Present

mainly by variations in Earth's orbit, but other factors are involved as well—volcanic eruptions and continental drift, for example.

Continents have been on the move ever since land first formed. Powered by volcanic heat, they creep across Earth's surface at the rate of around one inch or so every year. This movement is much too slow for us to notice, but over millions of years it can completely change the way Earth looks. And because the continents move, the oceans change shape as well.

Oceans play a key role in shaping the world's climate because they store heat from the Sun. Most of the heat is stored in the tropics and then carried north and south by warm currents. But if continents move and block these currents, the far north and south start to cool down. This cooling may be enough to trigger an ice age, which can last for hundreds of thousands of years.

STRANDED BY TIME

The last ice age ended around 10,000 years ago when Earth warmed up and glaciers began to retreat. Since then the global climate has been fairly stable, but it has not stayed exactly the same. Average temperatures have risen and fallen, and rainfall patterns have changed too. In places such as the Sahara Desert these changes have had some dramatic effects.

Today the Sahara is one of the driest and least fertile regions in the world. But 5,000 years ago its climate was much more moist. At that time elephants and antelope fed in open woodlands, and hippos lived in the region's lakes and rivers. Over the next 3,000 years the Sahara's climate became steadily drier. The desert began to expand, and many of the region's plants and animals withered away and disappeared. But they did not all vanish. Hidden away in the Sahara's mountains where the climate is slightly more moist, olive trees and freshwater fish still manage to survive.

△ ▽ *The Tassili Mountains in southern Algeria are in the heart of the Sahara Desert. Rock engravings—such as of the antelope below—show that this dry and remote region was full of wildlife a few thousand years ago.*

◁ *Polar ice works like a diary of the world's climate because it traps dust, pollen, and bubbles of air. By drilling down through the ice, scientists can collect samples dating back thousands or millions of years.*

△ As the days lengthen in the spring, this English oak tree suddenly starts to grow. Its buds burst open, producing thousands of bright-green leaves.

△ By midsummer the oak's leaves have turned dark green and have finished growing. Among them the year's acorn crop is starting to form.

△ During the fall the leaves change color from green to yellow and begin to drop. The acorns are almost ripe—soon they will start to drop as well.

△ In the winter the tree is leafless, so it is not harmed by the cold. It will stay like this until the winter is over and the warmer days of spring arrive.

SEASONS AND WEATHER

INSTEAD OF BEING UPRIGHT, EARTH TILTS AT AN ANGLE AS IT CIRCLES AROUND THE SUN. THIS TILT IS SMALL, BUT IT HAS A HUGE IMPACT ON LIVING THINGS BECAUSE IT IS THE REASON WHY THE SEASONS CHANGE.

Along the equator at noon the Sun is almost directly overhead, and every day is almost exactly 12 hours long. But farther north and south the Sun is lower, and the Earth's tilt has much more effect. In the winter Earth tilts away from the Sun, so the days are short and cold. In the summer it tilts in the opposite direction, so the days are long and warm. Near the poles it never gets warm, but summer days are so long that the Sun never sets.

◁ Earth's tilt means that the Northern and Southern hemispheres experience the same seasons, just six months apart. This diagram shows a complete year—with the northern summer on the left and the southern summer on the right.

A YEARLY DELUGE

In the tropics there is no such thing as winter, so plants and animals never have to face real cold. But they do have to cope with changing weather, as the seasons often switch between wet and dry. During the wet season the rain can be incredibly heavy. For example in Cherrapunji in northeast India, over 30 ft. (9m) of rain has fallen in a single month—15 times more than London, England, receives in an entire year. But at the height of the dry season, places such as Cherrapunji often have no rain at all.

Tropical plants and animals have to adapt to this topsy-turvy weather. Grazing animals feed up in the wet season, when there is plenty to eat. But during the dry season life becomes much tougher, as many plants stop growing and lose their leaves. Predators and scavengers, on the other hand, may do better in the dry season, as prey that is hungry or thirsty finds it harder to escape.

THE FOUR-SEASON WORLD

In the world's temperate regions there are usually four seasons— spring, summer, fall, and winter. In the spring the days lengthen rapidly, and plants put on an impressive burst of growth. This is also a busy time for animals, with millions of migrating birds arriving to breed. By midsummer most plants have stopped growing and are producing seeds. Fall is a time of preparation, with the days shortening and temperatures beginning to drop. By the time winter arrives the migrant birds have gone, and most of the trees have lost their leaves.

Temperate regions never get very hot or very cold, but their weather is often changeable and difficult to predict. Dry summers may be followed by wet ones, and warm spring weather can often be followed by frost and snow. Plants and animals have to be ready for these changes so that they can survive whatever the weather brings. Many of them use changes in day length as a guide to when to start growing or when to begin hibernating. Unlike the weather, day length always varies exactly along with the seasons—so it is a perfect way of keeping time.

ENDLESS LIGHT

Along the Arctic and Antarctic Circles the Sun never sets on a midsummer's day, and it never rises in the midwinter. Beyond here spring and fall become shorter and shorter, and the difference between summer and winter becomes more extreme. At the poles the Sun shines for six months without a break and then sets for a six-month winter rest. In midwinter the Moon is often below the horizon too, so the only light comes from the stars.

As well as coping with darkness and cold, polar wildlife has to put up with extremely strong winds. In Earth's windiest place, on the coast of Antarctica, gales can gust at over 186 mph (300km/h), and they keep blowing for days on end. Fortunately most polar animals live in the seas, where they are sheltered from this icy blast.

△ *These wildebeest may look miserable, but they depend on rainy season downpours to survive. If the rains are light, they will not have enough food to last through the year.*

▽ *This 24-hour sequence was taken on a midsummer's day just north of the Arctic Circle. The Sun sinks low in the sky around midnight but rises again before it has set.*

DEALING WITH DISASTER

IN NATURE DISASTER CAN STRIKE AT ANY TIME.
UNLIKE HUMANS, PLANTS AND ANIMALS CANNOT
CALL FOR OUTSIDE HELP—INSTEAD THEY HAVE
TO DEAL WITH DISASTERS THEMSELVES.

On August 27, 1883, the biggest volcanic eruption in
history blasted apart the Indonesian island of Krakatau.
On nearby islands forests disappeared under 246 ft. (75m)
of burning ash, while on Krakatau itself not a single plant or animal
is believed to have survived. Fortunately for Earth's wildlife this type
of catastrophe is very rare. But every year living things have to cope
with many different hazards—from extreme weather to forest fires.

△ *In the Midwest tornadoes cause severe
damage every year. Amazingly insects and
other small animals may survive even when
they are sucked up inside a tornado's funnel.*

DEADLY STORMS

When a storm is on its way, the air
pressure drops. Some wild animals
can sense this, but unless they
can fly they have little chance of
escaping. For plants the situation is
even worse, as they are stuck in one
place. So what happens to wildlife
when a really powerful storm strikes?

The answer is that it survives
surprisingly well. Animals instinctively
seek shelter to avoid the worst of the
weather, and unlike people they do
not venture out until the storm is
over. Floods are more of a problem,
as it can be difficult to find high
ground. For plants being flexible is
often the key to survival. Some palm
trees can bend almost horizontal
without snapping in two. After
the storm they gradually recover,

◁ *This lava flow in Hawaii buried
a village and obliterated roads. Animals
can usually escape slow-flowing lava, but
plants are incinerated before being engulfed.*

▽ *At this wildlife refuge in California lakes
often dry up in the summer, so animals have
to be prepared. Many freshwater animals
lay their eggs in the mud—these hatch
when the water returns.*

sprouting new leaves to replace the ones that have been torn away.

EARTHQUAKES AND FIRE

For humans earthquakes can be deadly, striking without warning and causing buildings to collapse. But despite their awesome power, they are much less dangerous for wildlife. This is because earthquakes rarely do much damage out in the open.

Fire is a much more serious hazard, so most wild animals take emergency action as soon as they smell smoke. Grazing mammals run away, while burrowing animals head underground. Honeybees return to their nests to

▽ *When floodwaters rise, grazing mammals can find themselves in trouble. Wild mammals can swim to safety, but these farm animals will have to be rescued.*

collect as much honey as they can before abandoning their home.

Compared to animals, plants are often better at surviving the flames, even though their leaves may be burned away. In dry habitats, such as scrublands (see pages 204–211), some plants actually depend on fire to keep other species in check.

DROUGHT BUSTERS

Natural disasters do not always strike suddenly. Drought is one of the most serious hazards, building up over months or years. Most dryland species—such as cacti and camels—are good at collecting and conserving water, but they cannot keep going forever if their supplies run out. The champion drought busters are tiny animals that dry out themselves. Called water bears, or tardigrades

△ *With flames flickering behind them, a group of mules and horses heads away from a fire. Most animals react instantly to the smell of smoke, waking up if they are asleep.*

(see page 155), they can survive droughts that last for years.

WINNING FORMULA

Even after a catastrophe as big as the Krakatau eruption, wildlife eventually recovers. Within five years Krakatau's shattered remains were coming back to life, and today the island is covered by forestland once again. Plants and animals can do this because they are good at producing young and because their young are designed to spread. For living things breeding is the best type of insurance, as it gives each species the best chance of survival.

THE EVOLUTION OF LIFE

BY EXAMINING FOSSILS SCIENTISTS CAN LOOK BACK AT LIFE IN THE DISTANT PAST. THIS RESEARCH SHOWS THAT LIVING THINGS GRADUALLY CHANGE—OR EVOLVE— AS TIME GOES BY.

Evolution happens extremely slowly, so it is hard to see it taking place. But it has left behind a wealth of telltale clues. Fossils are the most important because they tell us about extinct species and about the way living things have changed. Today's living things also provide clues, as evolution shows up in many different features—from skeletons right down to genes.

THE GREAT DEBATE

Two hundred years ago most naturalists believed that the world was only a few thousand years old. They also thought that living things, or species, always stayed the same. But as scientists examined rocks and fossils all over Earth, it became clear that the planet is very old and that many types of species had lived in the past and then become extinct. In 1859 an English naturalist named Charles Darwin published a book that

△ *Prehistoric cave paintings, such as this one in Lascaux, France, show that our ancestors lived alongside animals that are now extinct.*

made sense of these discoveries. Called *The Origin of Species*, it discussed the evidence for evolution and also explained why it occurs.

Since then evolution has been at the center of a great debate. On one side some people reject the entire idea because it does not fit into their religious beliefs. On the other side many people—including the vast majority of the world's scientists—are just as convinced that evolution does occur.

CHANGE AND ADAPTATION

Two years after Darwin published his book, workers in a German quarry discovered one of the most famous fossils in the world. Known as *Archaeopteryx*, it had wings and feathers, but it also had teeth, fingers with claws, and a long bony tail. *Archaeopteryx* was an early type of bird, but its teeth, fingers, and tail make it different from any bird alive today. Paleontologists—scientists who study fossils—recognized that *Archaeopteryx* was an extraordinary find that backed up Darwin's ideas. It had clearly evolved from reptiles, but its features showed that it was not a reptile itself.

◁ *Like a crashed plane,* Archaeopteryx *lies spread out in a slab of limestone. This famous fossil is a classic "intermediate" species—one that links together different groups of living things.*

When species evolve, adaptations develop that make them better at particular ways of life. For *Archaeopteryx*, feathers were a key adaptation because they enabled it to glide or maybe to fly. They would also have kept its body warm, and they might even have been used to scoop up dragonflies and other flying insects that *Archaeopteryx* used as food.

WINNERS AND LOSERS

Adaptations are the nuts and bolts of evolution. They can shape almost any feature of a living thing—from the way it looks to how it behaves. But as Darwin realized, they do not appear in a single lifetime. Instead they evolve gradually over many generations through a process called natural selection. Adaptations build up extremely slowly, but given enough time they can become so important that new species are formed.

△ *Fossils not only show what living things looked like—they can also show when they lived. This paleontologist is studying the fossil of a* Titanosaurus, *a dinosaur that died out around 66 million years ago.*

Evolution started when life began and living things started competing with one another to survive. This process is still at work, creating new adaptations that can help living things succeed. Extinction is part of evolution, as it clears away the "losers" and gives new and better-adapted species a chance to prove themselves. Ninety-nine percent of the world's species—including *Archaeopteryx* itself—are now extinct. But although *Archaeopteryx* died out, other feathered fliers survived, and their descendants now fill the skies.

▽ *Chimpanzees and humans look very different, but we share the same ancestors. Around five million years ago the lines that led to humans and chimpanzees split apart.*

TIME LINE OF LIFE 1

IF EARTH'S ENTIRE HISTORY COULD BE SHRUNK INTO ONE SINGLE DAY, THE FIRST SIGNS OF LIFE WOULD APPEAR LONG BEFORE DAWN. BUT IT WOULD BE 9:30 IN THE EVENING BEFORE ANIMALS STARTED TO RESEMBLE ANYTHING ALIVE TODAY.

To make sense of Earth's incredibly long history, scientists divide it up into different stages. The longest of these stages are called eras. Eras are split into periods, and periods are sometimes divided into shorter stages called epochs. During each stage living things evolved, and they left behind fossils when they died. On these two pages you can find out how life evolved during the most distant part of Earth's history—from its beginnings until the end of the Paleozoic Era 245 million years ago.

THE ARCHEAN ERA

This part of Earth's history began around 3.8 billion years ago—the age of the oldest known rocks. It lasted for 1.3 billion years, just over one fourth of Earth's total existence. Life appeared early in the Archean Era, and the first definite signs of it are chemical traces found in rocks 3.7 billion years old. The microscopic organisms that left these traces were single celled, like bacteria today.

THE PROTEROZOIC ERA

Proterozoic means "earlier life." In this era microbes evolved that grew by collecting the energy in sunlight. Known as cyanobacteria or blue-green algae, their descendants are still alive today. Cyanobacteria lived in shallow seas. Some formed large mounds called stromatolites, which left fossils in Proterozoic rocks.

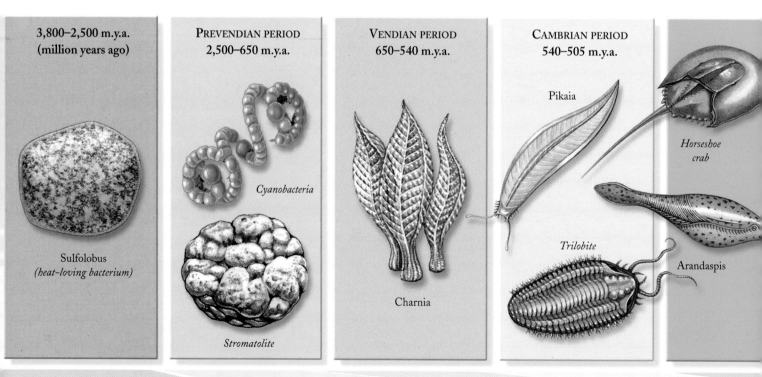

3,800–2,500 m.y.a. (million years ago)

Sulfolobus
(heat-loving bacterium)

PREVENDIAN PERIOD 2,500–650 m.y.a.

Cyanobacteria

Stromatolite

VENDIAN PERIOD 650–540 m.y.a.

Charnia

CAMBRIAN PERIOD 540–505 m.y.a.

Pikaia

Horseshoe crab

Trilobite

Arandaspis

Around one billion years ago life took a major step forward, when the first animals appeared. At first they were tiny, but they were more complex than earlier life-forms because their bodies contained many cells. By the Vendian period, at the end of the Proterozoic Era, animal life had become diverse. These early animals included *Charnia*, which looked like a feathery tuft on the seabed.

THE PALEOZOIC ERA

The Paleozoic Era—a word that means "ancient life"—is divided into six periods. The first one, called the Cambrian, was one of the most extraordinary times in Earth's history, when animals evolved shells and other hard body parts—a biological revolution that created many new ways of life. These animals included trilobites and other arthropods, mollusks, and chordates such as *Pikaia*. Chordates had a strengthening rod along their bodies and were the ancestors of all animals with backbones, including ourselves.

Marine life continued to expand in the Ordovician period. Some of the largest animals were nautiloids—a group of mollusks related to today's octopuses and squid. Horseshoe crabs and other arthropods were common, and at the end of the Ordovician some of these animals took their first steps onto land.

Sea scorpions were the giants of the Silurian period, at almost 10 ft. (3m) long. Fish such as *Jamoytius* were common. The first fish had no jaws, but during the Silurian fish with hinged jaws evolved. Unlike earlier types, these could bite off food.

By the Devonian period fish had taken over as the largest sea animals.

The 13-ft. (4-m) -long *Dunkleosteus* had platelike teeth that could slice prey in two. But this period brought even bigger changes on land. Four-legged amphibians that evolved from fish adapted to life out of the water. *Ichthyostega* was one of the first.

During the Carboniferous period huge forests were home to the first flying insects, including cockroaches and giant dragonflies. The first reptiles date back to this time, and during the Permian period they became the dominant land animals. *Dimetrodon* and *Edaphosaurus* were two of the biggest. Both had "sails" on their backs that helped regulate their body temperature. The late Permian saw the rise of therapsids—reptilelike animals that were the ancestors of mammals—but it ended with an extinction that devastated life on Earth (see page 51).

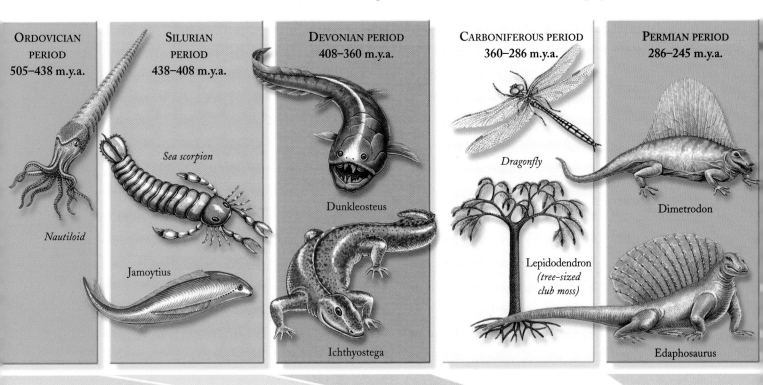

ORDOVICIAN PERIOD
505–438 m.y.a.

SILURIAN PERIOD
438–408 m.y.a.

DEVONIAN PERIOD
408–360 m.y.a.

CARBONIFEROUS PERIOD
360–286 m.y.a.

PERMIAN PERIOD
286–245 m.y.a.

Nautiloid

Sea scorpion

Jamoytius

Dunkleosteus

Ichthyostega

Dragonfly

Lepidodendron
(tree-sized club moss)

Dimetrodon

Edaphosaurus

PROTEROZOIC ERA

PALEOZOIC ERA

TIME LINE OF LIFE 2

OVER THE PAST 245 MILLION YEARS ANIMALS AND PLANTS HAVE LEFT A HUGE TREASURY OF FOSSIL REMAINS. THEY INCLUDE AWE-INSPIRING RELICS FROM THE AGE OF REPTILES AND FRAGMENTS OF EARLY HOMINIDS—APELIKE ANIMALS THAT EVENTUALLY GAVE RISE TO HUMAN BEINGS.

Compared to the time line on the last two pages, the one shown here is short. If Earth's history were squeezed into one day, it would cover just over an hour. But during this time an astounding variety of living things evolved—from flowering plants to the largest animals to ever exist on land. This time line covers two geological eras: the Mesozoic, which ended 66 million years ago, and the Cenozoic, which continues into modern times.

THE MESOZOIC ERA

The Mesozoic, or "middle life" era, is often known as the age of reptiles. Many other animals lived in this era, but reptiles became the largest in the sea, in the air, and on land. Scientists split the Mesozoic into three periods. The first one—known as the Triassic—started after the Permian mass extinction, a disaster that erased around three fourths of the animal species on Earth.

At the beginning of the Triassic most of the world's land was joined together in a supercontinent called Pangaea. The climate was warm, and tree ferns, conifers, and cycads were common plants. Triassic reptiles included some of the first gliding vertebrates. Evolution also produced bizarre animals such as *Tanystropheus*, which probably used its amazingly long neck to fish from the shore.

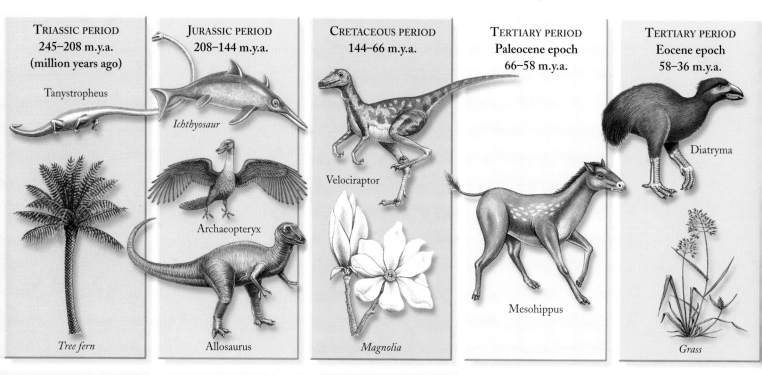

TRIASSIC PERIOD
245–208 m.y.a.
(million years ago)

Tanystropheus

Tree fern

JURASSIC PERIOD
208–144 m.y.a.

Ichthyosaur

Archaeopteryx

Allosaurus

CRETACEOUS PERIOD
144–66 m.y.a.

Velociraptor

Magnolia

TERTIARY PERIOD
Paleocene epoch
66–58 m.y.a.

Mesohippus

TERTIARY PERIOD
Eocene epoch
58–36 m.y.a.

Diatryma

Grass

Dinosaurs evolved toward the end of the Triassic, but the Jurassic period marked the height of their reign. As the climate became more moist, some plant-eating species reached incredible sizes. These herbivores provided prey for some equally impressive predators, including *Allosaurus*, which weighed up to three tons. Birds evolved from feathered dinosaurs, and the first ones date back to Jurassic times.

Flowering plants appeared in the Cretaceous period, triggering a burst of evolution in the insect world. Flying reptiles, called pterosaurs, soared through the sky on leathery wings. One species, *Quetzalcoatlus*, had a wingspan of 39 ft. (12m), making it probably the largest flying animal ever. Among the dinosaurs, small hunters, such as *Velociraptor*, lived alongside tyrannosaurs, the largest land predators of the time. But 66 million years ago Earth was hit by a giant meteorite, bringing the age of reptiles to a cataclysmic end.

The Cenozoic Era

During this era life recovered from the Cretaceous mass extinction. Mammals began to fill the roles that reptiles had taken before, becoming so successful that the Cenozoic is often known as the mammal age.

The first mammals fed on insects and other small animals, but in the Tertiary period large plant-eating types evolved. Grasses developed early in the Tertiary, enabling some mammals to adopt herding lifestyles in open grasslands and wooded savanna. These animals included the forerunners of today's horses, as well as much bigger animals, including *Brontotherium* and early elephants.

Birds also gained from the disappearance of the dinosaurs. The large, flightless *Diatryma* was most likely a predator, ripping prey apart with a massive hooked beak. Toward the end of the Tertiary, primates called australopithecines appeared in Africa. One of these apelike animals was our direct ancestor.

During the early Quaternary period the climate became colder, and a long ice age began. Mammals adapted to the changing conditions, and some highly specialized types evolved. One was *Smilodon*, a saber-toothed cat that killed its prey with serrated teeth up to 7 in. (18cm) long. Humans first appeared around 500,000 years ago. They collected wild food and hunted at first, but by the end of the ice age, 10,000 years ago, they began farming. Since then our species has changed the world.

TERTIARY PERIOD
Oligocene epoch
36–23 m.y.a.

Brontotherium

TERTIARY PERIOD
Miocene epoch
23–5.3 m.y.a.

Deinotherium

TERTIARY PERIOD
Pliocene epoch
5.3–1.6 m.y.a.

Australopithecus

QUATERNARY PERIOD
Pleistocene epoch
1.6 m.y.a.–10,000 y.a.

Smilodon

Irish elk

QUATERNARY PERIOD
Holocene epoch
10,000 y.a.–present

Modern human

Domestic dog

CENOZOIC ERA

HOW EVOLUTION WORKS 1

FOSSILS SHOW THAT LIVING THINGS
EVOLVE, BUT THEY DO NOT EXPLAIN HOW
OR WHY EVOLUTION OCCURS. AS CHARLES
DARWIN DISCOVERED, THE ANSWERS TO
BOTH QUESTIONS CAN BE FOUND BY TAKING
A CLOSE LOOK AT THE NATURAL WORLD.

In the mid-1800s when Charles Darwin wrote *The Origin of Species*, he discussed that evolution takes place, and he also explained why it happens. Darwin's breakthrough came when he realized that living things struggle to survive, and that in this struggle some will be better than others at surviving and producing young. Because these "winners" leave more offspring, their features will become more common. In other words their species will slowly change.

TOUGH TIMES AHEAD

A female common frog lays around one thousand eggs, and from the moment the eggs hatch an intense struggle for survival begins. Some of the tadpoles die within hours, either because they are attacked by waterborne fungi or because they cannot find enough food. Others die when they are swallowed by fish or other predators. By the time the tadpoles have turned into frogs, only a few dozen will be left. But even for the survivors life is not simple. Some will die of hunger, while those that wander too far from the water will die by drying out. Even if they avoid these fates, they still run the risk of being eaten by foxes or birds. After four years only a handful of frogs will still be alive and ready to become parents themselves.

But who are these winners? The answer is simple—they are those that are the "fittest" and have what it takes to survive.

INHERITED VARIATIONS

To us one common frog looks very similar to another. The same is true of almost all living things. But because most things have two parents they inherit a mixture of genes (see page 42). This gives them different features so that they have a variety of strengths and weaknesses in the struggle to survive. Useful genes are likely to be passed on because their owners are more likely to breed.

On the other hand unhelpful genes are less likely to spread because many of their owners will not survive to breed at all.

▽ *Because life is hazardous, parents in nature always produce plenty of young. A dandelion plant can grow up to 30 seed heads, or "clocks." Each one contains enough seeds for over 100 new dandelion plants.*

△ For lynx and hares speed is essential for survival. Lynx have developed muscles for sprinting, but hares have extremely sharp eyesight and hearing, so they often have a head start in the race to escape.

Although Darwin knew nothing about genes, he knew a lot about the variations in living things. He realized that these variations could be inherited and that useful ones could build up over time. Variations create adaptations—features that help living things survive. As these adaptations build up over time, species evolve.

NATURAL SELECTION
In the struggle for survival, nature favors those that are good at taking care of themselves and producing young. Darwin called this process natural selection. Natural selection works automatically without having anything behind the controls. Sometimes natural selection favors individuals that are extrastrong or extrafast. For example lynx have been "selected" for their speed, as they sprint to catch their food. But being strong and fast is not always a recipe for success. Many insects are successful because they are so small. They often succeed by staying still instead of running or flying away.

Natural selection can also favor different ways of raising a family. Many species—from oak trees to frogs—put all of their energy into producing plenty of young but none into helping them survive. Mammals are the opposite. They have smaller families, and they work hard to give their young a successful start in life.

NEW SPECIES
Natural selection is constantly picking its way through all of the tiny variations in living things. In the short term the changes are so small that they do not have a noticeable effect. But given more time they can have a much bigger impact. For example one species can evolve into several, each adapted for a different way of life.

Charles Darwin stumbled across a famous example of this when he visited the Galapagos Islands in 1835. He found one dozen species of finches that were all different, but at the same time they were suspiciously similar. As Darwin later realized, the finches had all evolved from a single species that had become stranded on the islands long ago.

▽ Near the remains of a fallen tree a young coconut sprouts its first leaves. Like all living things, its chances of survival will depend on two things—the genes that it inherited from its parents and luck.

▽ Female scorpions carry their young until they are ready to live on their own. Caring for a family makes life harder for parents, but it improves the chances that some of their young will survive.

HOW EVOLUTION WORKS 2

UNLIKE A HUMAN DESIGNER, EVOLUTION NEVER STARTS FROM SCRATCH. INSTEAD IT TAKES FEATURES THAT ALREADY EXIST AND ADAPTS THEM TO NEW WAYS OF LIFE. AS A RESULT EVERY LIVING THING CONTAINS REMINDERS OF ITS EVOLUTIONARY PAST.

Humans are great planners. Before we make something we decide how it is going to work, and then we select the best possible materials for the job. But evolution works in a very different way because the force that drives it—natural selection—cannot plan ahead at all. As a result evolution follows an unpredictable path. It can turn one adaptation into many different ones, and it can also backtrack, dropping something that it has previously made.

△ *The speed at which evolution works varies. The coelacanth has changed very little in the past 65 million years. Slow-changing species, known as "living fossils," include plants, microbes, and animals.*

LOOKING AT LIMBS
One of the best examples of the ingenuity of evolution can be seen in vertebrate limbs. Vertebrates are animals with backbones, and their limbs include legs, flippers, fins, and wings. From the outside these limbs look very different, and they work in different ways. But vertebrate limbs are all built on the same plan, and in scientific terms they are said

to be "homologous." This means that they all contain the same underlying skeleton inherited from the same distant ancestor that lived long ago—regardless of whether they are long, short, fat, or flat. Homologous structures provide strong evidence that different species are related.

Analagous structures are ones that do similar jobs but that are built in different ways. For example both birds and bees have wings, but birds' wings are made of bones and feathers, while bees' wings are made of a filmy substance called chitin. These two very different patterns show that birds and bees are not close relatives.

▽ *Unlike some flightless birds, ostriches still use their wings. They raise or lower them to adjust their body temperature. Male ostriches also spread them out to attract females.*

DROP IT!

In evolution adaptations have to pull their own weight. When an adaptation stops being useful, natural selection starts acting against it, and it falls out of use. Eventually an adaptation can stop working altogether, although it takes a long time for it to disappear.

This is exactly what happened with ostriches and other flightless birds. Millions of years ago their ancestors could fly, but as time went by they developed lifestyles that involved less time in the air. The forerunners of ostriches lived on Africa's open plains, and instead of flying away from danger they started running away. Over many generations natural selection built up their leg muscles and shrank the muscles that flapped their wings. Today ostriches have very weak wing muscles, and their flight feathers are soft and fluffy instead of stiff and strong. Even with its wings outstretched an ostrich has no chance of getting off of the ground.

PRECISION ENGINEERING

The natural world is full of adaptations that have been discarded in this way. Some reptiles have no legs, while many cave-dwelling animals have only tiny eyes. Humans also have a collection of evolutionary leftovers—for example some of our scalp muscles were originally used to move our ears.

But how did really complicated organs, such as eyes and ears, evolve in the first place? Could natural selection ever produce something as sophisticated as these? The answer—most biologists believe—is a definite "yes." Like all other adaptations, eyes and ears would

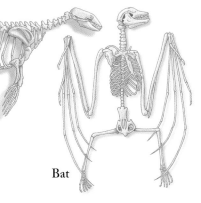

Seal

Bat

△ *Although seals and bats are very different from one another in appearance, and their bones are also different in shape and size, they both have skeletons that follow the same underlying plan. This similarity in skeleton shows that they have evolved from the same ancestors, which lived long ago.*

have evolved in a series of tiny steps, and at each stage they would have been a useful feature to have. A look at today's animals shows that eyes vary enormously—some are so simple that they can only tell light from dark. But in the distant future natural selection could convert these into eyes just as complex as our own.

△ *Some lizards have gradually lost their legs to suit a burrowing lifestyle. The giant legless skink from southern Africa can reach a length of 21 in. (55cm). This adult female is flanked by two of her young.*

GENES AND DNA

WHEN SCIENTISTS FIRST STUDIED EVOLUTION,
THEY HAD NO IDEA HOW LIVING THINGS
INHERIT FEATURES FROM THEIR
PARENTS. TODAY, AFTER 50 YEARS
OF GROUNDBREAKING RESEARCH,
WE KNOW THAT IT IS THROUGH
GENES AND DNA.

You do not have to be a scientist to know that cats produce kittens and that hens produce chicks and not the other way around. But what makes young animals—or plants—like their parents? And why are some features, such as eye color, passed on without being blended together and mixed up? Until the 1950s these questions were difficult to answer because no one knew how cells store the "instructions" needed to make living things. Then in 1953 scientists unraveled the structure of DNA, and the answers fell into place.

Nucleus

▽ The two strands in a DNA molecule spiral around each other like a twisted ladder. Each rung in the ladder is made by chemicals called bases, which fit together in pairs. The bases work like letters, spelling out the instructions that the DNA contains.

HOW DNA WORKS
DNA, or deoxyribonucleic acid, is a remarkable substance. It is the only chemical that can copy itself, and it is also one of the few that can store information. DNA is found in all living cells, and it copies itself when cells divide so that its instructions can be handed down.

Most chemicals always have the same structure—in other words their atoms are always arranged in exactly the same way. But DNA is different. Its molecules have a "backbone" of two spiral strands held together by chemicals called bases. The spiral strands are always the same, but there are four different types of bases, and they can be arranged in any order. These bases work like a four-letter alphabet, spelling out instructions. Before a cell divides the two strands unwind and each one makes a new partner strand. In this way the instructions are passed on.

FOLLOWING INSTRUCTIONS
Unlike a set of printed instructions, a DNA molecule is not divided up by paragraphs or headings. But DNA does have its own punctuation. Special sequences of bases act like start and stop signs.

△ Animals inherit a set of genes from each of their parents. This cat has inherited genes for a tabby coat and ones for green eyes. It will pass them on when it breeds.

△ This cat has inherited a gene that gives high levels of melanin in its coat. Melanin is a black pigment that is common in fur, feathers, and skin.

◁ *In most cells DNA is stored inside the cell's nucleus, or control center. Each cell has several DNA molecules, packaged up in X-shaped structures called chromosomes.*

Cell

△ *These trees belong to the same species, but each one has inherited slightly different versions of the same genes, giving each tree different chances in the struggle for survival.*

showing where each instruction begins and ends. These instructions are known as genes. There can be several thousand genes in one single DNA molecule. Together a complete set of genes contains all of the information needed to build up a living thing and keep it running.

The instructions programmed by genes are extremely varied. Some genes decide physical features

inherit a unique collection of alleles, which are slightly different versions of the same genes. As a result they have their own different characteristics. This type of variation is very important because it allows species to evolve.

The same cat might also inherit white paws from one of its grandparents, even though neither of its parents has white paws themselves. This happens because some alleles can be masked by others, disappearing for a generation or more until they are unmasked again.

THE FULL STORY
Genes control a huge range of features, but they do not decide exactly how everything looks and lives. The outside world plays a part as well. For example if an animal is well fed, it will reach its maximum possible size, but if it goes hungry it will be underweight. Animals inherit instinctive behavior, which is programmed by their genes. But many animals also learn some of their behavior, and this depends on their experience. Plants are even more variable. Their shape depends partly on their genes but a great deal on the conditions where they grow.

such as the color of eyes or skin. Many control the speed of chemical processes, while some act as "master" genes by turning other genes on or off. A few come into action only in emergencies—for example suicide genes make cells self-destruct if they come under attack by a virus.

NATURAL VARIATIONS
If two animals or two plants have the same genes, they will be identical in almost every way. This does happen in nature, but it is not common. Instead most living things

Genetic variation comes about mainly through sexual reproduction. In this type of reproduction alleles from two parents are combined and shuffled, creating a new combination that is handed down. For example a cat may inherit black fur from one parent and green eyes from the other.

▷ *Unlike most cells, bacterial cells have a single, looping, DNA molecule. This bacterium has been specially treated to make its DNA spill out of its single cell. DNA molecules are extremely slender, but they can measure a few inches long.*

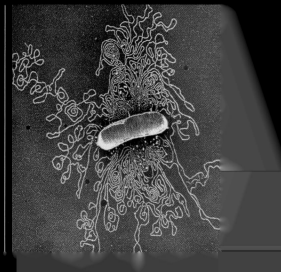

ADAPTING TO SURVIVE 1

THERE ARE MORE THAN TWO MILLION TYPES—
OR SPECIES—OF LIVING THINGS ON EARTH,
AND NO TWO ARE EXACTLY THE SAME. THAT
IS BECAUSE EACH ONE HAS FOLLOWED ITS
OWN PATH IN EVOLUTION AND DEVELOPED
DIFFERENT ADAPTATIONS FOR SURVIVAL.

If living things were perfectly equipped for their way of life, they would never need to change. But in nature nothing is ever perfect. Instead natural selection works all the time, giving a boost to any feature that helps in the struggle for survival. It has been doing this for over three billion years, so it has had plenty of time to come up with an amazing variety of adaptations. Wherever you look in the natural world, these adaptations exist. Some are eye-catching and easy to understand, but others are harder to spot and work in unexpected ways.

△ *The silversword plant has developed adaptations for life high up, where the sunlight can be intense. Because of these, silverswords can live in a habitat where few other plants are able to survive.*

LIGHT WORK
The ash-strewn slopes of a volcano and the swirling waters off a rocky coast could hardly be more different habitats—which is why their plants and animals have evolved in

▷ *Each one of a giant kelp's leafy fronds has a built-in, gas-filled float. The floats hold up the whole plant, which can be dozens of yards long.*

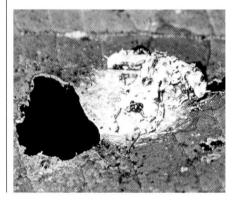

△ *Crouching on a leaf, this spider looks exactly like a bird dropping. This type of adaptation makes the spider less likely to be eaten.*

different ways. In the Hawaiian Islands the silversword plant grows on some of the highest volcanoes on Earth. Its leaves are covered with furlike hairs that keep it from being burned by the dazzling sunshine. But off the rocky coast of California, a seaweed called giant kelp has the opposite problem. To reach light it needs to grow up through 164 ft. (50m) of water. How does it do this? By forming gas-filled floats that keep the plant upright as it grows.

ANIMAL ADAPTATIONS

Evolution has been even more inventive in the animal world. Unlike plants, animals move, and they also eat food, so natural selection has been able to develop

△ *Aye-ayes use their unusual fingers to forage for food after dark. Like many highly specialized animals, they are easily harmed when humans interfere with their habitat.*

some very specialized adaptations for their different ways of life.

Our fingers are one example, as they allow us to pick up and hold things in numerous different ways. But when it comes to fingerwork, even we do not match up to the aye-aye—a strange-looking primate from the forests of Madagascar. Like us, the aye-aye has four fingers and a thumb. But the middle finger is much longer and thinner than the rest, and the aye-aye uses it like

△ *Protected by its portable armor, an armadillo takes a stroll. The armor is made up of small, bony plates that cover most of its body—except for its underside.*

a bony drumstick, tapping on branches as it climbs through trees. If the sound is promising, the aye-aye picks away the wood and pulls out insect grubs living inside.

HIDING AWAY

Natural selection has created many types of unusual body parts—from skinny fingers to mouthparts that work like harpoons. But it can work with entire bodies too. The animal world is full of species that are incredibly well camouflaged due to specially adapted body cases, shells, or skin. Some species blend in with their background, while others mimic something that is either inedible or dangerous to eat.

Animal camouflage can be amazingly convincing, but it is not too hard to work out how it evolves. If an animal is better at hiding than its relatives, it is less likely to be spotted and eaten, so it will leave more young. In the next generation the best camouflaged animals will also be best at surviving. Repeated thousands or millions of times, this process has created the extraordinary disguises that animals have today.

ANIMAL ARMOR

Over the history of life, armored animals have evolved many times. Today they include animals such as pangolins, armadillos, and tortoises.

In the past they included much bigger species, such as glyptodonts, which were built like living tanks. Because animal armor has evolved so often, scientists say there is a strong selection for it. In other words this is an adaptation that gives an animal a very good chance of success.

But unlike armor, some animal adaptations are shown by only a few species, or even just one. The aye-aye's fingers are one example, and so are the shells of mollusks called piddocks. The shells have sharpened edges, and a piddock uses them like a drill bit to bore a tunnel through wood or rock. Humans use drills all the time, but as the piddock shows, nature got there first.

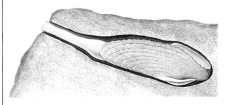

△ *Piddocks filter their food from seawater, and they use their sharp-edged shells to drill themselves a safe home. An adult piddock cannot leave its burrow because its shell is wider than the entrance.*

ADAPTING TO SURVIVE 2

ADAPTATIONS DO NOT ONLY
AFFECT THE WAY LIVING
THINGS LOOK. IN ANIMALS
SOME OF THE MOST IMPORTANT
ADAPTATIONS ARE ONES THAT
INVOLVE BEHAVIOR.

△ *Hibernation is an adaptation of behavior. It helps dormice survive through the winter, when food is scarce.*

Unlike longer legs or sharper teeth, behavior may not sound like an adaptation. You cannot pick it up and examine it, and it does not fossilize when animals die. But behavior can be inherited, which means it may change or evolve over time. This type of behavior is known as instinct, and it is programmed into an animal's genes. Like all other adaptations, instinct has developed over millions of years, and it helps animals survive.

FITTING IN
When animals first evolved, their behavior was extremely simple. They moved toward food and away from anything that might be dangerous. But as animals started becoming more complicated, their behavior became more complicated too. They evolved sense organs to find out about their surroundings and patterns of behavior that gave them the best chance of survival.

Millions of years later these patterns—or instincts—still control the way most animals live. Spiders rush toward struggling flies, but if they are threatened they head for somewhere dark. Honeybees fly toward the smell of flowers but away from the smell of smoke. In the fall many animals go into hibernation—a deep sleep that

▽ *Spiders use complicated behavior to spin their webs and catch prey. This orb weaver has caught an insect and has stopped it from struggling by wrapping it up in a bag of silk.*

lasts until the following spring. Animals do not have to learn this type of behavior because it comes built-in.

Just like other adaptations, behavior often reveals glimpses of a species' past. For example pet dogs often walk around in a circle before lying down—behavior inherited from their ancestors, which used it to flatten plants into a comfortable bed.

BEHAVIOR AND BODY PARTS
In the animal world behavior and body parts often evolve together.

▽ *A Weddell seal's breathing hole is its lifeline—without it survival is impossible. The seal starts the hole when the ice is shallow, but by the end of the winter it can be up to 6.6 ft. (2m) deep.*

△ *Beavers seem to understand a lot about dam building, but they work entirely by instinct. They can make a tree fall in exactly the right direction by chewing through the opposite side.*

Sometimes evolution creates new uses for standard animal equipment. This has happened with the Weddell seal. Its ancestors moved into the seas off of Antarctica around 15 million years ago, when the climate was much warmer than it is now. As Antarctica became colder, more and more of the sea became covered by winter ice. The Weddell seal survives in this frozen habitat because of its teeth, which it uses for gouging out breathing holes in the ice. Without this behavioral adaptation, most Weddell seals would die out.

BRANCHING OUT

Evolution also affects the way animals build. The first animals built nothing, but as time went by their descendants evolved special construction skills. Today's animals build many different shelters, nests, and traps—find out about some on pages 150–151. Just like body parts, these building skills have evolved as well. When birds first appeared, for example, they almost certainly laid their eggs on the ground—just like most reptiles do today. But as time went by and birds became more agile, some of them started nesting off of the ground. Today, over 100 million years later, birds include some of the best builders on Earth.

This makes a lot of sense because without the right behavior, many body parts would be no use at all. Complicated behavior controls legs and wings, but some of the most intricate types are used for catching food. Spiders, for example, use several different types of silk to make their webs, but they do not have to be taught which type goes where. When they make a catch they identify their prey by its movements, instinctively recognizing the difference between a fly and a wasp with a dangerous stinger.

▷ *Sometimes an animal's behavior allows it to make use of new opportunities. White storks originally nested in trees, but in Europe they often nest on rooftops. Many other birds— including swallows and swifts—nest inside of buildings.*

SHARED SOLUTIONS

IN THE LIVING WORLD SPECIES THAT LIVE IN SIMILAR WAYS OFTEN DEVELOP SIMILAR ADAPTATIONS. THIS CREATES SOME REMARKABLE LOOK-ALIKES—ONES EVEN SCIENTISTS MIX UP.

Take a close look at the two plants in the center of this page. Both have a barrel-like shape and are protected by spines. They both live in deserts and store water in their stems. Unless you are an expert on desert plants, you would think that they are close relatives. In fact they are very different. One is a cactus from Mexico, while the other is a baseball plant from southern Africa. They look the same because they have adapted to a very similar way of life.

△ *Mantis flies (top) and praying mantises (bottom) both have front legs that grab and stab prey, but they are not closely related. They have developed the same leg design separately through convergent evolution.*

NATURE'S COPYCATS

Like an inventor that never runs out of ideas, evolution is good at creating adaptations. It can even produce the same adaptation in two very different things. This usually happens when different species share a similar lifestyle, so that natural selection works on them in similar ways. The result is called convergent evolution— a gradual change that makes two species look more and more alike.

The cactus and the baseball plant are two examples of species that have "converged," even though they live thousands of miles apart. Their rounded shape helps them conserve water, while their spines keep hungry animals at bay. They have other similarities too—both have long roots, and neither grows leaves. Together these adaptations help them survive in a habitat that can be dry for months at a time.

▽ *The baseball plant (top) and the golden barrel cactus (below) are amazingly alike. But the baseball plant comes from southern Africa—a part of the world where wild cacti do not exist. It is short and squat, but some of its relatives from wetter places grow into scrubs and trees.*

HIDDEN HISTORIES

The world is full of convergent species— some are illustrated on these two pages. Many look only slightly similar, while others are close enough for people to confuse them. For example whales and dolphins look very much like fish because they have streamlined bodies and flippers instead of legs. Several hundred years ago most people thought they were all the same.

Deep down, however, convergent species are always different because they have evolved from different starting points. Fish are cold-blooded, and they breathe by collecting oxygen through gills.

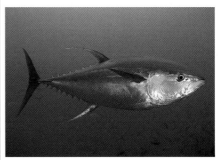

◁ *Limpets (left) and barnacles (right) both live in exposed places where they are often pounded by the waves. Limpets are protected by a shell, but barnacles have a case made up of separate plates. Although it is not built like a shell, the barnacle case does the same job.*

But the ancestors of whales and dolphins were warm-blooded land mammals that moved into the sea. Over millions of years these mammals adapted to their new habitat, and they gradually developed a fishlike shape.

But evolution could not hide their past. That is why whales and dolphins still raise their young on milk and why they come to the surface to breathe air.

CAUSING CONFUSION

Convergent evolution can create problems when scientists try to classify living things. It is not too difficult to work out that a dolphin is a mammal, but some look-alikes are more convincing than this. For example barnacles spend their adult lives attached to rocks, and they have pointed shells that protect them from the waves. They look like mollusks, and early naturalists believed that was what they were. However young barnacles start life in the open sea, and they have many legs. A closer look shows that barnacles are actually crustaceans—in other words relatives of lobsters and crabs.

Things get even more tricky when related species evolve in the same way, as they have a lot in common to begin with. To unravel their ancestry, scientists cannot rely on appearances—instead they often track the path of evolution by looking at their DNA.

CONVERGENCE PAST AND PRESENT

Today's look-alikes are only part of the story, as convergent evolution has been at work for a very long time. In prehistory animals called pyrotheres looked very similar to elephants, while further back in time reptiles called placodonts looked just like turtles because they developed the same rounded, scale-covered shells. But some of

the best examples of convergence occur in pouched mammals, or marsupials. Saber-toothed marsupials from South America looked just like saber-toothed cats, and marsupials called borhyaenids looked amazingly similar to wolves and bears. The most recent of these

△ *A dolphin (top) and a tuna (below) both have streamlined, muscle-packed bodies, and both feed on fish in open water. But dolphins are relative newcomers to life in the sea. The fact that they breathe air shows that their ancestors once lived on land.*

carnivorous look-alikes died out in the 1930s. Called the Tasmanian wolf, or thylacine, this unusual animal was the largest marsupial predator to survive into modern times. To see what it looked like, turn the page.

EXTINCTION

When something dies, its descendants usually live on. But when the last member of a species dies out, that species vanishes forever. Extinction is a natural part of evolution, and extinct species outnumber living ones by roughly one hundred to one.

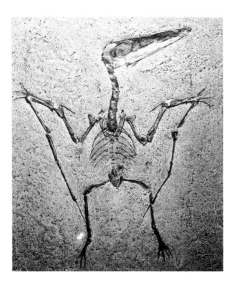

△ *For over 130 million years pterosaurs were the world's largest flying animals, with wingspans of up to 39 ft. (12m). Despite conquering the skies, these leathery-winged reptiles died out at the same time as the dinosaurs, around 66 million years ago.*

During the history of life on Earth, millions of species have evolved, and millions have become extinct. Extinction is normally a slow process, so there is plenty of time for new species to evolve. But occasionally huge numbers of species die out together when disasters or climate change strike. Today extinction is a hot topic because human activities are making species extinct at an ever-increasing rate.

FINAL EXITS

In the early 1800s the thylacine was a common animal. This wolflike marsupial lived in Tasmania, where it fed on wallabies, birds, and other wild prey. But when farming began on the island, thylacines developed a taste for sheep. Farmers fought back to protect their flocks, and by the 1880s thylacines were becoming rare.

▽ *Although thylacines have vanished forever, we have a good idea of what they looked like. Some were stuffed and put in museums. One was even recorded on film.*

By 1933 the situation reached a crisis point. The thylacine population was down to one—an animal in Hobart Zoo. When this sole survivor died three years later, Tasmania's marsupial "wolf" became extinct.

In North America the passenger pigeon suffered an even more dramatic fate. In 1810 it was the world's most numerous bird—one single flock was estimated to contain two billion birds. These gigantic flocks migrated across the continent to feed, and when the pigeons roosted or nested their weight could bring branches crashing to the ground. But passenger pigeons made easy targets, and large-scale hunting soon began. The last known specimen died in 1914.

◁ *Before they were wiped out, passenger pigeons mainly fed on acorns and nested in giant colonies up to 19 mi. (30km) across.*

These two stories show how easy it is for a species to die out. The thylacine and passenger pigeon were both well adapted and had existed for hundreds of thousands of years. But evolution could not prepare them for a new enemy— humans carrying guns.

FADING OUT

In nature it is very rare for species to die out as quickly as this. Instead they normally go into a slow decline, which gives better-adapted species time to take their place. In the

Clustered around a female, male golden toads fight for the chance to mate. This photograph was taken in the 1980s in the Monteverde cloud forest of Costa Rica. A few years later the species mysteriously disappeared.

MASS EXTINCTIONS

Two possible explanations for why the golden toad vanished are disease and water pollution. But every so often hugely catastrophic events have wiped out a large slice of the living world. The most famous of these mass extinctions occurred around 66 million years ago, when a 6-mi. (10-km) -wide meteorite slammed into Earth. Dinosaurs and pterosaurs died out completely, creating new opportunities for mammals and birds.

A greater mass extinction took place around 245 million years ago. Almost three fourths of the world's species disappeared. This extinction was probably caused by several factors, including volcanic eruptions, climate change, and a record drop in sea levels. Life eventually recovered, but it took millions of years.

Despite the ever-present threat of extinction, the living world harbors some surprising survivors. Scientists were stunned to discover a living coelacanth (see page 40) in 1938, as this fish was believed to have been extinct for millions of years. In the plant world a tree called the dawn redwood was discovered in 1944—another example of an "extinct" species coming back to life.

[Image of dawn redwood tree]

△ *The dawn redwood was discovered by a forestry official in a remote part of China in the 1940s. Since then examples of this "living fossil" have been successfully grown in parks all over the world.*

elephant family, for example, dozens of different species have evolved and become extinct over the past 50 million years. They included giant mammoths, mastodonts, and dwarf elephants just 3.3 ft. (1m) high. The most recent elephantine extinction involved the woolly mammoth, which died out only 6,000 years ago. It evolved during the last ice age but did not manage to adapt when warmer times returned.

Species that live in small areas are especially at risk if life gets tough or if humans change their habitat. This is what happened to the dodo, a giant flightless pigeon from the island of Mauritius. It was hunted by human settlers, and its young were eaten by introduced animals such as cats. It became extinct in 1681. Species that live on "islands" inland can also suffer. In Costa Rica, for example, the golden toad lived in one small patch of forest high up in the mountains. During the breeding season hundreds of toads used to gather in forest pools, but in the early 1990s the species disappeared.

▷ *This chart shows how extinction rates have varied over the past 545 million years. Not all mass extinctions happened quickly— some probably took tens or even hundreds of thousands of years. Species in the sea were often hit harder than ones on land.*

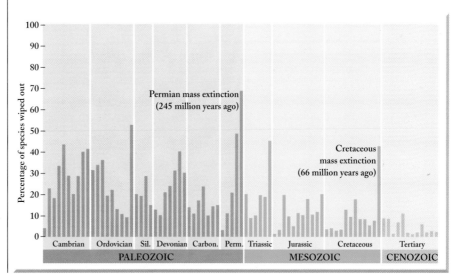

Percentage of species wiped out

Permian mass extinction (245 million years ago)

Cretaceous mass extinction (66 million years ago)

| Cambrian | Ordovician | Sil. | Devonian | Carbon. | Perm. | Triassic | Jurassic | Cretaceous | Tertiary |

PALEOZOIC · MESOZOIC · CENOZOIC

WILDLIFE UNDER THREAT

TODAY'S PLANTS AND ANIMALS LIVE IN A FAST-CHANGING WORLD. THERE ARE MORE PEOPLE THAN BEFORE, AND WE ARE HAVING AN EVER-INCREASING EFFECT ON OTHER LIVING THINGS. AS A RESULT MANY SPECIES ARE FINDING IT HARD TO SURVIVE.

Fifty years ago there were probably 100,000 black rhinos in Africa. Today there are around 3,000. In 1900 there were eight different subspecies of tigers. Today there are only five. Altogether over 5,000 types of animals are in serious danger of extinction, with at least as many plants. Numbers like this make difficult reading. They explain why many people are concerned about the world's wildlife—and why we need to act urgently.

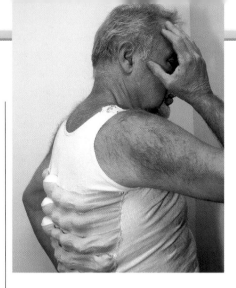

△ *An Australian customs agent demonstrates an undershirt that has been specially adapted for smuggling parrot eggs. The shirt keeps the eggs warm during their journey overseas.*

▽ *Every year millions of sea horses are caught, dried out, and then exported to the Far East. They are easy to catch, and many tropical species are disappearing fast.*

△ *In England the swallowtail butterfly once thrived in marshy places. But when marshes were drained to make way for fields, the swallowtail began to decline.*

▽ *Harpy eagles eat monkeys and sloths. They can survive only in undisturbed tropical forests with tall nesting trees.*

SHRINKING HOMES

The greatest threat facing wildlife is habitat change. Forests are cut down, marshlands are drained, and open spaces are covered by buildings and roads. One third of Earth's surface has already been changed in this way, and more is swallowed up every year.

All across the world changes like this have hit animals and plants. Small animals, such as butterflies, are easily harmed by habitat change, but the real losers are animals like the harpy eagle, which need an immense amount of space.

Harpy eagles are huge birds, and each breeding pair needs up to 98 sq. mi. (250 sq km) of forest to find enough food. At a time when tropical forests are being cut down, that much space is not easy to find.

THE WILDLIFE TRADE

People, as well as animals and plants, need living space. As the human population increases, we will need even more farmland to grow enough food. But habitat change is not the only problem facing the world's animals—many species are also targeted by the wildlife trade. Sometimes the victims are living animals, which are sold as performing animals or pets. But more often the trade is in body parts, which include many different things—from horns and bones to skins and eggs.

At one time spotted cats were high on the list of targets because their fur was in demand for making coats. Fortunately fur is not as fashionable now, but the demand for body parts still claims millions of animal lives every year. Black rhinos are killed for their horns, while elephants are hunted for their ivory. Tiger bones, bear paws, sea horses, and snakes are all used in oriental medicine. Birds' eggs are bought by collectors who are more interested in eggs than in living birds. Most of these trades are illegal, but high prices on the black market make them hard to prevent.

ANIMAL INVADERS

Poachers and collectors are usually aware that they are breaking the law. But wildlife can also be harmed accidentally when people move plants or animals between different parts of the world. This is what happened in Australia when European settlers introduced cats, rabbits, and foxes around 200 years ago. These mammalian invaders spread quickly, and they had a devastating impact on small marsupials in Australia.

Many nonnative animals are introduced deliberately, but some

▷ *On the island of Borneo, a wildlife worker looks after a baby orangutan. The orangutan's mother was killed when her forest home was set on fire.*

species hitch a ride instead. In North America one of the most problematic is a small, striped mollusk called the zebra mussel, which arrived from Europe in 1985. It traveled on board a ship heading for the Great Lakes, and it was flushed out when the ship emptied its ballast tanks. Since then zebra mussels have managed to spread throughout the Great Lakes, clogging up the intakes of power plants, sinking buoys, and swamping the feeding grounds of fish. If they spread much further, scientists believe that several types of freshwater fish could eventually become extinct.

ENDANGERED PLANTS

Compared to animals, plants do not often hit the headlines, but many of them are endangered too. If anything, they are even more important because animals often rely on particular plants for their food. Plants are threatened by being cut down or collected, and they can be at risk from other plants as well. In remote places, such as the Hawaiian Islands, introduced plants are a beautiful but deadly menace. Over 95 percent of Hawaii's native plants are found nowhere else in the world, but already some are on the verge of extinction, as green invaders take over their homes.

▷ *Dark areas show the black rhino's range today compared with its range in 1900 (light purple).*

◁ *Wildlife rangers examine the body of a black rhino that has been killed by poachers. The poachers started to cut off the rhino's horn but were disturbed before they finished.*

BACK FROM THE BRINK

WHEN A SPECIES IS ON THE EDGE OF EXTINCTION, EMERGENCY ACTION CAN SOMETIMES SAVE IT FROM OBLIVION. IT IS DEMANDING WORK, BUT RESCUE PROJECTS ARE NEVER SHORT OF VOLUNTEERS.

△ *Once common, prairie dogs now depend on human protection for survival.*

△ *Two Japanese cranes dance on a frozen lake. Japan's national bird, the crane almost died out in the 1950s, when most of its wetland habitat disappeared. Today special refuges help it survive.*

In 1980 there were just five Chatham Island black robins left on Earth. Fortunately the single female turned out to be good at laying eggs. Today Chatham Island robins number around 250 birds, so for now at least the species has survived its knife-edge scrape with extinction. No other animal has come back from such an all-time low, but many species are down to a few dozen or a few hundred animals. When populations become this small, great care is needed to bring them back from the brink.

△ *A wildlife worker helps baby turtles on their way to the sea. By raising turtle eggs in special hatcheries, many more of their young are able to survive.*

LAST CHANCE
Today almost 200 species of birds are classified as critically endangered. Cranes, ibis, and eagles all feature high on the list, but one of the rarest species—and certainly the strangest— is a parrot called the kakapo. Kakapos live in New Zealand, and they are the only flightless parrots in the world. Unfortunately their ground-based lifestyle makes them easy prey for stoats and cats, which eat their young and eggs.

In the 1970s the kakapo appeared to be doomed. A handful of birds were collected and kept in captivity, but none survived. During the 1980s all surviving kakapos were transferred to offshore islands that were free from introduced mammals so that the birds could live without the threat of attack. The gamble seems to have worked, because after several ups and downs the total population now stands at around 80. But everyone who works with kakapos knows that they are still not in the clear. For a species to be really safe, it needs to be able to survive on its own.

△ *Gripped by its neck and feet, an adult kakapo is given a checkup. Although they cannot fly, kakapos are good climbers. They use their beaks and toes to clamber into scrubs and trees.*

▷ *Pandas often give birth to twins, but it is rare for both of them to survive.*

very difficult to breed in captivity—scientists have been trying to improve their success rate for over 40 years.

Today there are a few hundred giant pandas in the wild in China and around 150 in captivity. Many have been loaned to foreign zoos in the hope of breeding young. Because pandas are popular, this also helps raise funds. But some specialists think that the best way to conserve pandas is to protect their habitat so that they can live and breed in the wild.

PROBLEMATIC PANDAS

Saving species can involve some difficult decisions. Moving kakapos might have harmed them rather than helped, which is why the operation had to be taken step by step. With other critically endangered species, another tactic is to breed animals in captivity so that they can eventually be released. In some cases this has been a big success. For example there are now almost 200 California condors, compared with 27 in the 1980s. But not all animals deal well with life in zoos. Giant pandas are

WINNERS AND LOSERS

Whales have a special place in the story of wildlife conservation. For hundreds of years they were ruthlessly hunted—between 1904 and 1939 over half a million blue, fin, and humpback whales were killed in the Southern Hemisphere alone.

But as whale stocks plunged, whaling quotas were agreed. Finally in 1986 a complete ban on commercial whaling came into force. Since then the world's largest whales have started to recover, prompting disagreements about what to do next. Many countries feel that whales should be granted permanent protection, but some are pressing for whaling to be resumed. For some species, however, the ban may have come too late. The northern right whale, for example, is down to around 300 whales. Because whales breed very slowly, most experts doubt that it will survive.

WORLDWIDE WORK

Most people are concerned about endangered mammals and birds. But threatened wildlife also includes many less glamorous species, such as snails, earwigs, and ferns. All over the world conservationists are working to protect these animals and plants, even though their efforts often go unnoticed. So why do they do it? The answer is because they are a part of nature, just like all species on Earth. Conservation is not only about protecting the species that we like or those that look good on television. Instead it is about protecting the entire natural world.

▽ *Visitors come face to face with a gray whale off the coast of northwest Mexico. Gray whales were given protection in 1946. Since then their population has risen to more than 20,000.*

Magnified over 20,000 times, these bacteria look harmless, but they can cause a dangerous lung infection called Legionnaire's disease. No one knows where this bacteria lives in the wild, but it thrives in water tanks and air-conditioning units, and it spreads to people when contaminated droplets get into the air. Fortunately, outbreaks of the disease are rare.

PART 2
THE LIVING WORLD

KINGDOMS OF LIFE

TO MAKE SENSE OF THE NATURAL WORLD, SCIENTISTS CLASSIFY
LIVING THINGS INTO GROUPS. THE SMALLEST GROUPS
ARE SPECIES. THE LARGEST, CALLED KINGDOMS,
ARE THE ULTIMATE "DEPARTMENTS" OF LIFE.

During the early days of science most naturalists believed that all living things were either animals or plants. But when microscopic life was discovered, it became clear that life is much more varied than this and that two kingdoms were not enough. Since then the number of kingdoms has expanded to five, but even this may not be the end of the story.

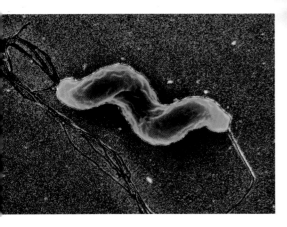

◁ *Many bacteria spend their lives attached to one place, but some can glide or swim. This spiral-shaped swimmer is* Campylobacter jejuni, *a bacterium that causes food poisoning in humans.*

▷ *Magnified over 600 times, this intricate object is the skeleton of a radiolarian. Radiolarians are protists that live in the sea. They use sticky threads to trap their microscopic prey.*

SMALL-SCALE LIFE

The world's smallest living things are bacteria. They are simpler than all other kinds of life, which is one of the reasons why they are classified into a kingdom of their own. Each one has a single cell containing only the bare essentials needed for staying alive. Around this is a tough wall that protects the cell from the outside world. Compared to other organisms, bacteria are not diverse, but they are incredibly abundant. Together they greatly outnumber all other living things on Earth.

The next kingdom, called the protists, also contains microscopic life along with some species that can be seen with the naked eye. Like bacteria, most protists have only a single cell, but theirs are more complicated and contain a range of different working parts, just like our cells. Protists usually live in the water, and some behave like tiny

▷ *Some fungi grow mushrooms and toadstools when they reproduce and are easy to see. But many others are microscopic and spread invisibly through their food.*

◁ *Plants are vital for life because they create food that other living things can eat. Some plants—like this barrel cactus—can survive without rain for months at a time.*

THE WORLD OF ANIMALS

The last of the five kingdoms contains all of the world's animals— a wide-ranging collection of living things with varied lifestyles. Like plants, animals contain many cells, but they need food to survive. Animal diets are almost as varied as the animals themselves. Many eat plants or other animals, but the animal kingdom also includes a host of scavengers and recyclers that live

△ *Two fake "eyes" make this moth caterpillar look a lot more dangerous than it is. Tricks like this are common in the animal kingdom, where animals run the risk of ending up as something else's prey.*

animals, while others are like miniature plants. Over 100,000 species have been discovered, and they are so varied that some scientists think that they should be classified into several kingdoms instead of just one.

FUNGI AND PLANTS

The next two kingdoms contain fungi and plants—living things that seem to have a lot in common. Most of them sprout out of the ground, and all of them spread by scattering spores or seeds. But fungi and plants are actually very different from each other. Fungi live by digesting substances around them, while plants do not need food at all. Plants collect energy directly by soaking up sunshine through their leaves. Scientists have identified over 100,000 kinds of fungi, but the plant kingdom contains at least 400,000 species and probably many more.

◁ *No one knows exactly how many species there are on Earth, but this chart shows how many have been identified so far. Animals make up the biggest slice by far because they have evolved into so many different ways of life.*

on nature's leftovers and on dead remains. Many living things can move, but animals move farther and faster than anything else. Some animals spend almost all their lives in one place, but most move around to find food. They crawl, run, fly, or swim through every habitat on Earth, using an amazing assortment of body parts—from muscular suckers and jointed legs to fins and feathery wings. Around two million species of animals have been found so far. Many scientists think the total could be five or ten times that number.

Plants 400,000

Fungi 100,000

Protists 100,000

Bacteria 10,000

Animals 2,000,000

CLASSIFYING LIVING THINGS

OVER THE NEXT 25 YEARS A TEAM OF SCIENTISTS IS PLANNING TO DRAW UP A DATABASE OF ALL THE WORLD'S LIVING THINGS. IT IS A GIANT TASK BECAUSE NO ONE KNOWS JUST HOW MANY SPECIES THERE ARE.

△ *By comparing DNA from different species, scientists can see how closely they are related. This chemical evidence helps in piecing together how different species have evolved.*

Long before science even existed, people recognized that living things fall into different groups. Birds, for example, have feathers and wings, while insects usually have six legs. Scientific classification continues this type of work but in a much more precise and orderly way. Once something has been classified, scientists can see how it is related to similar species and where it belongs in the living world.

FINDING A NAME

When a new species is discovered, scientists compare it with already known species to make sure it is a genuine new discovery. If it passes this test, the next step is to give it a scientific name. Unlike everyday names, scientific names are written in Latin, and they have two parts. The first part is the name of a genus—or group of species—to which the new discovery belongs. The second name identifies the species itself. For example the North American swift fox is called *Vulpes velox*. The first part of this name means "fox," while the second part means "fast."

Names like this sometimes look long and complicated, but they have

◁ *There are at least 20,000 species of crickets and grasshoppers and probably many more. This museum collection shows just some of the species that live in the rain forests of Central America.*

several big advantages. One is that they are unique, so two different species can never get mixed up. Secondly they can be recognized by scientists all over the world, whatever language they speak. The third advantage is that they work like signposts, showing how living things are related. This is easy to see using the Internet: search for the word *Vulpes*, and links to all the world's typical foxes will appear. In the plant world the name *Quercus* produces links to all the world's oak trees.

LIFE'S FILING SYSTEM

Scientific names are like fingerprints because no two species share the same one. But classification does not stop there. Individual species are organized into larger groups that work like folders containing computer files. The first folder is the genus, and the next one up

is called a family. After this come order, class, and phylum folders and finally, the top folder—a kingdom. Some folders contain just one single species, but the insect folder holds at least 800,000.

This filing system is very important because it shows how closely different species are related. If two species are in the same folder, that means they have shared the same ancestors at some point in the past. In other words they have evolved from the same branch of the living world.

CHANGING TRACK

If scientists could see back into the past, they would be able to classify all the species in the world in exactly the right way. But as this is not possible they have to work with different types of evidence, including fossils and the features of living things. Classification is updated all the time as the evidence is examined and new discoveries are made.

MICROLIFE

MORE THAN 99 PERCENT OF EARTH'S LIVING
THINGS ARE INVISIBLE TO THE NAKED HUMAN EYE.
TOGETHER THEY MAKE UP THE CROWDED
AND BUSTLING WORLD OF MICROLIFE.

Without help the smallest things that the human eye can see are around 0.2mm across—that's around one fifth of the width of an average human hair. This may seem small to us, but it is actually much bigger than many living things. These miniature life-forms are known as microbes or microorganisms. Some microorganisms are just barely visible, while others are so small that they can only be seen if they are magnified more than one thousand times. But small does not always mean simple, and microorganisms include some surprisingly complex creatures as well as the most basic living things on Earth.

WHO'S WHO

There are microorganisms in all of the kingdoms of the living world, and micro size is often the only thing they have in common. As a rule bacteria are the smallest and most numerous of them all, followed by larger, single-celled

▽ *Amoebas live in watery habitats, and the largest ones can be almost 1mm long. In theory these can be seen without a microscope, but because they are transparent they are actually very difficult to see.*

organisms known as protists. The microworld also contains microscopic fungi as well as thousands of species of microscopic animals and plants.

Although bacteria are the smallest living things, even smaller things sometimes show signs of life. These are viruses and viroids—packages of chemicals that survive by attacking living cells. Unlike other microorganisms, viruses and viroids cannot grow, and they cannot reproduce unless they manage to get inside a suitable host. For this reason—and several others—most scientists do not consider them to be fully alive.

A QUESTION OF SIZE

Where size is concerned, different kinds of microorganisms often overlap. For example the world's

smallest animals are much smaller than the largest bacteria, though they have complicated bodies with many moving parts. These animals are called rotifers, and they live in freshwater and the sea. Head-to-tail it would take over 5,000 of the tiniest species to stretch

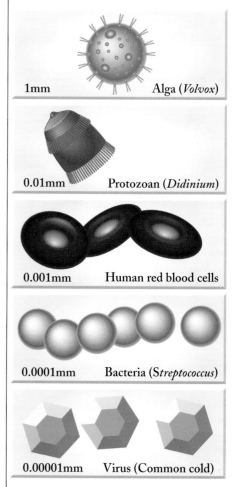

1mm   Alga (*Volvox*)

0.01mm   Protozoan (*Didinium*)

0.001mm   Human red blood cells

0.0001mm   Bacteria (*Streptococcus*)

0.00001mm   Virus (Common cold)

△ *This chart shows some average sizes of microorganisms and other living cells. From the top each step in the chart is ten times smaller than the one above it. Volvox is large enough to see with the naked eye.*

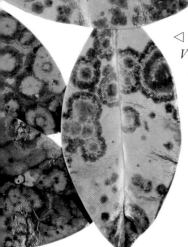

◁ The rings on these leaves are a sign of viral attack. Viruses are a serious problem for farmers and gardeners because they infect many types of plants. Some viruses simply weaken plants, but others eventually kill them.

across this page. At the other extreme some protozoans (animallike protists) are so big that they do not qualify as microorganisms at all. One of the bulkiest specimens alive today is a giant freshwater amoeba that can be easily seen with the naked eye. But even this is not a record because millions of years ago some single-celled protists managed to grow to the size of a grapefruit.

MICROHABITATS

One of the great advantages of being small is that the list of possible habitats is almost endless. Microorganisms are found in all of them. They find their way into the most remote and inaccessible places and into every part of human homes. In general most microorganisms live in the water or in places that are damp. One of their particular favorites is soil, especially when it contains plenty of dead remains. Other choice habitats are the moist surfaces and insides of larger living things. In animals these include skin, mouths, and teeth and also the entire alimentary canal—the tube that absorbs water and digests food.

For animals many of these microorganisms are harmless, while others are a positive help. Together they make up an animal's "microbial flora," which is the collection of microbes that lives on or in the animal when it is healthy. But microorganisms also include species that target living things and use them as food. These invaders are often pathogenic— in other words they cause diseases. Over millions of years animals in particular have developed defenses against these microattackers. Without these defenses they would soon be overrun.

LIVING IN THE MICROWORLD

For microorganisms the world is a very different place from the one that humans inhabit. For example gravity has almost no effect on them because there is so little for it to attract.

▷ Like ants on the surface of a space rocket, hundreds of bacteria are clinging onto the head of this pin. Bacteria like these often feed on microscopic patches of sweat left behind by human hands.

If a microorganism moves, it reaches full speed almost right away, but the moment it stops pushing it comes to an instant halt. On land microorganisms sometimes get blown into the air. Because they are so lightweight it can take days or weeks for them to come back to the ground. This means that it is difficult to keep anywhere completely microbe-free. In places where it really matters, such as operating rooms, the air is kept slightly pressurized to prevent any microbes from drifting inside.

MILLION-YEAR SLEEPERS

Microorganisms hardly ever build homes, and because they are small very little stands between them and the outside world. However many have a tough streak that helps them survive. They often cope with hard times by "shutting down," and they can do this for years on end. Some microanimals can stay dormant for ten years or more, but bacteria can do even better than this. In the right conditions their dormant spores can survive for millions of years—much longer than the entire history of the human species.

BACTERIA

FOR SHEER TOUGHNESS AND
ENDURANCE, BACTERIA BEAT ALL OTHER
FORMS OF LIFE. THEY EXIST IN EVERY
IMAGINABLE HABITAT—FROM HOT SPRINGS
AND DEEP-SEA MUD TO THE SURFACE OF HUMAN
TEETH. IN GOOD CONDITIONS THEY REPRODUCE
FASTER THAN ANYTHING ELSE ON EARTH.

△ *These* Clostridium *bacteria normally live harmlessly in the soil. However if they get into the human body, they can have deadly effects because they release one of the most powerful nerve poisons known.*

WHAT ARE BACTERIA?
Bacteria are the smallest fully living things and are also the most ancient forms of life on Earth. Each one consists of a single cell that is usually round, rod-shaped, or spiral.

Bacteria have a bad reputation because some types can cause diseases. But if bacteria disappeared overnight, most other living things—including ourselves—would soon find it very difficult to survive. This is because bacteria are nature's main recyclers. Many of them eat dead remains, and the warmer it is the faster they work. When they break down their food, they release nutrients that other living things need.

The cell has a tough wall, and it is often surrounded by a type of glue or by sticky hairs that help anchor it in place. To reproduce most bacteria simply divide in two. At top speed they can do this every 20 minutes, which means that a single bacterium can quickly turn into many millions of bacteria.

△ *These slender strands are formed by* Anabaena, *a cyanobacterium fueled by sunlight.* Anabaena *and its relatives collect nitrogen gas from the air, helping enrich or fertilize the soil.*

MAKING A LIVING
Compared to other forms of life, bacteria make their living in many different ways. Some get their energy from sunlight, while a few use chemicals from rocks— a trick that dates back to the

◁ *Individual bacteria are microscopic, but bacterial colonies can often be seen with the naked eye. This petri dish contains many colonies growing on a thin layer of nutrient-rich jelly.*

earliest days of life on Earth. But most bacteria absorb nutrients from dead matter, which can include anything from animal corpses to leftover food. Pathogenic bacteria are different because they invade living things. These invasions, called infections, often cause diseases.

VIRUSES

VIRUSES ARE THE SMALLEST THINGS THAT SHOW SOME SIGNS OF BEING ALIVE. THEY ARE MUCH SIMPLER THAN BACTERIA, AND THEY CAN ONLY SURVIVE WITH THE HELP OF OTHER LIVING THINGS. VIRUSES ARE GOOD AT SPREADING, AND THEY CAN BE DIFFICULT TO CONTROL.

Most viruses are much smaller than bacteria, and they are more like machines than living things. Instead of cells they have an exact number of chemical components that fit together in a specific way. Viruses do not eat or grow, and they cannot reproduce on their own. Instead they hijack living cells and force them to make copies of themselves. Viruses attack all kinds of hosts—including bacteria, plants, and animals—and many of them cause diseases.

INSIDE A VIRUS

Viruses are built like containers, and they carry an unusual cargo. This is a collection of genes— chemical instructions that build living things and make them work. Normally a virus' genes are switched off, but if the virus comes into

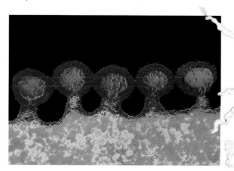

△ *Looking like a row of mushrooms, these human immunodeficiency viruses (HIV) are about to break out of their host cell. HIV causes AIDS—a disease that has swept the world in the last 20 years.*

contact with the right type of cell, that can quickly change.

First the virus inserts its genes into the cell, often leaving the empty container outside. The viral genes then switch on and begin taking

control. Within minutes the host cell stops its normal work and begins assembling viruses instead. Once these are complete, the cell often bursts, allowing the new viruses to escape. Viruses cannot move, so they rely on outside help to travel. Some are passed on by touch, while a few, including flu viruses, are passed on when people cough or sneeze.

△ *Tobacco mosaic viruses (TMV) look like slender rods. Each rod consists of a coil of protein molecules protecting a packet of genes that is hidden away inside.*

◁ *These bizarrely-shaped objects are bacteriophages, viruses that attack bacteria. They help keep bacteria in check.*

HALF ALIVE

Viruses are impossible to avoid, and most living things are attacked by them every day. Fortunately most viruses do little harm, but some can cause serious diseases. In humans these include yellow fever and AIDS. Exactly where viruses came from no one knows. One theory is that they are renegade genes that have managed to escape from living things and develop a "lifestyle" of their own.

The Grand Prismatic Spring in Yellowstone National Park gets its rainbow colors from cyanobacteria and other microbes. These bacteria live by collecting energy from the sunshine, and they are experts at coping with sizzling surroundings. The center of this giant pool is a piping-hot 187°F (86°C) because of volcanic heat from rocks below the surface of the ground.

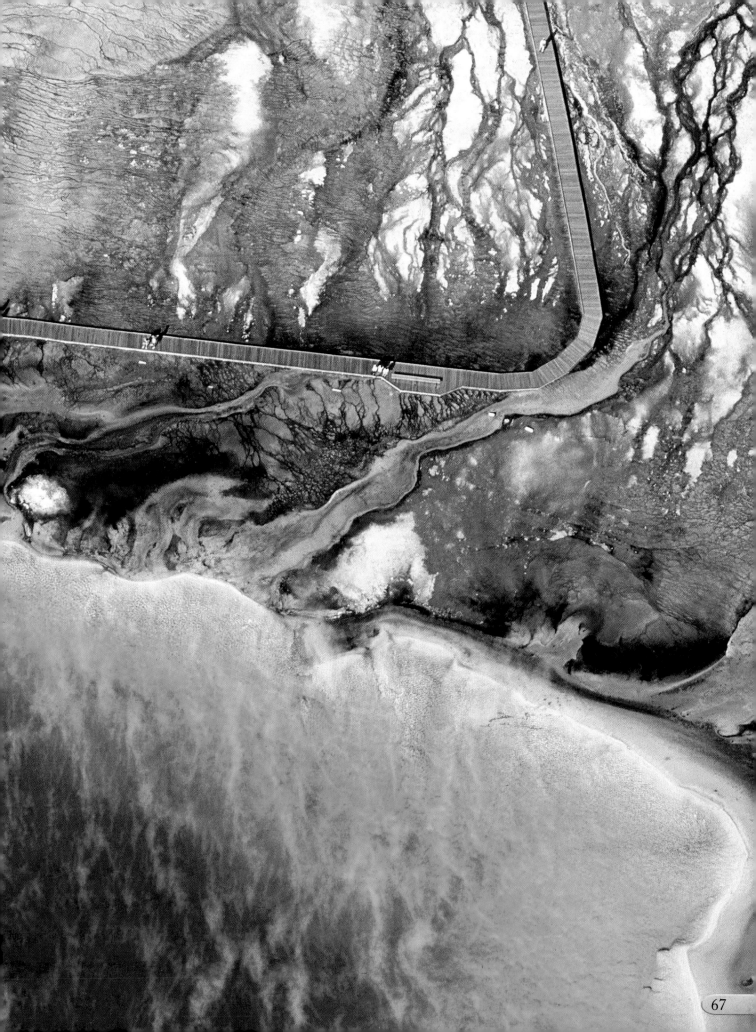

PROTOZOANS

DESPITE THEIR TINY SIZE, PROTOZOANS
INCLUDE SOME OF THE MOST VORACIOUS
PREDATORS ON EARTH. MOST PROTOZOANS
LIVE IN THE WATER, BUT SOME ARE FOUND
INSIDE OTHER LIVING THINGS.

Seen through a microscope, protozoans
often look like minute animals living
at breakneck speed. Many of them
swerve around obstacles and zoom away
from danger, and they quickly figure
out where there is a chance of finding
food. But protozoans are not animals,
and they do not have eyes, mouths, or
even brains. Instead they are protists—
microorganisms with just one single cell.
Unlike algae (pages 70–71), protozoans need
to eat, and they get their food in different ways.
Many are active predators and hunt for their
food, while others stay in one place and eat
anything edible that drifts nearby. Some form
partnerships with much larger living things,
but a few cause dangerous diseases.

Trichonympha, the hidden helper

Most plant-eating animals use
microorganisms to help them
digest their food. *Trichonympha*
is one of these hidden helpers.
It lives in the intestines of
cockroaches and termites,
and it eats tiny specks
of wood that its host has
swallowed. In return for this
food it produces energy-rich
chemicals that its host can
use. Without *Trichonympha*
most cockroaches and termites
would starve to death.

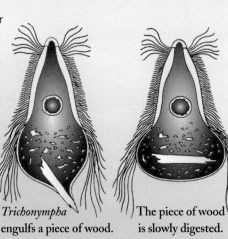

Trichonympha
engulfs a piece of wood.

The piece of wood
is slowly digested.

△ *Looking like a prickly sculpture, this
is the skeleton of a radiolarian—a protist
that lives in the sea. In a living radiolarian
jellylike threads reach out from the skeleton
and catch tiny creatures drifting nearby.*

LIFE ON THE MOVE

Protozoans are much too small to
have legs or fins, but they are still
amazingly good at getting around.
Amoebas move by changing shape,
a skill that is particularly useful for
squeezing through tight spaces such

times this speed. One of the fastest of all is *Paramecium*, a slipper-shaped organism that is covered with silky "fur." Unlike real fur, *Paramecium*'s hairs—called cilia—can move, beating in waves to speed this protozoan through its watery home. In fact *Paramecium* moves so quickly that it is hard to see under a microsocope unless a thickener is added to the water to slow it down.

PROTOZOAN PARTNERS

Most protozoans live in the sea or in watery habitats on land. They often form part of the plankton, which makes them important in food chains. But some live in a very different environment—the intestines of plant-eating animals. Here they help their host break down its food. These protozoans can be incredibly abundant: an elephant, for example, can have several billion of them living inside of its gigantic stomach.

Living inside an animal has many advantages. The protozoans have an almost nonstop supply of food, and they are kept safe and warm. But there is one important drawback: like water in a river, their food is always on the move, and the protozoans eventually get washed

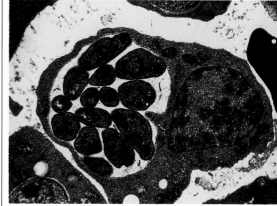

△ *This photograph shows a cluster of malaria parasites inside a human red blood cell. These parasites climb on top of mosquitoes, which suck them up when they eat blood.*

downstream. Many of them end up being digested by their host, but some pass out of its body unharmed.

PROTOZOAN PARASITES

Protozoan partners are useful to animals, but parasitic types are not. These unwelcome guests often live in water that animals drink, although some are injected by insects that eat blood. Protozoan parasites affect almost all wild animals, and many only cause minor harm. But they also include dangerous species such as the ones that cause malaria. This serious disease affects humans and many other mammals, as well as reptiles and birds.

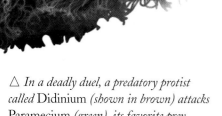

△ *In a deadly duel, a predatory protist called* Didinium *(shown in brown) attacks* Paramecium *(green), its favorite prey.* Didinium *can stretch like a balloon, allowing it to swallow prey even bigger than itself.*

as the gaps between particles of soil. When the amoeba has tracked down its prey, it flows around it and engulfs it—a process like being swallowed by living Jell-O™.

Even when the amoebas are in a hurry, they cannot travel faster than 0.8 in. (2cm) an hour. However in ponds and lakes some protozoans zip along at more than 30 or 40

▷ *Slime mold amoebas are some of the strangest inhabitants of the microworld. They spend most of their lives on their own, but they gather together to reproduce. Over 50,000 amoebas may join together to form a "slug" (right) that slowly creeps across the ground. When a slime mold "slug" finds a suitable spot, it begins to change shape. Some of the amoebas form a slender stalk, while the ones on the top of the stalk make spores (far right). Eventually the spores are scattered into the air. When they land, they hatch into new amoebas, and the cycle begins again.*

ALGAE

WHEREVER THERE IS WATER AND SUNLIGHT, ALGAE MAKE THEMSELVES AT HOME. THESE MICROPLANTS MAY BE SMALL, BUT THEY ARE SO NUMEROUS THAT THEY CAN SOMETIMES BE SEEN FROM SPACE.

△ *Volvox is a freshwater alga that lives in ponds. Shaped like a hollow ball, it contains many cells together with "babies" that swim around inside of it. The parent colony eventually breaks open to release the babies.*

Most algae are tiny green specks of living matter that drift in open water. They are simpler than real plants, but they live in the same way by soaking up energy from sunshine. Although they are small, algae are vital for water life because they make food that animals need to survive.

GOING GREEN

Long before true plants first appeared on Earth, algae were already flourishing in rivers, lakes, and seas. Today they thrive in many artificial habitats as well—from ponds and ditches to bottles filled with rain. In ideal conditions they can multiply very rapidly, turning the water bright green.

Algae belong to the protist kingdom, and most of them have a single cell. But unlike protozoans, algal cells often stick together to form groups called colonies. Algal colonies can look like microscopic space stations, stacks of miniature coins, or even mats of slimy hair.

MAKING BABIES

Algae do not have flowers, and none of them makes seeds. Instead the smallest ones often reproduce by dividing in two. This breeding technique is quick and efficient, and it boosts their numbers in record time. Algae divide most rapidly in the spring when the days are bright and long. This results in millions of tons of extra food that fish and other animals can use.

The bigger the algae the more cells they contain, and the harder this dividing technique becomes. To get around this problem, larger algae reproduce by making spores. Spores are like seeds, but they are much smaller, and they can drift far away through water or through the air. One ball-shaped alga, called *Volvox*, behaves like a floating nursery. It contains miniature "babies" that swim around inside of it until they are ready to begin living on their own.

△ *Green pond scum is often formed by* Spirogyra, *an alga whose cells grow in slender threads. Each cell contains a spiral band that collects energy from sunlight.*

ALGAE ON THE MOVE

Algae may be simple, but they have one remarkable talent: many of the smallest types can swim.

These micromovers swim in the same way as protozoans by beating tiny hairs to drive them through the water. They are too small to swim far, but they can propel themselves to where the light is the brightest. Because bright light means more energy, this simple reflex helps them thrive.

Many algae also have built-in floats that often come in the form of microscopic bubbles of oil. These floats keep them drifting near the surface—the best place to bathe in the Sun. Together these surface drifters make up the phytoplankton, a nutritious soup that protozoans and animals use as food.

LIVING IN A CASE

Most algae have tough cell walls, but some are also protected by a case. These cases are extremely small, but they include some of the most intricate and beautiful

△ Many diatoms are flat, but this species—called Campylodiscus—*has a built-in twist. In some parts of the ocean the empty cases of dead diatoms form layers of ooze that are many feet deep.*

Dinoflagellates: dangerous drifters of the seas

Most algae are quite harmless, but one group—called dinoflagellates—includes some of the most lethal organisms afloat. Many of them produce powerful poisons that can kill anything nearby. When conditions are good, billions of dinoflagellates can build up in warm water along shallow coasts, forming swarms called red tides. As well as poisoning animals directly, red tides suffocate fish and seabed life when their algae die and rot away.

Dinoflagellates are often armor-plated, and some species have sharp spines. In *Ceratium*, which is shown here, the spines are extra long, making the alga harder for animals to swallow. Like all dinoflagellates, *Ceratium* swims by beating two long hairs. One of the hairs pushes it along while the other one makes it revolve—like a microscopic bullet spinning through the sea.

objects in the microworld. One group of algae, called diatoms, makes cases that have two almost equal halves. One half fits tightly over the other like a box with a snap-on lid.

Diatoms build their cases from silica, the same substance that is used to make glass. But instead of heating the silica and then shaping it, they simply grow it into the

▽ Seaweeds often live in the zone between the tides where they have to withstand dry air as well as pounding waves.

right shape. Diatoms collect silica from the water around them, and they are incredibly good at gathering it up. Sometimes there is less than one part of silica to every million parts of water, but diatoms still manage to collect what they need.

OCEAN GIANTS

The algal world also includes some species that definitely do not qualify as microlife. These are seaweeds—algae that look like plants. Unlike real plants seaweeds do not have roots or leaves. Instead they keep themselves in place with a holdfast—which often looks like a rubbery clamp—and they absorb sunshine through their leathery fronds.

Some seaweeds are quite delicate, but others are amazingly strong. Called wracks and kelps, they live on stormy coasts where they have to withstand the pounding waves.

Seaweeds can be just a few inches tall, but some are many feet long. The longest of all is giant kelp, which grows along the west coast of North America. This huge seaweed is one of the fastest-growing living things on Earth. The record depth for a seaweed is 880 ft. (268m). At this depth sunlight is 500,000 times weaker than at the surface.

FUNGI

WHEN PEOPLE THINK OF FUNGI, MUSHROOMS AND TOADSTOOLS ARE USUALLY THE FIRST THINGS THAT COME TO MIND. BUT THESE COLORFUL, EYE-CATCHING OBJECTS ARE JUST A SMALL PART OF THE FUNGAL WORLD.

△ *These mushrooms have sprouted from a fungus that lives in the ground. They enable the fungus to spread while the underground part of it concentrates on collecting food.*

After bacteria and protists fungi are the most common living things on Earth. Most of them are microscopic, but they also include the largest single organisms that scientists have ever found. They live in all of Earth's habitats—from forests and deserts to the bottom of the sea—and they even form part of the teeming microworld that flourishes on human skin. Unlike plants, fungi can grow in the dark, but they need food to survive. Most eat dead leftovers, but some have a taste for living things. Despite this fungi often go unnoticed, and very few have everyday names. That is because most of them live inside their food and only become visible when they reproduce.

NATURE'S MISFITS

The reproductive parts of fungi include some of the strangest objects in the living world. Mushrooms and toadstools are odd enough, but other fungi look like nests, tufts of hair, or almost perfect replicas of human ears. They often sprout from the ground or from trees, and their job is to spread a fungus' spores.

Hundreds of years ago naturalists thought that these objects were plants, even though they do not have leaves. But since then scientists have made a remarkable discovery: far from being plants, fungi are more closely related to animals instead.

△ *The red cage fungus produces sticky spores on the inside of its struts. Flies are attracted by its strong smell, and they carry the spores away on their feet.*

FEEDING THREADS

There is no such thing as a typical fungus because they come in so many different sizes and shapes. But fungi all have one thing in common—they survive by absorbing food. Unlike

△ *Orange peel fungus often sprouts on gravelly soil. Its eye-catching color makes it very difficult to overlook.*

animals, fungi do not swallow food and then digest it. They do things the other way around. A fungus digests its food immediately and then soaks up the nutrients that are released. The structures that do this work are minute threads called hyphae, which spread throughout a fungus' food.

△ *Bird's-nest fungus, which is only 0.02 in. (5mm) across, produces clusters of spores that look like tiny eggs. When it rains the raindrops fall into the nest, throwing the "eggs" up to 3.3 ft. (1m) into the air.*

▷ *Yeast are microscopic fungi that consist of single cells. This is baker's yeast—the species that is used in the production of wine and beer and to make dough rise.*

Hyphae can be incredibly fine, but they can spread for amazing distances. They often reach from the ground right to the tops of trees, and they form immense networks in the soil. Some wood-eating fungi can even spread from house to house all the way down a street.

DRUGS AND POISONS

Some fungi are good to eat, but others contain foul-tasting chemicals or even deadly poisons. It takes skill and experience to tell which is which because safe and dangerous species sometimes look alike. Stranger still, being poisonous does not "run in the family" because some groups of fungi contain both safe and dangerous types. The world's most poisonous fungus is a species called the death cap, which lives in woodlands across the northern hemisphere. Death caps look a lot like edible mushrooms, but each one of them contains enough poison to kill an adult human being. To make matters worse, death cap poisons—called amatoxins—take up to 12 hours to start working. By the time someone starts to feel sick it is often too late to save

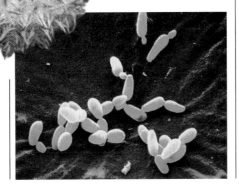

them. But strangely enough fungi that are poisonous to humans are often harmless to other animals. Slugs, for example, love toadstools, and they eat many poisonous kinds without suffering from any problems at all.

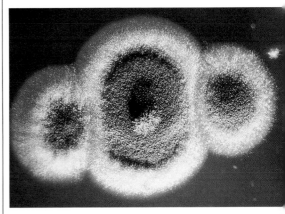

△ *In the wild* Penicillium *mold often lives on rotting fruit. It is one of the world's most famous fungi because it was the original source of penicillin— the first antibiotic to be discovered.*

FUNGI AT WAR

Scientists do not really know why some mushrooms and toadstools are poisonous, but they do understand why poisons are produced by some molds. These fungi often have to compete with bacteria, and they use poisons to stop their microrivals from taking over their food. Their poisons are known as antibiotics. They are some of nature's most effective chemical weapons.

The first antibiotic was discovered in 1928 when a Scottish biologist, Alexander Fleming, noticed mold in a laboratory dish. The dish was being used to grow bacteria, but the mold had killed all of the bacteria growing around it. From the mold— *Penicillium*—scientists later managed to isolate the chemical—penicillin— that it uses to keep bacteria at bay. It is now one of the world's most important medical drugs.

HOW FUNGI FEED

FUNGI CANNOT MOVE, BUT THEY ARE EXTREMELY GOOD AT FINDING FOOD BY STEALTH. THEIR DIET INCLUDES ALL TYPES OF FARE—FROM FRUIT AND ROTTING WOOD TO FEATHERS AND HUMAN SKIN.

For fungi feeding is a slow process. Instead of catching food, they normally grow through it. Their feeding threads—or hyphae—spread into their food and absorb the nutrients that it contains. Fungal threads are usually hidden away, but they can occasionally grow to be enormous. Some fungi feed on living plants and animals, while others spread through the soil. From time to time fungi also grow on something else—ourselves.

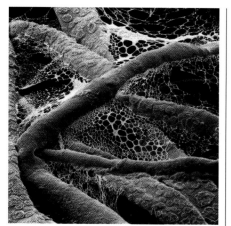

△ Enlarged over 1,000 times, this photograph shows fungal threads, or hyphae, growing through their food. Together the threads have a huge surface area—exactly what is needed to absorb nutrients.

FEEDING TIME

When animals feed, they usually swallow their food and then digest it. After this they absorb the food's nutrients. Fungi are different because they cannot swallow food at all. Instead a fungus releases digestive enzymes that break down the food on the spot. Once the enzymes have done this, the fungus absorbs the substances that it needs.

A fungus' enzymes are specially designed to deal with its food. Many fungi have enzymes that break down cellulose—the most important building material in plants. Some can also digest lignin, an even stronger substance that gives wood its strength. Fungal enzymes also include chemicals that can break down fats and proteins, helping enable fungi to attack animals and their remains. Some highly specialized fungi produce an enzyme that breaks down keratin. This extratough protein is the main ingredient in fur, feathers, claws, and nails and the outermost layer in skin. Fortunately our skin is protected from fungal attack. If keratin-eating fungi do get a hold, they rarely cause any long-term damage.

ATTACK FROM WITHIN

Fungi are not fast feeders, but they can develop huge appetites once they begin growing. As they feed they often change the appearance of their surroundings. They can turn ripe fruit soft and squishy and turn fallen leaves into a mushy paste. Fungi even attack other fungi, causing mushrooms and toadstools to rot away. When fungi feed on dead wood, they can weaken it so much that it falls apart. At first the wood slowly cracks and splits as its lignin is gradually destroyed. Eventually—often years later—it crumbles away completely, leaving nothing behind but a pile of dust.

Wood-eating fungi carry out an important task by breaking down fallen trees and branches so that their nutrients can be recycled.

△ In some fungi hyphae join together to form much thicker strands. These black strands belong to a honey fungus that is feeding on dead wood. Each strand is as thick as a shoelace.

But if they get into houses, they can cause serious damage. One notorious fungus—called dry rot—feeds on damp wood, and its long hyphae spread through gaps in bricks and concrete like invisible tentacles in search of food. Dry rot is a common problem in some parts of the world, but strangely enough it has hardly ever been found in the wilderness.

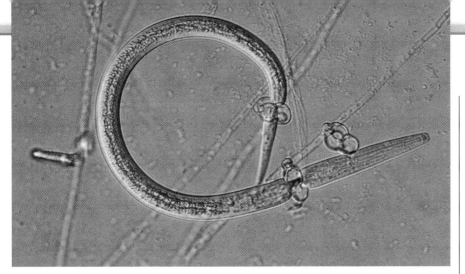

◁ *With its head trapped in a fungus' noose, this roundworm has no chance of escape. Its body will be digested as the fungus grows into its prey.*

HOW LICHENS LIVE

In a lichen the two partners work in different ways. The fungus collects minerals and other nutrients and also anchors the lichen in place. Meanwhile the algae gather energy from sunlight. They use it to carry out photosynthesis, which produces

△ *Spreading over an ancient gravestone, these lichens may be hundreds of years old.*

food that the fungus can use. Most lichens reproduce by releasing small granules that are scattered by the wind or rain.

Lichens grow extremely slowly, but they make up for this by having very long lives. In extreme habitats like Antarctica they can be hundreds of years old, but they often grow under one tenth of a millimeter per year.

On bare rocks lichens often dry out completely for weeks or months at a time. Plants cannot cope with this, but lichens adapt to it very well. When it rains, they soak up the water like pieces of paper towel and almost immediately spring back to life.

DEADLY SNARES

Many fungi attack living animals, often homing in on their skin. But some of the world's strangest fungi actually catch and kill their prey. Most of these fungal hunters live in the soil, where they trap microscopic worms. To catch their victims the fungi use special snares shaped like tiny rings. Each ring is made up of three curved cells that are very sensitive to the touch. If a worm accidentally wriggles into a ring, the cells instantly respond. They swell up, gripping the worm so that it cannot escape. Once the worm is dead, the fungus grows into its body and digests it from the inside.

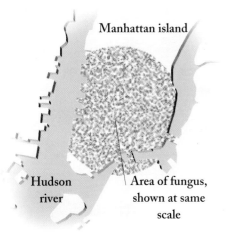

Manhattan island

Hudson river

Area of fungus, shown at same scale

△ *In 1992 scientists discovered a network of fungal threads covering 1,480 acres of forest floor in Washington state. It is the largest single organism ever found. This map compares its size with downtown New York City.*

Predatory fungi do not only live in the soil. Some species live in freshwater and go fishing for food with sticky lures. If an animal tries to feed on the lure, it gets glued into place. Once the animal is dead, the fungus digests the prey.

LICHENS

Fungi often hunt for food on their own, but they can be even more successful when they team up with living partners. These partners are often microscopic algae. When fungi and algae team up, the result is a lichen—a living mixture that is much tougher than either of the partners on its own. Some lichens look like small bushes, but most are flat and grow by spreading over surfaces like a living crust. Unlike plants, they do not have roots or leaves, and they never flower.

There are over 10,000 types of lichens living in an amazing range of habitats. Some grow on tree trunks, fallen branches, or fences, while others live on windswept hillsides or along the shore. Many of them grow on bare rocks in deserts, but they are just as much at home in cities, where they spread over pavement, concrete, and bricks. Several types manage to cling to life in Antarctica's mountains just a few hundred miles from the South Pole. Here the wind can reach 93 mph (150km/h), and winter temperatures drop to −76°F (−60°C), making it impossible for plants or animals to survive.

HOW FUNGI REPRODUCE

INSTEAD OF MAKING SEEDS, FUNGI REPRODUCE BY SCATTERING MICROSCOPIC SPORES. THESE SPORES WORK LIKE SEEDS, BUT THEY ARE MUCH SMALLER AND SIMPLER. THEY CAN DRIFT FAR AND WIDE THROUGH THE AIR, OR THEY CAN TRAVEL IN OTHER WAYS—FOR EXAMPLE BY CATCHING A RIDE ON AN INSECT'S FEET.

△ *Every time it rains these tropical puffballs release clouds of spores. Puffballs are common in woodlands and grasslands all over the world.*

Compared to animals and plants, fungi are some of the most prolific parents on Earth. An ordinary mushroom can produce 10 billion spores as long as it is not picked too early. Some fungi are even more productive than this. Puffballs can produce over five trillion spores—laid out end to end, enough to reach around Earth! So why is the world not swamped by fungi? The answer is that each spore has only a tiny chance of survival.

△ *A spore print like this is easy to make. Cut the cap off of a toadstool, lay it on a piece of glass or paper, and then cover it with a bowl. One day later the spores will form a print showing the toadstool's gills.*

SPORE FACTORIES

A mushroom is like a living factory, and it does its work in record time. In just one week it emerges from the ground, ripens its spores, and sheds them into the air. The spores float away on the breeze, often landing nearby. Some travel hundreds of miles before touching down.

Edible mushrooms make their spores in thin flaps called gills that are easy to see when a mushroom is turned upside down. Operating at full force, they can release up to half a million spores per minute. The cap works like an umbrella, making sure that the gills stay dry. With so many spores on the move, it is important that they do not collide or stick together. Scientists have discovered that each one has a minute electrical charge. This works like a magnet in reverse, keeping all the airborne spores apart.

LIFTOFF

Fungi have many different ways of sending spores on their way. Mushrooms shed their spores down, but puffballs give theirs a flying start by blowing them up into the air. When a puffball is newly grown, it feels hard and rubbery like a ball. But as its spores begin to ripen, it dries out. The top of the puffball then opens up, forming a hole so that the spores can be released. If the puffball is hit by raindrops, the "bag" is squashed, and a cloud of spores puffs out.

Most puffballs are not much bigger than a golf ball, but some reach gigantic sizes. One of the largest specimens ever known, found in New York in 1877, measured over 5.2 ft. (1.6m) wide. Giant puffballs tear open when they are ripe, releasing their spores into the air. Sometimes large chunks of them break away like pieces of sponge blowing around in the breeze. Remains of giant puffballs have been found in archaeological digs. Long ago people may have used them to carry fire because they smolder for several hours if they are lit.

FUNGAL ARTILLERY

To survive and grow, spores have to land near food. The chances of this happening are extremely small, and many of them perish during their journey. But some fungi have ways of improving the odds. *Pilobolus* lives on cattle dung and spreads by shooting packages of spores a few feet into the air. These packages stick on nearby blades of grass, where they are in just the right place to be eaten by cattle. If one of them is swallowed by a cow, it passes through its body unharmed and emerges perfectly planted in a new home.

△ *Inky cap fungi have caps that digest themselves, turning into a jet-black liquid. In this picture the tallest inky cap has almost finished self digesting.*

CLEANING UP

Animal dung is a favorite habitat for fungi, and many types live on this kind of food. Most of them have special spores that need to pass through an animal's body before

△ *This electron micrograph picture shows* Pilobolus *growing on cattle dung. Each body is around 0.4 in. (1cm) tall and ends in a swelling topped by a package of spores.*

they will begin to grow. One dung dweller grows on the droppings of mice and produces clusters of spores with long, sticky strands. If a mouse comes nearby, these strands glue themselves to its whiskers, and the mouse swallows the spores when it grooms itself.

SMELLY FUNGI

Mushrooms have a pleasant smell, but some fungi really reek. The most putrid are the stinkhorns. These woodland fungi grow long stalks that are topped by a mass of greenish slime. The slime attracts flies, and it sticks to their feet and mouths, ensuring that the spores are carried away.

Truffles also use smell to spread their spores, but their smell is much more appealing to humans. These woodland fungi grow underground, and they need animals to help them spread. Ripe truffles attract

▷ *These flies are feasting on the slime produced by a stinkhorn fungus. They will "plant" the spores when they land on the ground next.*

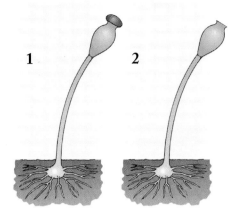

△ *1. Ripe* Pilobolus *fruiting bodies bend toward the light, and pressure builds up inside. 2. The package of spores blasts off, traveling up to 6.6 ft. (2m) into the air.*

wild boars, which dig them up and scatter their spores. For hundreds of years truffles have been highly prized by chefs, and in Europe professional truffle hunters use specially trained dogs or pigs to track them down.

◁ *This soldier termite is guarding a fungus garden deep in an underground nest. The white objects are the parts of the fungus that the termites eat.*

FUNGI AND ANIMALS

FOR ANIMALS FUNGI CAN BE EITHER USEFUL ALLIES OR DEADLY ENEMIES. SOME TYPES OF FUNGI PROVIDE ANIMALS WITH THEIR FOOD, WHILE OTHERS ARE STEALTHY INVADERS THAT ATTACK ANIMALS AND DIGEST THEM FROM THE INSIDE. BECAUSE THEY SPREAD BY USING SPORES, THESE KILLER FUNGI CAN ATTACK ALMOST ANYWHERE.

Compared to plants, fungi do not play a huge part in human life, although we would miss them if they disappeared. But for some animals fungi are vital to their survival. Mushrooms and toadstools are eaten by slugs and insect grubs, but the real fungus specialists are animals that cultivate fungi as food. They harvest fungi, but they also work as their partners by protecting them and helping them spread. Unfortunately for animals not all fungi are this useful or this well behaved. Some find food by breaking into animal bodies, and they can spread through them as quickly as mold through a slice of bread. A brush with one of these fungi can have fatal results.

THE FUNGUS GARDENERS

In warm parts of the world termites chew their way through wood and grass and carry millions of tons of it underground every year. Like most animals, the termites cannot digest this kind of food by themselves. Instead they rely on the help of tiny microbes that live in their intestines—one of these, called *Trichonympha*, is shown on page 68. But some species of termites are even more efficient because they

▽ *Slugs often eat mushrooms and toadstools. They tear away at the fungi with a radula—a mouthpart that contains hundreds of microscopic teeth.*

△ *This female wood wasp—or horntail—is drilling into a tree to lay her eggs. Wood wasps carry fungi with them, but they usually pick trees that have already been damaged by fungal attack.*

have developed an extra way of getting nutrients from their food.

In their underground nests these termites swallow their food and then gather up their own droppings. These droppings contain partially-digested remains, and the termites build them into a spongy mass that can be over 24 in. (60cm) wide.

▽ *This Peruvian grasshopper has been killed by a fungus. The fungus has sprouted tiny "mushrooms" that will soon scatter their spores.*

This is the termites' underground garden. It is a perfect habitat for a particular fungus that the termites grow and eat. As long as the termites take care of the fungus, it stays inside its underground home. But if they desert their nest, the fungus grows to the surface and produces mushrooms, enabling it to spread.

MOLDY TUNNELS

Many insect grubs bore their way through wood, using it as food. As they tunnel along they often swallow fungi that are already in the wood. For them fungi are like side dishes that help make up a meal. But some wood-boring insects go further. Fungi make up most of their diet, while wood takes second place.

Wood wasp larvae grow up in this way. They often tunnel through conifers, and foresters dislike them because they can damage and weaken trees. Their burrows are lined with a fungal "fur," and the grubs graze on the fungus as they crawl around in the wood. When adult wood wasps emerge from their burrows, they take some of the fungus with them. Females infect new trees when they lay their eggs, making sure that their grubs have the fungus that they need to survive.

THE INSECT KILLERS

Humans sometimes suffer from fungal infections. Athlete's foot, for example, is one that people often catch at school. It is caused by a fungus that feeds on the surface of the skin and thrives in the warm and moist conditions inside sweaty tennis shoes and other tight-fitting footwear. Usually these infections do little harm, although they take time to clear up. For wild animals fungi are more of a threat. They can kill mammals, birds, and fish, and they are particularly deadly to insects.

One way to identify these fungi is to look for insects that seem to be stuck on windowpanes or blades of grass. If an insect does not run or fly

△ *Fruit flies eat sugary sap and yeast—microscopic fungi that feed on sugar themselves. Yeast forms a thin layer around some fruits, giving them a waxy feel.*

away, it may have been a victim of fungal attack. The attack begins when a single microscopic spore lands on an insect's body. Once it has dissolved its way through the body case, the fungus spreads inside, dissolving the insect's internal organs as well. Once an insect is infected, the fungus often changes the way it behaves. It forces the insect to settle out in the open—the perfect place for the fungus to spread its lethal spores.

FUNGI AND PLANTS

MOST TREES ARE EVENTUALLY KILLED BY FUNGI,
AND FUNGI ALSO ATTACK MANY OTHER PLANTS.
BUT FUNGI AND PLANTS ARE NOT ALWAYS ENEMIES.
WITHOUT FUNGAL PARTNERS, MANY PLANTS
WOULD FIND IT DIFFICULT TO SURVIVE.

△ *These tiny orange mounds are produced by a rust fungus living in a leaf. Each one will release thousands of spores.*

Plants are tempting targets for fungi because they are full of food and cannot run away. Fungi attack plants above and below ground, seeking out any weak points in their defenses. They break into roots, grow through gashes in bark, and enter through the microscopic pores or breathing holes that all plants have in their leaves. Once a fungus is inside a plant, the stage is set for a serious and sometimes lengthy struggle. Some fungi damage parts of plants, leaving their host weakened but alive. Others are much more dangerous because they go in for the kill.

▷ *Fungi attack living trees and break down dead wood after a tree has died. These mushrooms are sprouting out of a decaying branch in the Amazon rain forest.*

△ *This peach tree has been infected by a rust fungus. Although the fungus will not kill the tree, it will reduce the crop and will probably spread to other trees nearby.*

MORTAL COMBAT

For plants fungal warfare starts from the moment they germinate from their seeds. One fungus, a mold called *Pythium*, is often lying in wait for them in the soil. *Pythium* breaks into tender young shoots and quickly dissolves their cells. In less than one hour the shoot often topples over like a fallen tree—ending a plant's life almost before it has begun.

At the other extreme duels between fungi and trees can go on for many years. This is because trees have many defenses that prevent airborne spores from getting at the living wood. If this shield is breached, trees can also use chemical weapons, including sticky resins, that make it harder for fungi to spread. Even if a fungus does take hold, trees can take a long time to die. Every year they surrender a little bit more of

themselves until finally no living wood is left.

When the battle is finally over and the tree is dead, different fungi move in. They slowly break down the dead remains, weakening the tree until it falls down. The trunk and branches then gradually turn to dust, and their nutrients are returned to the soil for future use.

FUNGUS EPIDEMICS

For farmers and gardeners fungi are a constant problem. Cultivated plants are attacked by hundreds of different species, including molds and mildews, wilts, rusts, and smuts. Their names may sound funny, but their effects are not. Despite modern fungicides, they can get out of control and cause tremendous damage to crops. Fungi can even change the landscape. In the 1920s, for example, a fungal epidemic killed most of North America's chestnuts, while in the 1980s Dutch elm disease killed most of the elm trees in the British Isles.

Further back in time fungal diseases have sometimes even caused greater disasters. One of these occurred in the 1840s when a fungus called late blight attacked Ireland's potato crop. Without this essential source of food, more than one million people starved to death.

UNDERGROUND ALLIES

With a record like this, fungi sound like nothing but trouble for plants. But fungi and plants have a strange relationship, and some fungi actually help plants thrive. These "good" fungi live in the soil, and they team up with plants by making contact with their roots. Instead of attacking the plant the fungus supplies it with mineral nutrients that it collects from the soil. It is something that fungi are very good at doing because their feeding threads spread so far.

△ *In woodlands and forests many toadstools are connected to nearby trees because their feeding threads spread underground to link up with tree roots.*

In return for this service the plant gives the fungus some of the sugary food that it makes.

Over millions of years this private arrangement has proven to be amazingly successful. Orchids have developed such close partnerships with fungi that they depend on them to survive. Many trees also rely on fungi, and even those that do not rely on them grow much better when they have these partners underground. This explains why some mushrooms and toadstools always grow near particular trees—together they make up some of nature's most effective teams.

▽ *Burnt orchids, which live in Europe's meadows and grasslands, can spend their first ten years hidden underground. During this part of their lives they get food from a fungal partner that wraps itself around their roots.*

PLANTS

IF ALIENS WERE STUDYING
EARTH FROM OUTER SPACE,
PLANTS WOULD BE THE
MOST VISIBLE SIGN OF LIFE.
PLANTS LIVE ON LIGHT
AND ARE THE CORNERSTONE
OF THE LIVING WORLD.

P lants are distant relatives of algae,
and they live in a similar way by
collecting energy from sunlight.
Most plants grow on land. Here they
have adapted to all kinds of habitats—
from dry deserts to the tundra near the
polar regions. Plants first appeared over
400 million years ago, and they have
evolved to include the tallest and most
colorful living things on Earth.

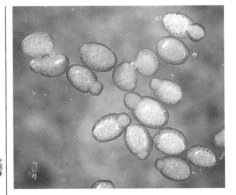

△ Duckweeds are the smallest flowering
plants in the world. The tiniest species can
fit through the eye of a needle, and their
flowers can only be seen with a microscope.

◁ A hiker peers inside a giant sequoia's
hollow trunk. These conifers are the world's
heaviest plants—up to 2,500 tons. Their
bark can grow over 12 in. (30cm) thick.

◁ Ant plants in southeast Asia have spongy stems that ants use as a home. The plant lives off of the ground and gets nutrients from the ants' droppings instead of the soil.

plants make their seeds with the help of flowers. There are 250,000 different types of flowering plants, many with amazing blossoms. Among them are all of the world's grasses and every single one of the world's broad-leaved trees.

GREEN ENGINEERING

Because plants cannot move around, they need equipment to survive. Their roots probe deep into the ground to search for water, and their leaves spread out to catch the Sun. A plant's stem carries out the vital task of transporting water up from the ground so that the leaves can do their work. If a plant's stem is cut or broken, the leaves soon shrivel and die. Some plant stems are short and stubby, but others tower over 164 ft. (50m) into the air. These giant stems are tree trunks—the heaviest pieces of engineering ever put together by

anything living on land.

Plants build themselves out of little more than water and air. This amazing trick is photosynthesis, and it is powered by energy from the Sun. Plants are not the only things that carry it out, but on land they are the only ones that use it on such a massive scale. Photosynthesis builds up every part of a plant, from tree trunks weighing thousands of tons to seeds smaller than dust.

△ The hammer orchid lives in western Australia. When a wasp lands on the red hammer, the flower suddenly folds up and dusts the visitor with pollen.

WORKING PARTNERS

Over millions of years animals and plants have become close partners. Many flowering plants depend on animals, but animals need plants even more. Without plants there would be no food for plant eaters, and without plant eaters predators would have nothing to hunt. But wild animals are not alone. Humans also depend on plants: without the food and raw materials that they supply, we would also find it impossible to survive.

GOING GREEN

The world's first land plants were just ankle high, and they reproduced by releasing tiny spores. Mosses still live like this, and like early plants they need to be damp to grow. As time went by plants became taller, tougher, and more varied. The new plants included giant horsetails and tree ferns, which grew in vast forests on swampy ground. The breakthrough came later when some plants evolved seeds. Seeds turned out to be one of nature's greatest inventions, allowing plants to spread to some of the driest and coldest places on Earth.

Today seed-bearing plants include coniferous trees, which make their seeds in woody cones. But far more

▷ The bird-of-paradise flower is pollinated by birds. If a bird lands on the blue perch, its feet collect pollen, and it carries this to the next flower.

△ *Using their leaves, plants collect about one percent of all the sunlight that shines on Earth every year. This energy drives almost all life on our planet.*

LIVING ON LIGHT

PLANTS LEAD THE WORLD IN USING SOLAR POWER. THAT IS BECAUSE SUNLIGHT SUPPLIES ALL OF THE ENERGY THAT THEY NEED TO SURVIVE AND GROW.

Every three seconds the Sun supplies Earth with as much energy as the entire human race uses in one day. We are only just starting to tap into this gigantic resource, but plants have been using it since they first evolved. Their secret is photosynthesis—a process that captures light and makes it work.

COLLECTING LIGHT
Light is pure energy. It cannot be eaten, and it cannot be stored, but it can be collected and used. This is exactly what plants do. Through their leaves they absorb the energy in sunlight, and they use it to power chemical reactions. These reactions work like digestion in reverse. They start with very simple substances and use them to build up ones that are more complex. This process is called photosynthesis—a word that means "building with light."

Plants first have to collect the energy in sunlight so that the cascade of chemical reactions can begin. They do this by using a substance called chlorophyll. Chlorophyll is good at collecting the blue and red parts of sunlight, but it is not as good at collecting the green. This unused light bounces back off of the leaves or shines right through them, which is why green is the color of the living world.

ESSENTIAL INGREDIENTS
As well as light, plants need two simple substances before photosynthesis can begin. One of these is water, which they normally get from the ground. Water travels up plants in a nonstop stream through their roots and stems until it arrives in their leaves. The other essential ingredient is carbon dioxide—a gas that is present in the air. Plants absorb carbon dioxide through their leaves. Once the gas is inside of a leaf, it seeps into the cells where photosynthesis occurs. These leaf cells are microscopic factories crowded with dozens of green blobs.

△ *Because plants use energy from the Sun, they do not need food. Their roots absorb water and small amounts of minerals but nothing else.*

These blobs, called chloroplasts, are where photosynthesis takes place. Inside of every chloroplast is a stack of transparent membranes that are packed full of chlorophyll molecules. When sunlight shines through the membranes, the chlorophyll starts capturing energy.

PERFECT PARTNERS

With the help of energy from the Sun, plants take water and carbon dioxide and use them to build a sugar called glucose. Glucose is packed full of energy, which means that plants can use it as a fuel. But even more importantly it is a stepping-stone toward making hundreds of other substances that plants need when they grow.

Most chemical reactions produce some waste, and photosynthesis is no exception. In this case the waste is pure oxygen that escapes into the air. This makes animals and plants perfect partners because animals need oxygen to survive. When animals breathe, they give off

carbon dioxide, and plants use this when they grow.

GOING FOR GROWTH

To grow, plants use building materials that can cope with tough conditions. In the plant world the number one building material is a substance called cellulose. Plants make cellulose by adding glucose molecules together to form long chains. A single chain can contain over 5,000 glucose molecules.

To use these chains as building materials, plants arrange them in special ways. They build the chains together into fibers, and then they lay the fibers down in crisscrossing sheets. The result is light but tough—exactly what is needed to keep plant cells in shape.

STORAGE FOR SURVIVAL

Plants need energy to keep going at night and to survive when the weather turns dry or cold. Many plants store energy by turning glucose into a powdery substance called starch. They stockpile starch

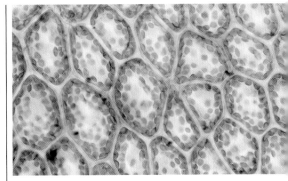

△ *Magnified over 500 times, this slice through a leaf shows chloroplasts inside of living cells. The more chloroplasts a cell has, the more light it can collect.*

in their roots or stems, and many also hold it in their seeds. In seeds this store gives young plants enough energy to germinate and grow.

Humans cannot digest cellulose, but starch is a vital part of our food. Wheat, corn, and potatoes are packed full of it. When we eat these we get a large helping of energy—one stored away by living plants using light from the Sun.

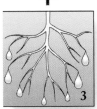
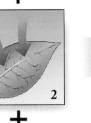
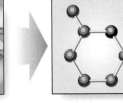
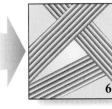
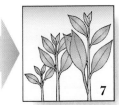

This diagram shows the main steps that take place during photosynthesis. The "ingredients" needed are shown on the left, and the results are shown below.

1 *Plant collects light energy through its leaves.*
2 *Plant collects carbon dioxide through its leaves.*
3 *Plant collects water through its roots.*

4 *Using solar energy, the chloroplasts combine water and carbon dioxide to make glucose.*
5 *Glucose is an energy-rich sugar, or simple carbohydrate. The plant can turn glucose into many useful substances. One of these is cellulose—a carbohydrate that is a strong building material.*
6 *The plant uses cellulose fibers to construct new cell walls.*
7 *New cells make the plant grow.*

LEAVES

Leaves are nature's answer to a tricky problem: how to collect light in the most efficient way. They have to stand up to all kinds of different conditions—from boiling-hot sunshine to torrential rains.

Leaves work like solar panels, and their job is to collect the light that plants need. Some are just a few millimeters long, while the largest palm leaves would barely fit inside of a bus. Leaves can be as soft and delicate as a piece of tissue paper or as hard as plastic with jagged edges, sharp points, or an armor of dangerous spines. These designs have developed over billions of years. They help plants adapt to different habitats and to very different ways of life.

△ Tropical plants often have big, floppy leaves because they live in places where the air is warm, damp, and still. In most other parts of the world leaves like this would get ripped to shreds by the wind.

▽ Like many freshwater plants, water crowfoot has two kinds of leaves—feathery ones underwater and rounded ones in the air.

◁ When leaves are held up to the light, their veins are easy to see. Leaf veins have two jobs: they support the leaf, and they carry water to its cells. This highly-magnified picture (above left) shows a single pore in a yew tree leaf. At night the brown guard cells close the pore to prevent the leaf from losing too much water.

HOW LEAVES WORK

No matter what they look like, leaves all work in a similar way. They gather energy from sunlight, and they use it to make substances that plants need when they grow. Leaves work by using photosynthesis (see pages 84–85). Photosynthesis needs carbon dioxide and water as well as sunlight, so these must be inside of the leaf for things to start. These substances get to the leaf by following two very different paths.

Leaves get carbon dioxide from the air through microscopic pores called stomata. These are surrounded by special guard cells that can make them open or close. Carbon dioxide flows in through these pores and then makes its way into the cells where photosynthesis takes place. At the same time oxygen flows out. It may sound like breathing, but plants do not have to put any effort into making it work. That is because their leaves are thin, so the gases can seep in or out without any help.

WATER ON TAP

Unlike carbon dioxide, water often has much farther to travel. It flows into a plant's roots and along a system of ultrafine pipelines, moving up the stem, into leaf stalks, and finally into leaf veins. Once it has arrived most of the water evaporates through the leaf pores, and this pulls more water up the

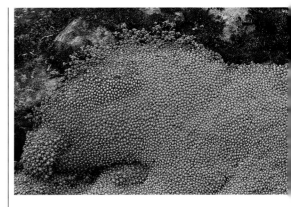

△ *Scabweed from New Zealand has just what it takes to survive on rocky mountain slopes. Its leaves are tiny and are packed closely together to protect them from the wind.*

plant to take its place. This water flow is called transpiration. The warmer, drier, and windier it is, the faster transpiration works.

Cacti often use only a few drops of water a day because they are specifically adapted to life in dry places. But most plants go through much more. A single corn plant can drink up to 52 gallons (200L) of water while it grows—enough to fill an average bathtub to the brim. Trees are even thirstier. A large oak can suck up over 130 gallons (500L) in one day. Poplar trees can dry out the soil so much that it shrinks, making buildings crack or collapse.

SPECIAL SHAPES
The ideal shape for collecting light is big and flat like a solar panel. But leaves are not made of metal and are not bolted to the ground. They have to combine lightness and strength, and they have to survive in all kinds of different habitats—from windswept mountainsides to dimly lit rain forest floors. This is one of the reasons why leaves are so varied and why no two species have leaves that are exactly alike.

Most plants grow simple leaves, which are ones with a single blade. Compound leaves are different because they are divided up into small leaflets that look like leaves themselves. To make things even more complicated, the leaflets may be compounds themselves, creating a mass of feathery foliage attached to a single stalk. Grass leaves are easier to recognize because they are long and narrow and do not have a stalk. In a grass leaf the veins are parallel, but in most other plants they spread through the leaf like a net.

LEAF LIFE SPANS
Leaves do not only differ in shape and size—their surfaces vary too. Some leaves are shiny and smooth, but others feel sticky or have a coating that feels like fur. A few are even dangerous to touch. Nettle leaves are covered in stinging hairs, while poison ivy leaves contain a toxic resin that can stick to skin and clothing. These different features help protect leaves against rain, strong sunshine, and drying

winds and also against animals that use leaves as food. In southwest Africa the welwitschia plant (see page 184) has only two leaves, and they are built to last for hundreds of years. But with most other plants, leaves have a much shorter life. Once their work is done the plant cuts off their water supply, and they flutter—or sometimes crash—to the ground.

FULL CIRCLE
Every year evergreen trees shed their leaves gradually, but deciduous trees lose all of them at the same time. In the fall leaves litter the ground, but by the following spring most of them have disappeared.

This vanishing trick is the work of bacteria and fungi that feed on dead leaves, turning them into smaller and smaller fragments that eventually mingle with the soil. These dead remains fertilize the ground, helping more plants—and more leaves—to grow.

◁ *The raffia palm has the world's biggest leaves. They can be up to 75 ft. (23m) long, and each one lasts for up to 10 years. Raffia fibers are made from the leaf stems.*

FLOWERS

PEOPLE ARE FASCINATED WITH FLOWERS. WE PAINT
THEM, PHOTOGRAPH THEM, AND OFTEN KEEP THEM IN
OUR HOMES. BUT FLOWERS DO NOT GROW JUST FOR US
TO ENJOY. INSTEAD THEY HAVE A DIFFERENT MISSION:
TO ENABLE PLANTS TO REPRODUCE.

It is difficult to imagine a world without flowers.
They grow in every natural habitat on land,
and a few very special kinds even "bloom"
beneath the sea. Flowers brighten up gardens
and roadsides, and some of the smallest ones
manage to survive in cracks in the sidewalk
right underneath passing feet. Flowers have
a bewildering variety of shapes and colors,
but they all carry out the same essential
tasks. They allow female cells to be
fertilized by male pollen. Once this
has happened they make a plant's seeds.

ANATOMY OF A FLOWER

The best way to find out about
flowers is a drastic one: start on
the outside and pull it apart. In most
flowers the first things to break off
are green flaps called sepals, which
protect the flower while it is still a
bud. Next come the petals. Usually
they are the most eye-catching parts
of flowers, and their job is to attract
animals so that pollen can be
transferred from plant to plant.
With the sepals and petals out of
the way, only the innermost parts
of the flower are left. First is a circle
of stamens. These are the flower's
male parts, and their function is to
produce pollen. In the very center
are the flower's female parts, or
carpels. Their role is to collect
pollen arriving from other
flowers and then use
it to make seeds.

*With its petals folded back,
this tropical passionflower is an
irresistible attraction for visiting
insects. Its intricate shape ensures
that insects get dusted with
pollen as they eat.*

2 *The bright-red flowers attract insects that bring pollen from other poppy flowers.*

1 *Poppy flowers open in the morning when their sepals fall off and their petals open up.*

3 *The petals drop off, leaving a case that contains hundreds of developing seeds.*

ANIMALS AND WIND

That, in a nutshell, is how most flowers are made. But because there are so many types of flowering plants, there are thousands and thousands of different flowers. Most flowers are like living window displays, and they lure animals with the promise of food. This food is usually sugary nectar, although some flowers reward their visitors with other things, such as pollen itself.

These flowers need to be noticed, which is why they are brightly colored and have tempting smells. But not all flowers are like this. Many plants do not need to attract animals because they spread their pollen through the wind. Their flowers are often green and small and are easy to overlook.

THE SEX LIFE OF PLANTS

Animals are usually male or female, but in the plant world things are not always as straightforward. Because most flowers have male and female parts, their owners are male and female at the same time. Plants like these usually swap pollen with their neighbors, but if they are forced to they can often pollinate themselves—a useful trick if they are growing on their own with no available partners nearby.

But many other plants, such as pumpkins, have separate male and female flowers. Their flowers grow on the same plant, but only the female ones produce fruit and seeds. Finally there are plants that are more like animals with separate sexes on separate plants. The kiwi fruit is one of these. To produce kiwi fruit, farmers have to grow male and female plants so that pollination can occur.

POLLINATION

UNLIKE ANIMALS, PLANTS CANNOT PAIR
UP TO REPRODUCE. THEY GET TOGETHER
IN ANOTHER WAY BY SWAPPING
MICROSCOPIC GRAINS OF POLLEN.

For plants reproduction is a tricky business. Male and female cells are needed, and if possible these need to come from different parent plants. But plants cannot move, so the parents can never meet. This is where pollen comes in. This dustlike substance contains a plant's male cells, and it is small and light enough to travel from plant to plant. When male pollen lands on the female parts of a flower, it fertilizes the female cells, or ova. Once this vital step has taken place the female cells can begin developing into seeds.

△ Pollen grains are as distinctive as fingerprints. Each plant produces its own type, and scientists sometimes identify plants by looking at their pollen alone.

△ In the summer a quick shake is enough to make a pine tree release clouds of yellow pollen. These pollen grains have microscopic sails that help them float away.

POLLEN ON THE MOVE

Pollen grains are made by stamens, or the male parts of flowers. Once their pollen is ripe, they release it so that it can travel from plant to plant. The journey may be as close as a plant next door or one mile away. Each plant has its own "brand" of pollen, and it can only fertilize plants with the same type.

Pollen gets around in two very different ways. Some plants simply shed their pollen into the air. The pollen floats away in the breeze, and with luck some of it lands on the female parts of other flowers. This method is used by all of the world's grasses and by many broad-leaved trees. It is also used by conifers, although they make their pollen in cones instead of flowers.

Because wind pollination is so hit-and-miss, a huge amount of pollen is needed to make it work.

On warm summer mornings wind-pollinated plants release billions of pollen grains into the air. The grains are much too small to be visible, but they give many people hay fever and itchy eyes.

POLLEN CARRIERS

The world's earliest seed-producing plants were all pollinated with the help of the wind. But when flowering plants appeared, some of them developed smarter ways of sending pollen on its way. They grew flowers that attract animals. In return for food these visitors act as a private delivery service, carrying pollen to its destination. The first pollinating animals were probably

◁ Bees help spread pollen, but they also use it as food. They scrape pollen off of their bodies and store it in special "pollen baskets" on their legs.

beetles, which shuffle around in flowers to find food. Today pollinating animals include many different types of insects as well as birds, bats, and marsupials. During their long partnerships flowers and their visitors have evolved so that they fit almost like a lock and key. When an animal arrives at a flower, the flower's male parts, or stamens, dust its body with pollen. The animal carries this to the next flower it visits, where the flower's female parts are waiting to collect it. Once a pollen grain arrives at its destination, it grows a slender tube into

▷ Hummingbirds are the only pollinating birds that hover as they eat. Pollen sticks to their faces and is transferred from flower to flower.

the flower's ovaries, which are the chambers where the female cells are held. Each pollen grain fertilizes a single female cell, and after this the cell grows into a seed.

ANIMALS AT WORK

By looking at a flower, it is often easy to figure out which animal pollinates it. Insect-pollinated flowers are usually brightly colored and sweet smelling because insects are attracted to vibrant colors and sugary smells. Flat flowers are often pollinated by flies and wasps, while tube-shaped ones are visited by butterflies and bees because they have longer tongues. They can reach down into the bottom of the flower where the reward of nectar is waiting. Moth-pollinated flowers—such as honeysuckles—have a similar shape, but they release their perfume at night when the most moths are flying around.

Because most insects are small, insect-pollinated flowers are also small. But birds and bats often use flowers as landing pads, so it is important that the flowers are strong. A bird or a bat can drink much more nectar than a bee, so their flowers produce nectar for days at a time, attracting plenty of visitors.

PARTNERS

Many pollinating insects visit a variety of plants, but some concentrate on just one type.

These insects get all their food from the plant as well as somewhere to raise their young. In return they provide the plant with a private delivery service. In warm parts of the world fig trees are pollinated in this way. There are over one thousand species of fig trees in the world, but amazingly each one has its own kind of pollinating wasp.

▽ Banana flowers have a musky smell that attracts bats after dark. Here a short-nosed fruit bat is lapping up nectar and is getting covered in pollen as it eats.

FLOWER HEADS

FOR PLANTS THE BEST WAY TO
ATTRACT ANIMALS IS TO PUT ON
A REALLY IMPRESSIVE SHOW. THIS IS
THE REASON WHY SO MANY PLANTS
GROW THEIR FLOWERS IN GROUPS.

On their own single flowers can be hard to spot—imagine searching for a single poppy in a field. But if a plant has hundreds or thousands of flowers, the combined display is much harder to miss. Plants put on this show by having many separate flowers or by growing the flowers in clusters known as flower heads. Flower heads are almost as varied as flowers themselves, and some of the world's best-known "flowers" are actually flower heads in disguise.

△ *Lotus plants have large, single flowers. Like the world's first flowers they are built on a simple circular plan, so their different parts are easy to see. Flower heads are more complicated, and their individual flowers are sometimes hidden away.*

FLORAL LOOK-ALIKES

To find one of the most common types of flower heads, look to the nearest patch of grassy ground. This is the favorite habitat of daisies—some of the most successful and widespread weeds in the world. Daisy plants look as though they have individual flowers, but each "flower" is actually made up of dozens of miniflowers, or florets. In this type of flower head the florets are arranged as if they were on a plate. The ones in the middle of the plate produce pollen and seeds, while the ones around the rim each have a single extralarge petal that makes the flower head bright and easy to see.

Daisies belong to a gigantic family of plants that is at least 25,000 species strong. Their relatives include dandelions, goatsbeards, thistles, and sunflowers, as well as many garden plants. Each species is different and unique, but their flower heads are all built on the same winning plan.

△ *Orchids have complicated flowers with colors and scents that attract particular animals. Some orchids grow single flowers, but most have eye-catching flower heads.*

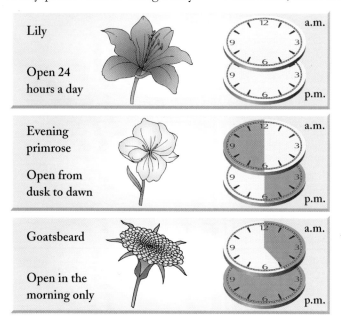

Lily		a.m. / p.m.
Open 24 hours a day		
Evening primrose		a.m. / p.m.
Open from dusk to dawn		
Goatsbeard		a.m. / p.m.
Open in the morning only		

◁ *Flowers often have different opening times, shown in yellow on these 12-hour clocks. Lilies never close. Evening primroses, which are pollinated by moths, open at night and close during the day. Goatsbeard flower heads have one of the shortest opening times—they open around sunrise but close by noon.*

△ *The titan arum's flower head can be over 8 ft. (2.4m) tall and up to 13 ft. (4m) around its rim. Rare in the wild, it has been cultivated in botanical gardens.*

SPIRES AND UMBRELLAS

Daisy florets are not much wider than a human hair. But many flower heads have much larger flowers spaced much farther apart. In foxgloves, for example, the flowers are as big as thimbles—the ideal size for bumblebees to squeeze their way inside.

In a foxglove flower head the lowest flowers open first. So when a bumblebee arrives to look for nectar, it starts at the bottom of the flower head and works its way up. Foxgloves take advantage of this behavior because the first flowers that a bee visits, at the bottom, contain only ripe female parts. These collect any pollen that the bee is carrying and use it to make seeds. Higher up where the flowers are younger, only the male parts are ripe. They dust the bee with pollen, and it flies away, carrying the pollen to another foxglove plant.

Many other plants have flowers in spires, but plants in the carrot family have flower heads shaped more like umbrellas. Each umbrella has a set of spokes topped with a set of flowers. For insects these flower heads make handy feeding platforms and also great places to bask in the sunlight. Hover flies are particular fans of them, and they guard their umbrellas fiercely, zooming toward rivals and chasing them away.

STATELY BUT SMELLY

The world's tallest flower head belongs to a plant called *Puya raimondii,* which grows in the Bolivian Andes. It can be over 33 ft. (10m) tall, and it contains nearly 10,000 small white blossoms. A *Puya* plant can take 100 years to grow, but it only blooms once for around three months and then dies. But for a combination of size and smell nothing beats the titan arum, or devil's tongue, which grows in rain forests on the Indonesian island of Sumatra. Its flower head sprouts from a giant underground tuber, and it looks like a soft, fleshy spire towering out of a leathery cup.

Unlike the *Puya* flower head, this colossal object only blooms for four or five days, and it produces a powerful odor that smells like a mixture between burned cooking and rotting fish. Flies love the smell, but people find it so repulsive that it can even make them faint. The titan arum's flowers are tiny and well hidden. The only way to see them is to take a deep breath, get up close, and peer inside.

▽ *When sunflowers blossom, their outer florets open first. Because they have many florets, they stay in bloom for many days.*

SEEDS AND FRUITS

INSIDE EVERY SEED IS AN EMBRYO PLANT JUST
WAITING FOR THE CHANCE TO GROW. SEEDS
PROTECT THIS IMPORTANT CARGO, WHILE FRUIT
HELPS SEEDS SPREAD FAR AND WIDE. SOME SEEDS
CAN BE SMALLER AND LIGHTER THAN SPECKS OF
DUST, BUT THE LARGEST FRUITS OF ALL CAN
WEIGH ALMOST HALF A TON.

Seeds are designed to last and are the toughest objects in the
entire plant world. If they are kept dry, they can survive for
years, and if they are deep-frozen, they can often survive for
over one hundred years. But as soon as outside conditions are right
a seed germinates, which means that the embryo inside it begins
to grow. A fruit is a container that holds seeds. It shelters the
seeds while they develop, and it often helps them spread.

SEED OR FRUIT?

Seeds and fruits are two very
different things, but they are easy
to mix up. Seeds are usually small
and hard, and each one always
contains a single embryo plant.
Most seeds also have a collection of
prepackaged food. This food keeps
the embryo alive until it germinates.
After this it helps a young
plant grow until it is
able to make food
on its own.

In everyday life a fruit is
something tender and juicy that
is good to eat. But to scientists
a fruit is anything that contains
seeds, as long as it is produced
by a single flower. That means
that fruits include not only
apples, oranges, and grapes but
also all types of other things—from
cucumbers, coconuts, and
tomatoes to pea pods

and poppy heads. The world's
heaviest fruits are pumpkins:
the largest on record weighed
a monstrous 1,063 lbs (481kg).

SEEDS IN STORAGE

Although seeds often look small
and fragile, they can cope with
conditions that would kill adult
plants. They do not need light,
and they can survive with almost
no water or air. Also seeds are
not harmed by the cold. Low
temperatures simply slow down
their chemistry, so putting seeds
in a refrigerator keeps them fresh.
Once they are brought out, warmed

◁ *Goosegrass
fruits have tiny
hooks that cling
to the fur of
passing animals.
These fruits break
off easily if the
animal brushes past*

◁ *These four pictures show a wheat seedling germinating. Seedlings need water, so their number one priority is to grow a root that collects water from the soil.*

△ *This is the winged fruit of a climbing plant,* Alsomitra macrocarpa, *which grows in the rain forests of southeast Asia. With "wings" that are 6 in. (15cm) across, it can take over a minute to flutter to the ground.*

up, and watered, they miraculously come back to life. Cold storage is a method used by conservationists to protect many of the world's endangered plants. In the past ten years seeds from thousands of rare plants have been collected, dried out, and stored in special seed banks in different parts of the world. They are kept at a temperature of around −4°F (−20°C), which is about the same as in a deep freezer. In these chilly conditions seeds can last a long time. Most of the ones in storage today will be alive and well in the year 2100 and beyond.

GERMINATION

Seeds need warmth and moisture before they can start to grow. But to be on the safe side, they wait for the right moment before breaking their dormancy, or sleep. In places where the winters are cold most seeds do not germinate until they have been "primed" by several weeks of frost. This means that they come to life when the winter is truly over, rather than during mild periods in between. In deserts many seeds are triggered into life by sudden storms, while on scrublands they are often primed by natural chemicals formed during bushfires. This ingenious system means that they start growing as soon as a fire is over, when the ground is covered with fertile ash.

AGAINST THE ODDS

Despite their toughness, individual seeds have only a tiny chance of growing into adult plants. For some disaster strikes early on when they get eaten before they have even left their parent plant. For many others a similar fate waits for them on the ground. Small birds often eat seeds, and rodents enjoy the taste of them as well. Seeds can also be attacked by diseases and by molds. With this long list of dangers, it is not surprising that so few survive.

To make up for all of these casualties, plants produce seeds on a massive scale. A single grass plant can produce hundreds of seeds, while an oak tree can grow more than 100,000 acorns a year. And unlike a grass plant, an oak tree goes on doing this for 200 years or more.

But the champion seed producers are orchids that grow high up on tropical trees. Just one of these plants alone can produce more than ten million seeds. These orchid seeds are the smallest and lightest in the world, and it would take almost one billion of them to weigh as much as a single pea.

SEEDS ON THE MOVE

YOUNG PLANTS NEED TO GET AWAY FROM THEIR PARENTS SO THAT THEY HAVE ENOUGH LIGHT AND SPACE TO GROW. OVER MILLIONS OF YEARS PLANTS HAVE COME UP WITH SOME AMAZING WAYS OF SCATTERING THEIR SEEDS FAR AND WIDE. SOME DO IT ALL ON THEIR OWN, BUT MANY RELY ON OUTSIDE HELP.

△ *These jackal-berry seedlings are germinating in a pile of elephant dung. Jackal-berry seeds are primed to germinate by being swallowed and then passed through an animal's intestines.*

△ *In the rain forests of Central America the quetzal eats fruits with large seeds or pits. The bird digests most of the fruit, but it drops the pits on the forest floor.*

Plants are incredibly good at spreading, even though they cannot move. They quickly take over newly cleared ground, whether it is in someone's backyard or on remote islands far out at sea. Plants set up home on other plants, and a few even manage to root themselves in walls and on rooftops high above city streets. Plants can get to these places because their seeds are natural travelers. Because of them hardly anywhere is beyond their reach.

CATAPULTS AND BOMBS
The world's heaviest seed belongs to the coco-de-mer, a rare palm that grows in the Seychelles (see page 155). Its seeds can weigh a massive 44 lbs (20kg). When they are ripe they crash to the ground, roll a few feet, and then come to a halt. But many seeds travel much farther than this. To get going they rely on fruits because these natural containers are designed to help seeds disperse.

Plants with dry fruits often get their seeds off to a flying start. For example, poppy heads work like miniature pepper shakers, scattering their seeds when the wind blows by. Pods are more like catapults. Once they have dried out in the sunshine they split open with a snap, flinging their seeds across the ground. One

unusual fruit, called the squirting cucumber, behaves like a miniature bomb. This bristly object explodes when ripe, blasting seeds and juice several feet into the air.

DRIFTERS AND FLOATERS
Snapping and bursting works well enough, but seeds travel even farther when they drift or float away. Many of the world's most successful weeds—including dandelions and thistles—have feathery fruits that are blown away by the wind. Each fruit contains a single seed and a bristly parachute that helps it along. In forests plants often have fruits with wings that helicopter their way to the ground. Some are not much bigger than a fingernail, but giant ones, such as *Alsomitra macrocarpa*

(see page 95), can have a "wingspan" as large as some birds.

Coastal plants, like the coconut palm, often have waterproof fruits that float. If a coconut gets caught in a current, it can drift across an entire ocean to germinate on a faraway shore. The same is true of a plant

△ *Common dormice feast on blackberries, helping to scatter the seeds. Soft fruit like these change color when they are ripe, letting animals know they are ready to eat.*

called the sea bean, which grows on coasts around the Caribbean Sea. Its heart-shaped seeds often cross the Atlantic Ocean and sometimes get washed up north of the Arctic Circle.

▷ *This ant has made a useful discovery—a seed with a special parcel of food. Back in their nest the ants eat the food parcel but abandon the seed, unintentionally "planting" it underground.*

ANIMAL HELPERS

These travels are impressive enough, but they are only half of the story. Just as plants use animals to carry their pollen, they also use them to spread their seeds. Many of their fruits have hooks or barbs that work by latching onto fur and skin. Some of these fruits are also good at sticking to socks or at fastening themselves to shoes. Fortunately most of these hitchhikers are small, but a few reach serious sizes. In Africa the devil's claw has hooks up to 3 in. (8cm) long—just the thing for snagging onto antelope hooves.

Juicy fruits also use animals, but they work in a more roundabout way. When these fruits are ripe they become brightly colored, which attracts animals looking for a meal. Animals are less picky than humans, and they do not bother to pick out the seeds as they eat. Instead they

swallow the entire fruit along with the seeds. The fruit's flesh soon gets digested, but the seeds are much tougher. Unless they get chewed they will pass through animals unharmed. Digestive juices often prime them to germinate, and without animals some of them cannot begin growing.

Fruit-eating animals include many types of birds as well as mammals and even some fish. Most of them make good seed spreaders because they are always on the move. For plants they are especially useful because they often scatter seeds in a readymade fertilizer: a pile of droppings or dung.

▽ *When tumbleweeds have finished flowering, their roots shrivel up and break away. The dead plants then roll along in the wind, scattering seeds as they go.*

PLANTS WITHOUT FLOWERS

No matter how hard you look, you will never find mosses or ferns in bloom. Plants like these breed without needing flowers— just like the earliest plants on Earth.

Until the end of the age of the dinosaurs, flowers did not exist. There was no grass—because grasses are flowering plants—and no broad-leaved trees. All plants bred by shedding tiny spores or by making primitive seeds. Since then the world has changed a great deal. Dinosaurs have vanished, and flowerless plants have been pushed aside by ones with blossoms. But flowerless plants still survive, and some are very successful.

◁ *Mosses grow their spores in slender capsules that are usually around one inch tall. One of these capsules has opened up so that it can scatter its spores into the air.*

MOSSES AND LIVERWORTS
One of the best places to see these flowerless survivors is by fast-flowing streams. The rushing water creates a cool and damp habitat—exactly the kind of place where mosses thrive. Mosses are basic plants without true leaves or roots. They often look like bright-green cushions,

△ *Filmy ferns get their name because their leaves are just one cell thick. These delicate plants can only grow in very humid places because they dry out easily.*

◁ *Liverworts spread by making spores and by growing cups containing miniature "eggs." The eggs jump out of their cups when they are hit by rain. Exactly the same technique is used by bird's-nest fungus (see page 73).*

although some underwater types look like hair. Unlike flowering plants, they are small and compact. The world's tallest species, from Australia, is only 23 in. (60cm) high.

To grow, mosses have to be wet, and many of them can hold water like a sponge. But although they like streamsides and marshy places, they do not have to be permanently damp. Some mosses grow on rocks and walls where they can dry out for weeks or months at a time. These dried-up mosses look gray and dead, but when it rains they quickly come back to life.

Streamsides are also a favorite habitat for liverworts—the simplest plants in the world. Some look like small green tongues, while others are more like ribbons with tiny leaves. Liverworts creep along instead of growing up, and they branch off by splitting in two. Many grow over damp rocks, but in rain forests they also live on other plants' leaves. They do not damage their host plant, but they do steal some of its light.

FERNS

There are over 11,000 species of ferns, making them the largest group of nonflowering plants. The smallest types could easily fit into an eggcup, but the world's tallest species—tree ferns—can grow up to 82 ft. (25m) high. Most ferns are rooted in the ground, but some clamp onto tree trunks, while a few float on the surface of ponds. Some species of ferns are rare, but one kind—called bracken—is a troublesome weed.

Compared to mosses and liverworts, ferns are more like flowering plants. They have true roots as well as stems and leaves, and they also have internal pipelines that carry water up from the soil. But ferns do not have flowers, and they spread by making spores rather than seeds. Their life cycles switch between two different types of plants (see page 101).

CONIFERS AND THEIR RELATIVES

Seeds and flowers usually go together, but in the history of plants seeds were actually developed first. That explains why conifers can have seeds although they do not have flowers. There are only around 550 types of conifers in the world compared with 250,000 types of flowering plants, but they are still very plentiful in places where it is dry or cold. In the far north they make up the boreal forest—the largest forest in the world.

Conifers also have some relatives that are harder to find. They include cycads—which look like palm trees—and the ginkgo, or maidenhair tree. This "living fossil" comes from the Far East and has leaves that look like bright-green fans. Another conifer relative, called welwitschia (see page 184), is a leading candidate for the title of the strangest plant in the world. It lives in the deserts of southwest Africa, and it often looks like a heap of garbage rather than something living.

△ *Conifers have two types of cones. Male cones make pollen, but female cones make seeds. These are young female cones from a larch tree. They are still soft, but they will turn hard and woody when they are ripe.*

PLANT LIFE CYCLES

TWO OR THREE TIMES EVERY CENTURY MILLIONS
OF BAMBOO PLANTS IN CENTRAL CHINA BURST INTO
BLOOM, DROP THEIR SEEDS, AND DIE. THIS FINAL SHOW
IS NOT AN ACCIDENT—INSTEAD IT IS JUST ONE OF THE
MANY WAYS IN WHICH PLANTS ORGANIZE THEIR LIVES.

Compared to animals, plants have amazingly wide-
ranging life spans. At one end of the spectrum some
live for only a few weeks, while bristlecone pines can
keep going for more than 5,000 years. Creosote bushes can
reach their 10,000th birthday because each clump keeps on
spreading long after its oldest part is dead. A few—including
many bamboos—bloom in a single, suicidal burst. But whatever
their lifespan, plants divide up their lives in different ways.

△ *Mulleins are biennial plants. During
the first year (top photograph) the plant
is low-growing and has a rosette of leaves.
In the second year it puts all of its energy
into growing an impressive flower head
that can be over 6.5 ft. (2m) high.*

A SPEEDY START
For most weeds the important
thing in life is speed. These plants
often grow on unsettled ground,
and they need to flower and seed
before larger plants push them out.
Instead of storing away food for
hard times they put all their energy
into flowering, and after this they
die. These plants are known as
annuals because they complete their
whole life cycle in less than one year.
Annuals include poppies and other
wayside weeds, as well as plants that
spring up in deserts soon after it rains.

A LIFE DIVIDED IN TWO
In places where the winters are
cold many plants follow a different
timetable. They live for two years, and
in the first year they concentrate on
growing and storing up food. In the
second year they use up all of their
food reserves to grow flowers. Then
their lives usually come to an end.
These plants are known as biennials.

△ *Field poppies are typical annual plants
with a life cycle lasting only a few weeks.
They do not live long as plants, but their
seeds can survive for many years in the soil.*

△ *In mountain pastures many perennial plants grow from tubers or bulbs. These orchids are flowering in the Pyrenees.*

Biennials store food in roots or tubers because there is less chance of being eaten underground. Carrots are biennials—they are dug up after their first year, before they have a chance to flower and seed.

PERMANENT PLANTS

Annuals and biennials are temporary plants. They are quick to appear, but they never grow in the same place for long. The reason that they keep on the move is that they have to compete against plants that are designed to last. These permanent plants are called perennials. They include ones that die down to ground level at the end of every year, as well as all of the world's shrubs and trees. Compared to annuals and biennials, perennials play a long-term game. They often grow slowly, and it can take them

years to reach adult size. But once they are mature, they keep faster-growing plants in the shade. Unlike their smaller rivals, most perennials keep flowering year after year.

GRAND FINALE

More than 99 percent of all of the world's plants follow one of these life cycles. The ones that do not are the plant world's real eccentrics, saving all of their energy for a once-in-a-lifetime explosion of flowers. These plants include many different types of

△ *Agave flower heads can be more than 50 ft. (15m) high. Something this big takes a huge amount of energy to grow, which is why agaves flower only once and then die.*

bamboos, as well as agaves, many bromeliads, and the famous talipot palm (see page 105). Talipot palms grow until they are around 75 years old, and then they produce one of the biggest flower shows in the world. Although the tree dies, this grand finale is not in vain because it produces a gigantic crop of seeds.

△ *The Australian Christmas tree is a woody perennial. As long as it gets enough water, it grows bigger every year. At Christmas it produces a stunning display of flowers.*

▷ *Ferns have complicated life cycles that involve two separate types of plants. "Adult" ferns release spores that germinate to produce plants called gametophytes. These make male and female sex cells that come together to produce the next generation of adult plants. Fern gametophytes are paper-thin and are often smaller than a stamp.*

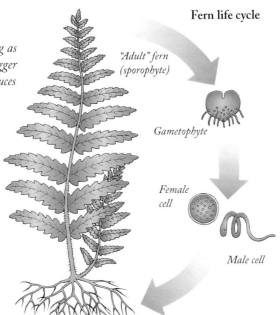

Fern life cycle

"Adult" fern (sporophyte)

Gametophyte

Female cell

Male cell

TREES

Trees are the tallest and heaviest living things that have ever existed on Earth. For thousands of years people have used them for their wood and for food, but even today new types are still being discovered in remote parts of the world.

△ *This picture shows magnified cells deep inside an oak tree's trunk.*

People often talk about trees and plants as if they were different things. It is easy to see why because trees grow to such impressive sizes. But trees are plants, even though they are built on a gigantic scale. The feature that makes trees special is that they have trunks and branches made out of wood. Wood is the plant world's strongest building material. It takes time and energy to make, but it enables trees to tower above other plants. This gives trees an unbeatable advantage in the struggle to collect light.

REACHING FOR THE SKY
The world's tallest trees are coast redwoods that grow in northern California. Helped by the mild and foggy coastal climate, these majestic conifers can be more than 360 ft. (110m) high. In the past some trees were even taller than this. In 1885 the giant trunk of a fallen mountain ash was discovered in Australia.

▷ *This giant fig tree from the Kakamega Forest in Kenya is held up by huge buttress roots that snake their way across the ground. Figs are broad-leaved trees, and they grow mainly in warm parts of the world.*

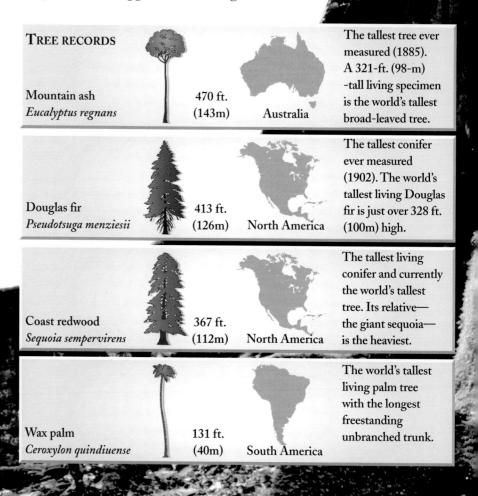

TREE RECORDS			
Mountain ash *Eucalyptus regnans*		470 ft. (143m)	Australia	The tallest tree ever measured (1885). A 321-ft. (98-m)-tall living specimen is the world's tallest broad-leaved tree.
Douglas fir *Pseudotsuga menziesii*		413 ft. (126m)	North America	The tallest conifer ever measured (1902). The world's tallest living Douglas fir is just over 328 ft. (100m) high.
Coast redwood *Sequoia sempervirens*		367 ft. (112m)	North America	The tallest living conifer and currently the world's tallest tree. Its relative— the giant sequoia— is the heaviest.
Wax palm *Ceroxylon quindiuense*		131 ft. (40m)	South America	The world's tallest living palm tree with the longest freestanding unbranched trunk.

When this tree was alive, it probably towered more than 460 ft. (140m) above the ground. But some dendrologists, or tree experts, believe prehistoric trees may have reached 574 ft. (175m)—around 25 stories high. When architects design skyscrapers, they know exactly how tall the finished building will be, but a tree keeps growing up until something stops it or makes it fall down.

The threats that trees face include lightning, drought, and wind, and the taller a tree grows the more dangerous these threats become.

△ *California's upright coast redwoods are a tempting target for loggers. Over the years conservationists have battled to keep these conifers from being cut down.*

TYPES OF TREES

With a few rare exceptions, all of the world's trees belong to just two groups of plants. The first contains conifers, which are trees that grow their seeds in cones. Most of these trees are evergreens with scaly or needle-shaped leaves. Conifers grow quickly and often have stick-straight trunks—something that makes them very useful as timber trees. There are only around 550 species of conifers, which is very few compared to the total number of plant species in the world. But conifers are very common, and because they are planted for their wood they are becoming more widespread all the time.

The second group contains broad-leaved trees. Not all of them actually have broad leaves, but they do all grow flowers. Some have flowers that are pollinated by the wind, but many have eye-catching blossoms that attract animal visitors. In the tropics broad-leaved trees are usually evergreen, but in places with dry seasons or cold winters their branches are bare for several months every year. Broad-leaved trees are amazingly varied, and they live in all types of habitats—from deserts to seashore mud. Over 10,000 species have been identified, but no one knows how many types there are.

1   2   3

△ *Broad-leaved trees all have flowers, but they are pollinated in different ways. Oak trees (1) have catkins pollinated by the wind. Judas trees (2) and horse chestnuts (3) have flowers pollinated by insects.*

◁ *Trees growing in exposed places often develop a lopsided shape. This happens because the prevailing wind kills buds on one side of the tree, making it grow in the opposite direction. This windswept shape protects the tree.*

SAPWOOD AND HEARTWOOD

Trees do not simply grow up: most of them grow out at the same time. This outward growth is produced by the cambium—a layer of living tissue just a few cells thick. The cambium is located right beneath the bark, and it covers the entire tree like an invisible film. Trees

HOW TREES GROW

TREES CAN KEEP GROWING FOR HUNDREDS OF YEARS, SO THEY HAVE TO BE BUILT FOR STRENGTH. MOST TREES STEADILY REINFORCE THEMSELVES AS THEY GROW, SO THE OLDER AND TALLER THEY ARE, THE STRONGER THEY BECOME.

In the tropics some trees rush up at a rate of 16 ft. (5m) per year—around 100 times faster than humans grow during their teens. In other parts of the world trees grow more slowly, but some still extend up a few feet every spring. For trees growing is a complicated business, and it has to be carefully managed. That is because every extra foot increases the risks of getting blown down or falling apart.

△ *Banyan trees sprout roots that can turn into extra trunks. The world's largest banyan tree has more than 1,700 trunks and covers an area bigger than a soccer field.*

▽ *In the mountains the higher up trees are, the more slowly they grow. The timberline marks the point where conditions become too tough for survival.*

△ *The traveler's tree from Madagascar grows a gigantic fan of leaves. The youngest leaves are on the top of the fan, and the oldest ones are on the sides.*

grow when the cells in their cambium start to divide. On the inside layer of the cambium the cells produce new wood that makes the trunk and the branches expand. On the outside layer they produce new bark that pushes out, making the old bark split or fall away. These two types of growth fatten up a tree, giving it the extra strength it needs.

Because the cambium stays near the surface, this is where a tree's youngest wood is found. Called sapwood, it is sometimes so full of sap that it feels slippery and wet if it is cut. But as each year's sapwood gets older, it gradually starts to change. It stops carrying sap because its cells become blocked with resins and oils. This turns it into heartwood—old wood that is heavy and hard. Heartwood strengthens trunks and branches like an inner skeleton. But unlike bone, heartwood cannot grow because almost all of its cells are dead.

GROWTH RINGS
In places where it is always wet and warm trees can grow all year-round. But where the winters are cold all the year's wood is formed in a single burst during the spring and early summer. These bursts of growth create rings in the wood that can be seen when the trees are cut down.

By counting growth rings, it is easy to figure out a tree's age. But growth rings can reveal much more than this. Because they are thick when growing conditions are good and thin when they are bad, they also show what the weather was like in the past. By examining growth rings from the world's oldest trees, dendrochronologists—or tree ring experts—have been able to piece together a climate record for the world dating back over 5,000 years.

△ *Talipot palms from Southeast Asia flower once and then die. Each tree can have more than 250,000 creamy yellow flowers.*

PALM TREES
Most trees have a "wraparound" cambium, but palms and their close relatives are built in a different way. They have just one single growing point at the very tips of their trunks. The growing point builds the trunk, and as it moves up, growth beneath it stops. If the top of a palm is cut off, the tree stops growing and dies.

This unusual growth technique means that palm trunks get taller without getting any wider—one of the reasons why they are such graceful trees. Palm trunks do not have true bark, which means that

they cannot heal cuts in the same way as other trees. People who harvest coconuts make use of this. The steps that they cut into a coconut palm in order to climb it last for its entire life.

CHANGING SHAPES
Palm trees never have branches, but with other trees new branches often shade out the old ones lower down. To deal with this problem, trees often carry out their own tree surgery by shedding the branches closest to the ground. This surgery starts when a tree is young, and it continues year after year. As a result, the remaining branches move higher and higher, and the tree develops a crown. Some of the world's greatest branch shedders grow in tropical forests. Here the tallest trees end up with smooth, branchless trunks up to 98 ft. (30m) high, soaring up like pillars from the forest floor.

Trees respond to their surroundings in other ways. They grow taller if they are crowded, and they often lean away from the prevailing winds. In shady conditions they often have larger leaves. These different growth patterns help explain why no two trees are exactly the same.

Conifers usually have short branches and keep their upright shape as they grow.

Palms have no branches. They grow taller, but their trunks do not become thicker.

Most broad-leaved trees change shape as they get older, developing a rounded crown.

PLANT DEFENSES

PLANTS CANNOT BITE BACK AT HUNGRY ANIMALS, BUT THEY HAVE PLENTY OF WEAPONS THAT CAN STOP THEM IN THEIR TRACKS OR EVEN KILL THEM.

△ *Stingers give nettles protection from plant-eating mammals. Cattle and horses eat many other wild plants, but they stay far away from nettles.*

△ *Poison ivy contains a chemical called urushiol, which causes skin inflammation. The poison can be spread on clothing and even in smoke if the plant is burned.*

In the animal kingdom vegetarians outnumber predators by at least 10 to 1. From insects to elephants they make up billions of mouths, all hungry for their share of food. Without protection the world's plants would be helpless, and every last trace of them would soon disappear. But plants manage to thrive. That is because evolution has given them ingenious—and sometimes painful— ways of fighting back.

SECRET SHIELDS

The most common weapons in the plant world can only be seen through a microscope. They are tiny hairs, and they cover many plants like miniature forests less than an inch high. Some of these hairs are branched and are designed to snap off and clog up insects' mouths. Others produce blobs of sticky substances that trap aphids and other sapsuckers before they have a chance to feed. Hairs are particularly important for protecting new stems and leaves, which is why they often have a silky or sticky feel.

To fend off much larger animals, bigger weapons are needed. On their stems and leaves nettles have hollow hairs made of silica, which work like hypodermic needles. If an animal— or person—touches one of these hairs, the tip snaps off and injects a collection of toxic chemicals, including formic acid, the same substance found in ant stings.

△ *Cholla cacti have brittle stems covered in spines. If an animal touches one of these plants, pieces of stem break off and attach themselves to its skin.*

▷ *Animals often use camouflage to avoid attack, but this tactic is much harder for plants. These living stones, found in the deserts of southwest Africa, masquerade as pebbles in their gravel-covered home.*

Stings from the common nettle hurt for a few hours and then fade away, but some species—such as the New Zealand nettle tree—have much more powerful stings that have been known to kill farm animals. However these stings are too large to bother insects, which is why many caterpillars grow fat on a diet of nettle leaves.

SPINES AND THORNS

In dry habitats animals use plants for water as well as for food. Here plants often defend themselves with an armor of vicious spines. Acacia trees have woody spines that are up to 6 in. (15cm) long, but the most painful spines belong to cacti. Some cactus spines have overlapping scales that point back toward the plant. If one of these gets into an animal's skin, the scales make it very hard—and uncomfortable—for the spine to work its way out. As if this were not enough, cacti also have another defense because their spines sit in tufts of slender hairs. These hairs look harmless, but they break off easily. Once they get into the skin, they cause an irritation that can last for days.

Spines give animals an instant warning, making them move away, but thorns often have the opposite effect. Because thorns are curved, they hook into an animal's skin, making it difficult for the animal to escape. While the animal struggles to extract itself, it learns a painful lesson. Hopefully it remembers not to tangle with the plant a second time.

CHEMICAL WEAPONS

If an animal does get through a plant's outer defenses, it may have an unpleasant surprise in store. This is because many plants use chemical weapons to avoid ending up as food. Some of these substances simply make leaves taste bitter or become difficult to digest, but they also include some deadly poisons. For example a common garden shrub called cherry laurel can produce cyanide in its leaves. Normally the leaves are quite harmless because they contain the ingredients for making cyanide rather than the poison itself. But if an animal starts to feed on them, cyanide starts to form. Its sickly sweet smell warns the animal that it is playing with death.

Most plant poisons have to be swallowed or breathed in before they work, but some are dangerous even if they touch the skin. Poison ivy is one of the most notorious because it produces a toxic resin that can stick to clothing and shoes. Even months later its effects can still be felt.

△ *Many plants produce latex—a milky sap containing defensive chemicals. Here latex is being tapped from a rubber tree by cutting into the wood.*

▷ *For plants animals can be allies as well as enemies. These South American ants live inside cecropia trees. In return for a home they attack anything that tries to eat the trees' leaves.*

CARNIVOROUS PLANTS

TO A CARELESS FLY A VENUS'S-FLYTRAP SEEMS
LIKE A GOOD PLACE TO LAND. BUT THIS IS
A DEADLY MISTAKE BECAUSE THE FLYTRAP IS
CARNIVOROUS, AND IT USES FLIES AS FOOD.

Plants grow by using sunlight, but they also need simple nutrients just like we need salt and other minerals. Most plants get these from the ground, but carnivorous plants get some of theirs by catching and digesting animals. These plants have developed sophisticated lures and traps, and most of them catch insects.

OPEN AND SHUT

The Venus's-flytrap is barely more than ankle high, but it is one of the strangest plants in the world. Each of its leaves is divided into two flat lobes bordered by a row of spikes. The lobes join at a hinge, but they are normally held wide open to make an inviting landing platform for passing flies. The platform has a special attraction: it produces sugary nectar that insects use as food. But if a fly lands to feed, it brushes against special trigger hairs, and the trap

springs into action. Within half a second the lobes snap shut, and the spikes lock the fly inside. No matter how hard it buzzes the fly is doomed, and within the next hour it dies.

Once the flytrap has caught its prey, its digestive enzymes get to work. They break down the fly's body so that the plant can absorb the nutrients it contains. Several days later the remains of the fly fall out, and the trap is ready for another catch.

STUCK FAST

Venus's-flytraps are amazingly sensitive, and they can tell the

◁ *Caught by a Venus's-flytrap, a fly is digested. Each trap catches up to four insects before withering away.*

◁▽ *Climbing pitcher plants have traps at the ends of their leaves. Each trap has a lid and a funnel. The pool of digestive fluid often contains dead remains.*

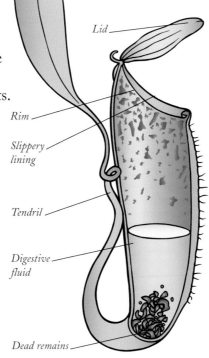

Lid

Rim

Slippery lining

Tendril

Digestive fluid

Dead remains

△ *There are over 100 species of sundews, which is about one fourth of all the world's carnivorous plants. This one—growing in a peat bog—has caught a damselfly.*

difference between appetizing insects and inedible objects that fall into their traps by chance. But most of the world's carnivorous plants "hunt" in a different way. They lure insects into sticky situations, making it very difficult for them to escape. Some of the most common of these plants are called sundews. They live all over the world, especially on mountains and in boggy places. A sundew's leaves are covered in sticky hairs that carry drops of gluelike fluid. If an insect lands on a sundew's leaf, the hairs fold over it until it cannot escape.

DEATH BY DROWNING
Insects are often attracted to sweet-smelling drinks, and sometimes they fall into them and drown. Pitcher plants use exactly the same principle to catch their prey. There are several types of pitcher plants, and they grow in many habitats—from marshlands to tropical forests. Although they belong to different plant families, their traps all work in a similar way. Each pitcher is like a vase, and it has a slippery rim that lets off a rotting scent. If an insect

lands on the rim to investigate the smell, it slips over and tumbles inside. The bottom of the pitcher contains a pool of digestive juices that turns insects into meals.

Some pitcher plants are barely one inch tall and have traps that sit on the ground. But the world's largest species—from Southeast Asia and Australia—can be over 20 ft. (6m) tall and climbs up through trees and shrubs. One of the rarest of these plants—*Nepenthes rajah*—lives in the rain forests of northwest Borneo. Its pitchers can hold over four cups (1L) of fluid, and they are so large that rats have been known to fall into them and drown.

BLIND EXIT
Most pitchers have flaps that work like umbrellas, stopping rainwater from getting inside. But a plant called the cobra lily, from California and Oregon, has hooded pitchers with protruding tongues. The tongues produce nectar that attracts flies searching for food. When a fly lands it walks along the tongue and into the pitcher's mouth. Here it sees a collection of tiny windows above it. The insect flies up toward the windows but finds it cannot escape.

△ *The Albany pitcher plant grows in southwest Australia. Its pitchers are close to the ground—the ideal place to catch beetles and ants looking for food.*

Soon it becomes exhausted and drops into the deadly fluid below.

UNDERWATER HUNTERS
The Venus's-flytrap reacts amazingly quickly, but some even faster hunters set their traps in ponds and lakes. These plants are called bladderworts, and they catch tiny water animals

△ *These balloon-shaped objects are a bladderwort's underwater traps. Although they look harmless, they are a deadly threat to small animals that come too close.*

such as worms and water fleas. Bladderworts drift across the water's surface, and as well as having upright stems they have curling underwater stems that look very similar to roots. These underwater stems carry the plant's hunting equipment. Each one contains dozens of traps that look like tiny balloons. Each trap has a small trapdoor that is normally kept tightly shut. To prime the traps the plant pumps out some of their water so that the pressure in them is lower than the water outside. If an animal swims too close to a trap, it touches a set of bristles that are attached to the door. The door flicks open, and the trap sucks in water, carrying the animal inside. The door then snaps shut. Once the victim has been digested, the trap is reprimed so that it is ready for another catch.

Peering out of its own private pond, this tree frog lives high up in a rain forest in Central America. Its home is a bromeliad plant, which is especially adapted for life above the ground. The bromeliad's scarlet-colored leaves collect rainwater, and they funnel it into a central tank. This water store keeps the plant alive, and it also gives the frog an unusual home.

PASSENGERS AND PARASITES

MOST PLANTS RELY ON THEIR OWN RESOURCES IN THE DAILY STRUGGLE TO SURVIVE, BUT SOME USE THEIR NEIGHBORS AS WELL. THESE PLANTS INCLUDE HARMLESS PASSENGERS, AS WELL AS SOME DAMAGING OR DEADLY PARASITES.

△ *Unlike most epiphytes, air plants can survive in places where the climate is dry. This one has managed to set up home on a telephone line.*

In the plant world light is the key to success. Individual plants grab as much as they can, but the competition is tough, especially if there are trees nearby. Plants called epiphytes have developed a way around this problem—they perch on other plants. Parasitic plants are more ruthless. They attack their hosts, stealing their water and food.

△ *There are around 20,000 types of orchids in the world, and over half of them are epiphytes that grow on other plants. This king orchid from Queensland, Australia, is growing on a tree trunk.*

FREE RIDES

Epiphytic plants are specialists in life off of the ground. Most of them live on trees because this gives them a solid perch where they can safely grow for many years. In temperate regions—such as North America and Europe—the most common epiphytes are mosses and ferns, but in the tropics trunks and branches are often draped with flowering plants as well. These high-rise flowerers include some of the world's most beautiful orchids, as well as spiky plants, called bromeliads, that can grow to be larger than a shopping cart and can weigh more than an adult man.

Despite their differences epiphytes share a number of interesting adaptations for their unusual way of life. They hang onto their hosts with specialized roots or stems, and they also use these for collecting water when it rains. They get nutrients from airborne dust or from dead leaves that fall on them from above.

UNWELCOME APPROACH

Epiphytes do not cause their host plants any harm, although if there are too many of them their weight can sometimes bring branches crashing to the ground. Parasitic plants are different because they

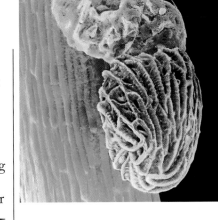

live at their hosts' expense. There are different levels to this sneaky lifestyle—some parasites merely steal from their neighbors, others grow on them, and a few actually spend their lives hidden away inside of them.

The Australian Christmas tree (see page 101) is an example of a parasite that robs its neighbors. Its roots break into ones grown by nearby plants so that it can siphon off

▽ Rafflesia plants have no roots and no leaves but gigantic flowers. Their seeds are spread by large forest animals, including elephants.

their water and sap. Its most common hosts are grasses, but it will try to break into almost anything that is shaped like a root, including buried cables.

Because roots are hidden away, it is difficult to recognize parasites that steal underground. Aboveground parasites are much easier to spot. One of the most common is a plant called dodder, which is found in many parts of the world. Its spaghettilike stems swarm over its host, producing small growths that steal water and nutrients by breaking into its stems. Dodder starts life on the ground, but its roots soon wither

△ Dodder stems wind around their host plants, seeking out places where they can break in and steal water and nutrients.

away. It can leap from host to host, creating a tangled web many feet wide.

PLANT INVADERS

Mistletoe is a parasite that many people have heard of because it is often gathered and hung up at Christmastime. It lives on trees and spreads by growing berries that contain sticky seeds. Birds eat the berries, but the seeds often stick in their beaks. When they clean their beaks on branches, the seeds are left behind. Dwarf mistletoe, from North America, spreads in

△ Witchweeds are parasites that attack many crops, including corn, rice, and sugarcane. Here a witchweed seed— colored orange—is germinating and has started attacking a plant.

an explosive way. Its berries burst open when they are ripe, firing their seeds sideways at speeds of up to 62 mph (100km/h). The world's most impressive parasite—giant rafflesia —lives in the forests of Sumatra. It attacks vines, and its flowers are the largest of any in the world. But this is the only part of the plant that is ever seen because the rest is hidden away inside its unlucky host.

△ This old poplar tree has been attacked by dozens of mistletoe plants. With so many parasites stealing its nutrients, the tree will find it difficult to grow.

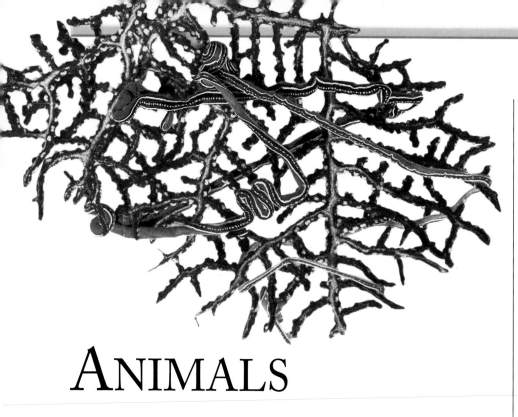

ANIMALS

THE WORLD IS FILLED WITH ANIMALS. THEY LIVE IN EVERY HABITAT—FROM TROPICAL FORESTS TO POLAR ICE. SO FAR SCIENTISTS HAVE IDENTIFIED AROUND TWO MILLION DIFFERENT TYPES, BUT MILLIONS MORE ARE STILL WAITING TO BE DISCOVERED.

There is no such thing as a typical animal because animals are the most varied living things on Earth. Some types are as soft as jelly and hardly look like animals at all, while many have much more complex bodies with tough skeletons, sharp senses, and weapons such as teeth, claws, or stingers.

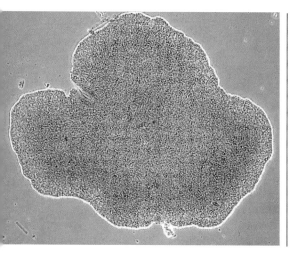

◁ *Placozoans were discovered in 1883 by a sharp-eyed scientist who found them in a saltwater aquarium. They are not the world's smallest animals, but they are the simplest. They have no close relatives.*

ANIMAL FEATURES
The world's simplest animals are so tiny that they can just barely be seen with the naked eye. Called placozoans, they are shaped like miniature pancakes, and their paper-thin bodies are only 0.08 in. (2mm) wide. Placozoans live in water, and

◁ *Ribbon worms are the longest animals in the world. One record-breaking specimen measured over 180 ft. (55m) from its head to the tip of its tail—making it over 50 percent longer than the biggest blue whale.*

they do not have eyes, fins, or even mouths. They creep over rocks and grains of sand, and they reproduce by breaking into separate pieces that take on life on their own.

It would take 15,000 placozoans lined up end to end to cover the full length of a blue whale. This seagoing mammal is the largest animal that has ever lived, weighing up to 190 tons. Despite this incredible difference in size, placozoans and whales do have some things in common. Like all animals, their bodies are made up of many cells. They have to eat to survive, and they are able to move around.

CELLS AND SKELETONS
Placozoans have just a few hundred cells, but most animals—including humans—have millions or billions. In an animal's body cells are divided into different types, and each type carries out different kinds of work. Some cells protect an animal's body from the outside world, while others help it absorb and digest its food. Most animals also have nerve cells that keep their bodies coordinated and muscle cells that enable them to move. Sensory organs are also part of the nervous system. They help animals keep track of changes around them, so they can escape from danger or find food.

▷ Mammals dominate life on land, but they make up less than three percent of all animal species on Earth. These gemsboks are experts at living in dry habitats—they can get all their water from their food.

Unlike plant cells, animal cells are soft and flexible because they do not have cell walls. But some animal cells produce hard substances that give them extra strength. These substances include chalky minerals, which make up shells and bones, and chitin, which makes insect body cases. Chitin looks and feels like plastic, and it is tough, waterproof, and extremely light.

◁ Sharp eyesight and spiky talons make the sparrow hawk a highly effective predator. This one is feeding on a bird that it has attacked and killed.

FOOD AND FEEDING

No matter how or where they live, all animals need food. Food provides them with energy and with the substances that they need to grow. Most animals either eat plants or other animals, but some have much more unusual diets based on leftovers or dead remains. For example museum beetles eat mummified corpses that have dried out in the sunlight. These scavengers do a very useful job in nature, but they can wreak havoc when they attack stuffed animals in museums.

Because animals do not need light to survive, they can live in many more places than plants. Many animals live in the darkness, either in the soil, in caves, or in the depths of the sea. Many more animals are active at night, when there is less of a chance of them being spotted and attacked.

ANIMALS ON THE MOVE

Compared to other living things, animals are expert movers. They run, crawl, burrow, or swim, and some of them can fly or glide. Whales, birds, and butterflies can travel thousands of miles each year, and even slow movers—such as snails—manage to cover an impressive distance during their lives. Some animals have a lot of stamina and can keep on the move for days. Swifts, for example, eat and sleep in the air and fly without a break until they are three or four years old. But on land many predators move in short bursts because they use speed and surprise to catch their prey.

Animals are not the only things that can move around—many microorganisms can as well. But animals are by far the biggest and fastest travelers in the natural world. However the animal kingdom also contains plenty of creatures that spend their adult lives fixed in one place. These animals include corals, barnacles, and giant clams. Because they live in the water, they can survive by just sitting and waiting for food to drift their way.

SHAPES AND SKELETONS

ALL ANIMALS NEED TO KEEP IN SHAPE. SOME OF THEM ARE AS SOFT AS JELLY, BUT MANY HAVE A HARD FRAMEWORK THAT HOLDS THEIR BODIES TOGETHER.

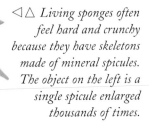

◁△ *Living sponges often feel hard and crunchy because they have skeletons made of mineral spicules. The object on the left is a single spicule enlarged thousands of times.*

The world's simplest animals are all soft-bodied. Most of them live in the sea, where the water helps keep them afloat. On land being soft is not as much of a good idea because gravity can make soft things collapse. This is one of the reasons why most large animals have hard skeletons. These hold their bodies together so that they can keep their shape and move around. Skeletons can also make an animal more difficult to attack.

ANIMALS UNDER PRESSURE

Soft-bodied animals are not difficult to find. They include many seashore creatures, such as sea anemones and jellyfish, and also a very common land animal: the earthworm. An earthworm has no hard body parts, but it has no trouble pushing its way through the ground. If it is picked up, it can squeeze its way between a person's fingers with surprising strength.

How does something soft manage to do this? The answer is that an earthworm's body is divided into dozens of compartments, and each one is under pressure like a tire. This pressure comes from a fluid, and it pushes out against the worm's skin, helping it keep its shape. When the worm wants to move, it makes its compartments stretch and contract. Normally this pushes the worm forward, although it can just as easily go in reverse.

SPONGY SKELETONS

When animals developed skeletons, they came up with several different types. Some of the most unusual ones belong to sponges. These primitive animals do not have heads or brains, but they do have internal scaffolding made up of microscopic particles of silica and other minerals. These particles are called spicules. Some spicules are straight, while others are shaped like hooks or even tiny stars. A single sponge has millions of them, and they are often linked together by fibers that help give a sponge its shape. A bath sponge is a complete skeleton without the sponge's living cells. Before it can be sold, it has to be cleaned because sponges often have sand and small animals inside them.

LIVING IN A CASE

Unlike sponges, the world's most successful animals are often on the

◁▽ *Flatworms (left) and sea anemones (below) have soft bodies. Like many soft-bodied animals they can move—but only slowly. Flatworms ripple through the water, while sea anemones creep over rocks.*

move. Called arthropods they include an incredible array of creatures that hop, scurry, run, swim, or fly. The most common arthropods are insects, but this huge group of animals contains many other species, such as spiders, scorpions, and crustaceans and also centipedes and millipedes.

Arthropods are extremely varied, but they have one feature in common—a skeleton that works like a case. The case is made of separate

△ *This spider has almost finished molting. It is hanging beneath its old body case, which is attached to a leaf by its empty legs.*

plates that meet at flexible joints. It fits around the animal's entire body, with tubular plates for legs and transparent ones for eyes. The case helps an animal keep its shape and stops it from drying out. Because it is flexible it lets its owner move.

Arthropod body cases are almost as varied as arthropods themselves. In crabs and lobsters they are like suits of armor, protecting them from attack. Scorpions also have tough cases, but because they live on land theirs combine lightness with strength. A mosquito's body case is ultrathin because it spends most of its life in the air.

SHELLS AND BONES

Body cases are one of nature's most successful "inventions," but they have two serious drawbacks. The first is that they are heavy and cumbersome if they are too big. That is why most of the world's arthropods are only an inch or so long. Secondly a body case cannot grow. Instead it has to be discarded or molted from time to time and a replacement grown in its place.

Shells do not have this disadvantage because they can grow along with their owners. They are very good at protecting the animal inside but not much help for moving around. But there is one type of skeleton that can move and also grow. It is the type that we have, and it is made of bone.

FLEXIBLE FRAMEWORK

Vertebrates are the only animals that can grow bones, so they are the only ones with bony skeletons. They include fish, amphibians, reptiles, birds, and also mammals—such as ourselves. Unlike body cases,

△ *The giant African land snail is the largest shelled animal that lives out of the water. Its spiral shell can measure over 10 in. (25cm) long.*

a vertebrate's skeleton is on the inside. It has flexible joints that allow it to move, but it is also very strong.

Bones contain living cells, and they grow along with the rest of an animal's body. This means that vertebrates do not need to molt. Better yet a bony skeleton can grow very large without making it difficult to move. That is why the world's largest animals are all vertebrates— on land, in the sea, and in the air.

▷ *A gibbon's skeleton contains over 200 separate bones. The joints in its arms are very flexible. It can swing from branches almost as fast as a person can run and can leap over 33 ft. (10m) from tree to tree.*

BREATHING

WHEN A WHALE COMES TO THE SURFACE
AFTER A DEEP DIVE, ITS NUMBER ONE PRIORITY
IS AIR. ON AVERAGE WE BREATHE AROUND
15 TIMES A MINUTE, BUT MANY WHALES CAN
HOLD THEIR BREATH FOR OVER AN HOUR.

Animals breathe, or respire, because their bodies need to take in oxygen and get rid of carbon dioxide. Some small animals, such as flatworms, simply let these gases flow through their skin. But most animals need much more oxygen, especially if they lead active lives. They get it with the help of respiratory organs, which include gills and lungs. These organs have a rich blood supply. Blood flows through them to collect oxygen and then delivers it to where it is needed.

△ *Like many freshwater insects, diving beetles have to come to the surface to breathe air. They store air under their wing cases, so they have to swim hard to dive deeper.*

△ *After diving a humpback whale blasts a jet of oily-smelling breath into the air. Most whales have a pair of blowholes, but sperm whales have just one on the left side of their snouts.*

BREATHING UNDERWATER

Water contains plenty of dissolved oxygen, especially if it is cold. Mammals cannot breathe this oxygen—even ones that are full-time swimmers such as seals and whales. But fish breathe it all the time because they are equipped with gills.

Gills are collections of flaps or filaments that are surrounded by water. They have a large surface, but they are also very thin, so oxygen can easily flow into them while carbon dioxide flows out. Most fish gills are hidden away in hollow chambers just behind their heads. When a fish swims, water flows in through its mouth, past its gills, and then out through slits or holes. The faster the fish moves, the more oxygen its gills take in. When a fish is still it often "gulps" water to keep up its oxygen supply. A few fish, such as the mudskipper, can survive in the air. But for most fish being hauled onto land spells certain death. Their gills stick together, preventing them from getting the oxygen they need.

BREATHING TUBES

Fish are not the only animals with gills—tadpoles have them too. So do lobsters, crabs, and clams, as well as some insects that swim or dive. But insects were originally land animals. This explains why most of them have to come to the surface so that they can breathe air.

Insects have a unique system for getting oxygen into their bodies. Instead of lungs they have a set of breathing tubes called tracheae. The tubes open to the outside through holes called spiracles that are along an insect's sides. Inside the animal each tube divides into thousands of microscopic branches that supply oxygen to individual cells. Small insects let oxygen flow through their tubes unaided, but large ones—such as grasshoppers—often contract

▽ *This newt tadpole breathes through a set of feathery gills. As it turns into an adult, it will slowly lose its gills and instead breathe through its lungs and its skin.*

their muscles to help it on its way.

When an insect sheds its skin, it has to shed the lining of all its breathing tubes as well. As the skin falls away the linings

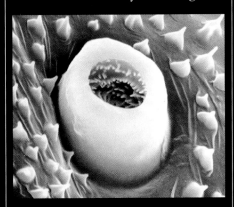

△ *Magnified hundreds of times, this picture shows a single spiracle belonging to a caterpillar. Spiracles are normally arranged in a line along an insect's sides.*

are pulled inside out, just like discarded socks.

TAKING A BREATHER

Tracheae work well for insects because their bodies are small. But animals with backbones, aside from fish, all breathe by using lungs. Unlike gills, lungs are hollow, and they are hidden away inside the body. They contain millions of small air spaces that make it easy for oxygen to flow into the blood. A shrew's lungs are smaller than peas, while a whale's are often bigger than a car. Despite this enormous difference in size, they work in a very similar way. When

a mammal takes a breath, muscles make its chest expand. This makes the lungs expand as well, and they suck in air from the outside. To breathe out the animal lets its chest muscles relax. As its chest contracts the lungs shrink, and used air is squeezed out. But if an animal is highly active, its chest muscles work much harder. They suck in up to five times as much air as normal and also force much more of it out.

HIGH FLIERS

After a two-hour dive elephant seals only need about five minutes at the surface to catch their breath. But the real experts at collecting oxygen are birds. A bird's lungs are connected to hollow chambers called air sacs that reach right inside their bones. Air flows through a bird's lungs in a one-way stream, allowing them to collect as much oxygen as possible. Birds need highly efficient lungs because flying uses up so much energy—up to ten times as much as when they are sitting on a perch. Extraefficient lungs also enable them to fly at high altitudes where the air is thin. Some birds can fly at altitudes of over 6 mi. (10km), a height that would leave human beings gasping for air.

▽ *Due to their extraefficient lungs, yellow-billed choughs manage to live at over 19,680 ft. (6,000m) in the Himalayas.*

HOW ANIMALS MOVE

FOR MOST ANIMALS MOVEMENT IS VITAL FOR SURVIVAL. SOME MOVE SO SLOWLY THAT THEY WOULD TAKE ONE HOUR TO CROSS THIS PAGE, BUT THE FASTEST CAN ACCELERATE FASTER THAN A CAR.

Animals are not the only living things that move, but nothing can beat them for stamina and speed. Some birds can fly over 620 mi. (1,000km) in a single day, while over a whole lifetime a gray whale swims double the distance to the Moon. Animals move by using muscles, and they control them with their nerves and brains.

△ *A frog's back legs work in two ways— they can be used for jumping and also for swimming.*

fastest swimmer of all is the sailfish, which can hit speeds of over 62 mph (100km/h). Its muscle-packed body is streamlined, and its powerhouse is a stiff, knife-shaped tail fin that slices its way through the sea.

△ *If it is threatened, the basilisk lizard can run across the surface of rivers and ponds. Once it has traveled a good distance away from the danger, it swims off.*

IN THE SWIM
Three fourths of the world is covered in water, so swimming is an important way of moving around. The tiniest swimmers are planktonic animals that live near the surface of the sea. Some of them simply drift along, but many move by beating feathery legs or minute hairs that work like oars. Planktonic animals cannot make much headway against the current, but many of them carry out daily journeys down into the sea's depths to keep out of the way of predatory fish.

FAST MOVERS
In the water most large swimmers move using fins or flippers. The

Compared to the sailfish, whales move much more slowly. The gray whale, for example, migrates over 7,440 mi. (12,000km) a year, but its average speed is not much faster than a person walking. But dolphins and porpoises can swim fast—some of them reach speeds of 34 mph (55km/h).

Fins and flippers are not the only way of swimming in a hurry. Octopuses escape from danger by sucking up water and then squirting it backward through a funnel. This makes the octopus zoom off in the opposite direction— a type of underwater jet propulsion.

MOVING ON LAND
Some ways of moving in water also work on land. For example land snails move in exactly the same way as their watery relatives by crawling on a single suckerlike foot. To make sure that its sucker sticks, a snail

◁ *Most fish beat their tails when they swim and use their other fins for steering. Sharks are different because they swim by bending their bodies from side to side.*

△ *Several desert snakes—including this African viper—move by "sidewinding." Instead of slithering these snakes throw themselves forward over the sand.*

groups of leg-bearing animals on land. The first are the vertebrates, which are animals with backbones like ourselves. The second are the arthropods—animals that include insects, spiders, and their relatives.

Vertebrates never have more than four legs. Arthropods often have six or eight, but some have many more. The record, held by a millipede,

is an amazing 750. At the other extreme some vertebrates have gradually lost some of their legs and move on their bodies instead. A rare reptile called the ajalote has just one pair of legs, but all the world's snakes have no legs at all.

QUICK MOVERS

Because arthropods are small, they do not reach high top speeds. The fastest are cockroaches, which can run at just over 3 mph (5km/h). But as these animals weigh very little, they can perform some remarkable feats. Almost all of them can run upside down, and some can jump dozens of times their own length. They can also start and stop almost instantly—one of the reasons why people find insects alarming.

By comparison vertebrates take longer to get moving, but they are much faster overall. For example a red kangaroo is able to cruise at 30 mph (50km/h). Cheetahs—the world's fastest land animals—can hit double this, although they cannot keep up this speed for more than 30 seconds at a time.

▽ *Although it is fast, this hare is no match for a cheetah. Cheetahs move too quickly to pounce on their prey—instead they trip it up with a blow from one of their front paws.*

produces a slimy mucus that forms a trail behind it as it moves. Snails can climb up vertical surfaces and can also move upside down. But this way of getting around is not fast—at top speed a snail moves at 0.005 mph (0.008km/h).

LEGS

Legs were developed by animals that originally lived in the water and later crawled out to begin life on the land. Today there are two very different

GLIDING AND FLYING

▽ The barn owl hunts small rodents and is a specialist at flying slowly. When searching for food, it moves at 6 mph (10km/h)—slower than a human jogger. Here an owl swoops down and opens its talons, ready to grab its prey.

ANIMALS FIRST TOOK TO THE SKIES OVER 350 MILLION YEARS AGO. TODAY THE AIR IS FILLED WITH ANIMALS GLIDING OR FLYING. SOME ARE LARGE AND POWERFUL, WHILE OTHERS ARE ALMOST INVISIBLE.

Many animals can glide, but only insects, birds, and bats can truly fly. They use muscle power to flap their wings, so they can take off and land whenever they like. Insects outnumber other fliers millions of times, and their small size makes them extremely good at maneuvering in the air. Bats fly far and fast, but birds are the best aviators in the animal world. Some of them carry out airborne journeys that actually cross the Earth.

△ Flying lemurs, or colugos, are some of the world's largest gliding mammals. With their legs stretched out, their skin flaps make them look like living kites.

◁ Flapping its delicate wings, a lacewing launches itself into the air. This slow-motion sequence shows the moment of takeoff, with two pairs of wings beating together.

GREAT GLIDERS
Gliding animals include an amazing array of creatures—from rodents and marsupials to snakes, frogs, and fish. Some glide just a few feet before dropping back to the ground, but expert gliders—such as flying fish—can stay in the air for 985 ft. (300m) or more. Many of these animals use gliding as an emergency escape, but for some, such as the flying lemur,

gliding is a practical way of moving around—even for mothers who have to carry their young on board.

Gliding animals do not have true wings. Instead they have flat body parts that cushion their fall once they have launched themselves into the air. Flying fish glide on one or two pairs of extralarge fins, while flying frogs use their outstretched feet, which work like small parachutes. Gliding mammals use flaps of elastic skin that stretch between their legs and often their tail. When not in use these conveniently fold away.

△ *Flying fish glide to escape from predators. They spread their fins like wings, and some species use their tails like an outboard motor, helping launch them into the air.*

In North America monarch butterflies often migrate over 1,860 mi. (3,000km) to breed, while in Europe clouded yellow butterflies often cross the Arctic Circle in the summer to lay their eggs.

FEATHERED FLIERS

Bats can fly up to 25 mph (40km/h), but that is slow compared to some birds. Geese can exceed 56 mph

from aircraft over 7 mi. (11km) up, and it is possible that they can fly even higher. Birds set these flight records because they have hollow, lightweight bones and very efficient lungs. But their feathers are even more important. They provide a streamlined shape and help them speed through the air.

Arctic terns travel up to 31,000 mi. (50,000km) a year, which is probably more than any other animal in the

AIRBORNE INSECTS

Unlike gliders, flying insects put a lot of muscle power into staying in the air. A dragonfly beats its wings around 30 times a second, while a housefly beats its 200 times or more. Flies have just one pair of wings, but most other insects have two. In butterflies and moths the front and back wings beat together, but in dragonflies they beat in opposite directions at once. This allows dragonflies to hover and even to fly in reverse.

Most insects do not fly far, and many are so small that they are easily blown off course by the wind. But the insect world does include some true long-distance travelers.

(90km/h) in flight, while peregrine falcons hit 125 mph (200km/h) diving after their prey. Vultures have been seen

world. But sooty terns are even more impressive. They can stay airborne for over five years. Their epic flights end on tropical islands, where they eventually land to breed.

▷ *For an earwig getting ready to fly is a lengthy job. The hind wings are packed away under the much smaller forewings (1), and they are folded up over 30 times to make them fit. Once the earwig has unfolded them, the wings are surprisingly big (2).*

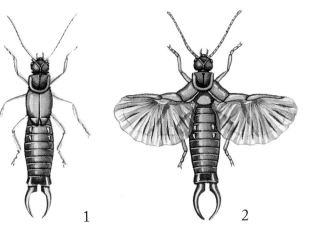

1

2

△ *Jumping spiders have four pairs of eyes. One pair is extra large and faces forward like a pair of headlights. The spider uses these eyes to judge distances before it jumps.*

ANIMAL SENSES 1

ANIMALS HAVE TO FIND FOOD, BUT THEY ALSO HAVE TO STEER CLEAR OF DANGER. THEY DO THIS BY USING SENSES THAT KEEP THEM IN TOUCH WITH THE OUTSIDE WORLD.

For humans vision and hearing are the most important senses in daily life. They tell us an immense amount about our surroundings and help us pinpoint things that are on the move. But we are not alone because many animals rely on these two senses as well. Predators often use vision or hearing to track down their prey, while prey animals often use the same senses to make a quick escape. Our senses may be sharp, but some animals' are even sharper.

SEEING AHEAD

A flatworm's eyes are so simple that they can only tell the difference between light and dark. Eyes like these are no good for finding food, but they give flatworms advance warning if a predator is lurking overhead. But most animal eyes do much more than this. They gather light and then focus it so that their owner can form an image of the surrounding scene.

Our eyes have a single lens that focuses light onto a curved screen called a retina. All mammals have eyes like these and so do other vertebrates or animals with backbones. Because we have two eyes we see the same scene from slightly different viewpoints, and this enables us to judge depth. This is very important for animals that hunt, which is why almost all of them have forward-pointing eyes as well. Plant eaters, on the other hand, often have eyes that point sideways. This allows them to keep on the lookout all around them so that they get the earliest possible

△ *For its size the tarsier has the largest eyes of any mammal. Each one is larger than its brain. Tarsiers live in tropical forests and hunt insects after dark.*

warning of approaching danger. Chameleons get the best of both worlds. Their eyes can swivel independently, so they can look in two different directions at once.

SEEING IN DETAIL

Eyes work because their retinas contain special receptor cells. These cells intercept light and convert it into electrical signals that travel to the brain. Some receptors respond to color, while others work in black and white. The more receptors there are, the more detail an eye can see.

A human eye has up to 200,000 receptors in each square millimeter of its retina, but some birds of prey have five times more. This gives them extremely sharp eyesight, allowing them to spot small animals from high up in the air. These birds are very good at seeing things that move, but they find it much harder to see things that are still. Many other predators are the same, which is why prey animals often "freeze" if they are seen.

COMPOUND EYES

When we look at other mammals, similar eyes look back at us. But facing an insect eye-to-eye is a very different experience. That is because insect eyes are built on an entirely different plan. Instead of having a single lens, they have hundreds or even thousands. Each one leads into a separate compartment, and these have up to 25,000. Its eyes are so big that they cover most of its head. Eyes this size are good at spotting movement—just what a dragonfly needs to snatch up other insects in midair.

PRIVATE CALLS

Vision has one serious drawback—it does not work in the dark. That is why many nocturnal animals rely on hearing instead. Hearing does not provide as much detail, but it works even when there are obstacles in the way. Many animals use sound to communicate because they can call while they are safely hidden away. In tropical rain forests cicadas produce deafening calls that can be heard from almost 0.6 mi. (1km) away. Despite this cicadas are extremely difficult to find. At the other end of the sound spectrum elephants communicate by rumbles that are too deep for humans to hear. These sounds carry far and wide, allowing different herds to keep in touch.

HUNTING BY SOUND

Some animals find their food by sound. They do this by producing high-pitched noises and then listening for the echoes that come back. If something is nearby the echoes return quickly, helping the hunter zone in on its food. This system is called echolocation, and it is most highly developed in bats. In one famous experiment a bat was released in a pitch-black room that was divided in two by a transparent fishnet. The bat flew through the net by closing its wings, showing that it could tell where the net was.

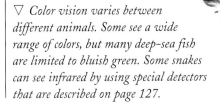

▽ To keep from being eaten some moths let off high-pitched sounds. These "jam" the echolocation signals used by bats, throwing them off course.

▽ Color vision varies between different animals. Some see a wide range of colors, but many deep-sea fish are limited to bluish green. Some snakes can see infrared by using special detectors that are described on page 127.

△ Aardwolves eat termites and search for them after dark. Their highly sensitive ears pick up the sound made by termites as they move across the ground.

combine together to produce the image that the insect sees.

These eyes are known as compound eyes, and their size and shape varies hugely throughout the insect world. Worker ants often have minute eyes with less than 50 compartments, but a dragonfly's eyes

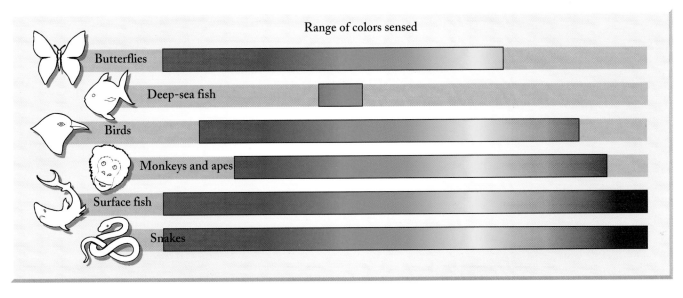

Range of colors sensed

Butterflies

Deep-sea fish

Birds

Monkeys and apes

Surface fish

Snakes

ANIMAL SENSES 2

WITHOUT VISION AND HEARING, HUMANS WOULD HAVE PROBLEMS DEALING WITH EVERYDAY LIFE, BUT IN NATURE MANY ANIMALS USE COMPLETELY DIFFERENT SENSES TO FIND THEIR WAY AROUND AND TRACK DOWN THEIR FOOD.

△ *Cave crickets use their long antennae, or feelers, to find their way through the darkness. Their antennae are very sensitive to air currents, warning the crickets if predators are nearby.*

Humans have five main senses—sight, hearing, smell, taste, and touch. We also have a sense of balance, which is often overlooked. Our sense of touch is good, but compared to many animals our senses of smell and taste are very poor. Many animals use smell and touch as they move around, and some have mysterious extra senses that detect things we cannot sense at all.

Animals use taste to test things they touch, but their sense of smell can work much farther away. Some male moths can detect the scent of a female when she is over 3 mi. (5km) away. At this distance the female's scent is so diluted that it makes up only one million billionth of the air. Regardless the male's antennae can pick up the scent molecules.

NAVIGATION BY SMELL

Animals use smell to stay in touch and often to find their food. Mammals are very good at this, and many species—from foxes to antelope—use scent to mark their territories. These scent marks cannot be seen, but they last for days or weeks, telling possible rivals that the area has already been claimed. On the whole birds do not have a good sense of smell, but there are some exceptions. American vultures are attracted by the smell of rotting flesh, for example.

For land animals smell and taste are two different senses, but in the water they merge. Most people can tell the difference between bottled and tap water, but fish and turtles can sense incredibly small variations in water's chemical composition. As well as tasting these differences, they also remember them so that they can use them like points on a map. Salmon use this sense to find their way across the sea and back into the very same rivers where they hatched.

△ *Butterflies, houseflies, and honeybees can all taste with their feet. These butterflies have settled on some animal dung and are sucking up the salts that it contains.*

TASTE AND SMELL

When a butterfly lands, it can taste what is underfoot without having to unroll its tongue. Butterflies can do this because they—and some other insects—have chemical sensors built into their legs. This remarkable system allows flies to home in on their food, and it also helps butterflies find the right plants on which to lay their eggs.

▷ *Male moths have feathery antennae that are good at collecting minute amounts of scent from the air. The females' antennae are much smaller and simpler.*

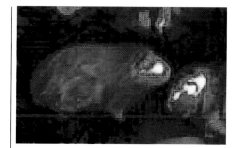

◁ △ *Rattlesnakes (left), boas, and pythons have heat sensors near their eyes. These enable snakes to hunt warm-blooded prey in the dark. The images above show the body heat of guinea pigs. In the wild this would show a rattlesnake where they were.*

snouts that detect fish hiding in seabed sand. But the most powerful animal electrician is the Amazonian electric eel. It uses an electrical field to sense its prey and then kills it with a shock of up to 600 volts. Experiments have shown that migrating birds probably use Earth's magnetic field to find their way. It is one of several senses that help them navigate, but scientists still do not know exactly how it works or how many other animals share it as well.

STRANGE SENSES

People can sense electric shocks, but we cannot sense electrical fields. Nor can we sense the magnetic field that surrounds the entire Earth. But for some animals both play a part of their everyday life.

Most animals have their own electrical field because they generate electrical impulses in their muscles and nerves. The elephant-trunk fish uses its field like a type of radar to help it find its way through muddy streams. Some sharks use electrical fields to hunt. They have electrical sensors around their mouths and

▷ *The elephant-trunk fish finds its way by using its own electrical field. Like most fish, it also has a line of pressure sensors along its sides.*

PLANT EATERS

HERBIVORES, OR PLANT EATERS, OUTNUMBER PREDATORS BY AT LEAST TEN TO ONE. THEY RANGE IN SIZE FROM THE LARGEST LAND MAMMALS TO TINY GRUBS THAT CAN FIT COMFORTABLY INSIDE OF A LEAF.

P lant food has two big advantages—it is often easy to find, and, even better, it cannot run away. For small animals there is another plus—plants make good places to hide from prying eyes. But eating plants does have some drawbacks, as this type of food takes a long time to eat, and it can be difficult to digest.

△ *In proportion to their weight, caterpillars eat more food than elephants. These tropical caterpillars have spikes to protect them from birds.*

SECRET ARMIES
Elephants can eat one third of a ton of food a day, and they often smash down trees to reach the leaves. Wild boars use different tactics, bulldozing their way through soil to reach juicy roots. But despite their size animals like these are not the most important plant eaters in the world. Instead insects and other invertebrates are far in the lead.

In tropical grasslands ants and termites often outweigh all other plant eaters put together. They collect seeds and pieces of leaves and carry them underground. In woodlands and forests many insects feed on living wood, while caterpillars chew through the leaves overhead. They have voracious appetites, and if they get into parks or plantations they can be serious pests.

Mammals often eat a wide range of plants, and so do slugs and snails. But small plant eaters are usually much more picky about their food. For example hazelnut weevils always feed on hazelnuts, while

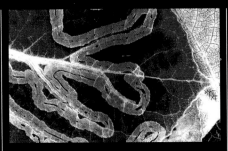

△ *This wandering trail shows where a leaf-mining caterpillar has chewed its way through a leaf. The dark patches in the trail are the caterpillar's droppings.*

▽ *Snails nibble away at plants using a set of microscopic teeth. They usually eat young plants because their leaves are thin and tender.*

red admiral caterpillars feed on nettle leaves. If these caterpillars are put on any other plant, they starve to death. Such pickiness might seem strange, but for plant eaters it sometimes pays off. This is because specialists are extraefficient at dealing with their normal food.

SEEDS AND STORES
There are very few plant-eating reptiles but many plant-eating birds. Only a small number eat leaves—instead

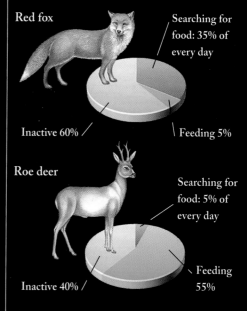

◁ Naked mole rats live underground and feed on plant tubers and roots. These African rodents are almost blind, and they hardly ever come to the surface.

most concentrate either on flowers or on fruits and seeds. Hummingbirds visit flowers to gather nectar, while some parrots collect pollen, which they lap up with their brush-tipped tongues. But fruit- and seed-eating birds are much more common, and unlike hummingbirds and parrots they live all over the world.

Seeds are an ideal food because they are packed full of nutritious oils and starches. That is why many birds and rodents feed on them. Seed-eating rodents are especially common in dry places where food can be difficult to find.

△ Like many other small rodents, kangaroo rats use their cheek pouches to carry seeds back to their nests.

Unlike birds, rodents are able to survive difficult times by collecting food and storing it underground. In central Asia some gerbils store up to 133 lbs (60kg) of seeds and roots. This massive collection can keep them well fed for months.

EATING GRASS

Seeds are easy to digest, which is one reason why they make up an important part of most people's diets. But grass and other leaves are not nearly as easy for animals

to break down. That is because they contain cellulose (see page 85), a substance that humans are not able to digest. We are not alone because grazing mammals cannot break down cellulose either, even though it makes up a large part of their food.

So how do these animals survive? The answer is that they use microorganisms to do this work for them. These organisms include bacteria and protozoans, and they have special enzymes that can split cellulose molecules apart.

Mammals keep these microorganisms in their digestive systems, where the warmth and moisture create ideal conditions for their work. Many grazing animals house them in a special stomach chamber, called the rumen, which works like a fermentation tank. These grazers, known as ruminants, include antelope, cattle, and deer. All of them "chew the cud," which means that they regurgitate their food after swallowing it and then chew it a second time. This mashes the food up, making it easier for the microorganisms to break it down.

△ Grazing mammals often live in herds because this gives them a better chance of spotting predators before they have the opportunity to attack.

FULL-TIME FEEDERS

Rumination is very efficient, but it takes a long time to work. Eating grass is also time consuming, since each mouthful has to be bitten off and then thoroughly chewed. As a result grazers do not have much

Red fox

Searching for food: 35% of every day

Inactive 60%

Feeding 5%

Roe deer

Searching for food: 5% of every day

Inactive 40%

Feeding 55%

△ Compared to predators such as the red fox, plant eaters spend much less time looking for food but much longer eating it. For example a roe deer usually feeds for over 12 hours every day.

time off. Instead they are kept busy collecting and digesting their food.

The same is true for plant-eating insects, although their feeding habits often change once they grow into adults. Caterpillars are busy feeders, but adult butterflies and moths spend most of their time looking for partners or laying eggs. Many of them visit flowers, but a few do not eat at all. Mayflies take things to even greater extremes—as adults they do not have working mouths.

▽ *In Alaska brown or grizzly bears wade into rivers to ambush migrating salmon. For a few weeks they feast on this high-protein food.*

PREDATORS

I**T IS DIFFICULT NOT TO FEEL ANXIOUS WHEN A PREDATOR CLOSES IN ON ITS PREY. BUT PREDATORS ARE AN ESSENTIAL PART OF THE NATURAL WORLD—WE ARE SOMETIMES PREDATORS OURSELVES.**

C**ompared to eating plants, being a predator is a gamble because there is always a chance that the prey will escape. To make up for this, meat is a highly nutritious food. To hunt successfully most predators have sharp senses and rapid reflexes. They overcome their victims by using specialized weapons such as poisonous stingers, powerful claws, or sharp teeth.**

△ *The crown-of-thorns starfish feeds on living corals. It crawls over coral reefs, digesting the soft parts of the coral polyps.*

SLOW-MOTION HUNTERS

When people think of predators, fast-moving animals—such as cheetahs—are often the first ones that come to mind. But many predators are not like this. For example starfish move more slowly than snails, but they prey on animals that cannot get away. For a starfish finding food is not difficult. The hard part comes when it has to pull a shell apart to get at the animal inside.

In water and on land many

▷ *With its jaws gaping open, a rat snake swallows a bird. Snakes always swallow their prey whole, so they need powerful digestive juices to break down their food.*

◁ *An African fish eagle carries off its prey after snatching it from the water's surface. It will swallow the fish after it lands on a perch.*

predators do not chase anything at all. Instead these hunters lie in wait for prey to wander within range. Many of them are perfectly camouflaged, and some improve their chances by building traps or using lures. Lie-in-wait hunters include anglerfish, praying mantises,

△ *Using its small but powerful jaws, a praying mantis feeds on a cricket. Large praying mantises sometimes catch lizards and even frogs.*

spiders, and many types of snakes. Most of them are cold-blooded, which means that they do not need much energy from their food. As a result they can survive without food for days or even weeks.

MAMMALS THAT HUNT
Birds and mammals are warm-blooded, so they need a lot of energy to keep their bodies working. For a brown bear that energy comes from all types of foods—including insects, fish, and sometimes other bears. Weighing up to 2,210 lbs (1,000kg), this animal is the world's largest land-based predator. Normally it steers clear of humans, but if it does attack the results can be deadly.

Mammalian carnivores—or meat eaters—have specialized teeth to deal with their food. Near the front of their mouths they have pointed canine teeth that are used to grip their prey. Once they have killed a victim, their carnassial teeth get to work. These teeth are near the back of the jaw. They have long, sharp edges, and they slice through flesh like a pair of scissors. Some carnivores, such as wolves, use them for cracking open bones so that they can reach the marrow inside.

AIRBORNE ATTACK
Birds of prey do not have teeth, and instead they hunt with their talons, or claws. Once they have made a kill they usually carry the victim back to a favorite perch or to their nest. Some of the largest species can lift amazing weights—in 1932 a white-tailed sea eagle in Norway carried off a four-year-old girl. Amazingly she survived.

Talons are good for catching prey, but birds of prey use their hooked beaks for tearing up food. Birds that hunt small animals have a different technique. They maneuver their

food until it is pointing headfirst down their throat. Then they swallow it whole.

MASS MURDERERS
Some of the world's most efficient hunters eat animals that are much smaller than themselves. In the Southern Ocean whales hunt shrimplike animals called krill by filtering them out of the water. Their giant catches are the largest made by any predator, and a single mouthful can weigh over one ton. Gray whales dig up mollusks on the seabed, while humpback whales ambush schools of fish by making "nets" out of bubbles. This forces the school into a small space, where it becomes much easier prey. But the best fishers of all are humans—we catch millions of tons a year.

▽ *By blowing air from its blowhole, a humpback whale surrounds a school of fish with a column of rising bubbles. The whale then swims up through the center of the column, swallowing the fish that are trapped inside.*

△ This giant earthworm from Australia is bigger than many snakes. Fortunately it is a harmless scavenger that helps improve the quality of the soil.

▽ Male fiddler crabs use their small pincer to pick up particles of food. Once they have chewed the particles they leave pellet-shaped leftovers on the mud. The large pincer is too clumsy for feeding—instead it is used to signal during courtship.

SCAVENGERS

THOUSANDS OF DIFFERENT TYPES OF ANIMALS FIND RICH PICKINGS IN WASTE AND DEAD REMAINS. THEY HELP RECYCLE MATTER SO THAT NUTRIENTS CAN BE REUSED.

In the animal world scavenging is a good way to make a living. That is because other animals generate a constant supply of dead bodies along with droppings, flaked skin, feathers, and fur. None of this appeals to us, but for scavengers it makes up a nutritious and reliable source of food. Without scavenging animals dead remains would still be broken down by microbes, but they would take much longer to be cleared away.

PARTICLE FEEDERS

To find some of the world's most successful scavengers, the place to look is the closest muddy shore. This is a prime scavenger habitat because it is full of tiny particles containing animal and plant remains. Many of these particles come from the sea itself, but others flow down rivers and then settle on the shore. The result is a rich layer of sediment—the ideal place for small scavengers to set up home.

Many of these particle feeders burrow through the sediment—

△ With its tentacles extended, a fanworm collects drifting particles from the sea. Each tentacle is covered in fine hairs that brush food toward the worm's mouth.

a good way to avoid hungry birds. These burrowers include shrimps and snails and also heart urchins, which have spines that look like fur. Fanworms have a different feeding technique—they collect the particles as they drift by. In warm parts of the world fiddler crabs emerge onto the mud when the tide goes out, picking up the particles with their claws. Every time the tide comes in it drops more particles, so the crabs rarely run out of food.

SCAVENGERS IN SOIL

On dry land scavengers are everywhere, living unseen in the soil. Many of them are microscopic, but in some parts of the world—such as South Africa and Australia—they include earthworms over 13 ft. (4m) long. Earthworms are very useful animals because they help mix up and fertilize the soil. Without them the ground would be much less fertile, making it more difficult to grow food.

◁ By shaping animal dung into a ball, dung beetles can roll it away to an appropriate spot for burial. They push the ball along with their feet.

Earthworms drag dead leaves into their burrows, but some insects bury other things underground. Burying beetles dig "graves" for small mammals and birds, and they lay their eggs on them before covering them up. When the beetle grubs hatch, they feed on the corpse. Dung beetles do the same thing, although their grubs hatch inside of a private ball of animal droppings that their parents have rolled up and then buried.

attract a scavenging marsupial called the Tasmanian devil. It has a formidable bite, allowing it to slice through dry skin, gristle, and even bones. But in many parts of the world the most important scavengers arrive through the air.

Many birds home in on dead remains. Crows and magpies, for example, often gather to feed on animals that have been hit by cars. Gulls feed on dead remains that have been washed up on the shore and also on waste food that humans throw away. But in the bird world vultures are the real specialists at the scavenging way of life. They fly by soaring high up on warm air currents—a technique that enables

them to scan enormous areas in their search for food. Vultures also keep a close eye on each other, and if one drops down to feed others soon follow from far around.

For a vulture survival depends on being able to eat a lot of food in a short amount of time. Sometimes these birds eat so much that they have to wait several hours before they can fly away.

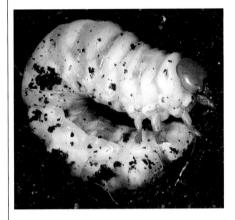

△ *Many insects feed on dead remains. This stag beetle grub will spend several years feeding on dead wood before it turns into an adult.*

▽ *In Africa's grasslands this carcass is surrounded by jostling vultures. Although they have weak claws, their powerful beaks can rip holes in rotting skin.*

WINGED SCAVENGERS

Burying beetles deal with small corpses, but large ones attract very different scavengers. In Africa hyenas are easily attracted to the scent of rotting flesh, while in Tasmania carcasses

ANIMAL DEFENSES

ONCE THEY ARE ADULT, SUPERPREDATORS SUCH AS THE GREAT WHITE SHARK HAVE NO NATURAL ENEMIES. BUT FOR OTHER ANIMALS DANGER CAN STRIKE AT ANY TIME, AND GOOD DEFENSES ARE VITAL FOR SURVIVAL.

In the animal world predators are always on the lookout for food. Compared to them prey animals often look vulnerable, but in fact things are not as one-sided as they may seem. Prey species have developed many types of defenses—without them they would not exist. These defenses are not totally foolproof, but for every animal that gets killed and eaten, plenty more outwit their enemies and escape.

◁ *Rodents keep out of danger by staying out of sight, often in dense vegetation. Caught out in the open by a bobcat, this mouse has only a small chance of survival.*

QUICK EXITS
When danger threatens, many animals react by trying to make a rapid escape. Some antelope can run at over 37 mph (60km/h), while hares can cruise at over 31 mph (50km/h)—an impressive feat for animals that weigh one tenth as much as a man. But for getting out of trouble, acceleration is sometimes as important as speed. Cockroaches have a top speed of only around 3 mph (5km/h), but they accelerate amazingly quickly from a standing start. As they scuttle away from danger, they often change direction—a trick that makes them even harder to catch.

Animals that cannot move quickly often use camouflage to blend in with their surroundings. Insects are especially good at this, which is fortunate for them because their predators include sharp-eyed birds. For camouflage to work an animal normally has to stay completely still, but some stick insects blend in even better by swaying slightly—just like twigs blowing in the breeze.

TRICKSTERS AND CHEATERS
One of the best ways to ward off an attacker is to carry a dangerous weapon. For example most predators will not touch wasps or hornets because these insects have

▽ *Few animals can beat insects when it comes to camouflage. This photograph shows two perfectly camouflaged katydids on the bark of a rain forest tree in Peru.*

△ *The hornet clearwing moth bears an astonishing resemblance to a real hornet. However despite its black-and-yellow warning colors, it does not have a stinger.*

dangerous stingers. But not all "wasps" and "hornets" are exactly what they seem. Some harmless flies and moths imitate these insects, and they do it so convincingly that few predators—or people—can tell them apart. The moths have transparent wings, and some of them even make a wasplike buzzing sound when they fly.

△ *With its mouth open and its tongue hanging out, this grass snake looks dead. Grass snakes are not poisonous, and they use this defense if they cannot escape.*

This defense technique is called mimicry, and it is widespread in the insect world. Spiders are also good mimics. Several types mimic stinging ants, and they move in an antlike way across the forest floor. Spiders have eight legs, while ants have six legs. But birds cannot count, so they are fooled by the spiders' disguise.

PLAYING DEAD

Scavengers are not picky about their food, but many predators only hunt prey that moves. They show little interest in animals that are still and even less in ones that are dead. This gives prey animals a remarkable last-ditch defense—if they can pretend to be dead, there is a chance that a predator might leave them alone.

Not many animals can do this, but those that can are some of the best actors in the living world. The grass snake lies on the ground with its mouth gaping open, while the Virginia opossum collapses on its side. It can stay like this for up to six hours and does not react in any way if it is touched. Once the coast is clear, the "dead" opossum comes back to life and runs away.

INEDIBLE MEALS

Another way to keep out of trouble is by being difficult or dangerous to eat. This is the defense used by tortoises and other animals that have hard shells. Tortoises pull in their legs and head if they are threatened, but box turtles can seal off their shells completely once they have withdrawn inside. Some armadillos roll themselves into a ball, while the porcupine fish inflates itself by swallowing water so that it swells up like a spiny ball.

All of these animals are edible, which is bad news for them if their defenses fail. But animals with built-in poisons do not need shells or spines. Some of the most potent poisons are produced by tiny arrow

△ *By baring its teeth and hissing, a wildcat tries to make itself look as dangerous as possible. If it is cornered, it responds by going on the attack.*

poison frogs that live in tropical forests. In one species a single frog contains enough poison to kill one thousand people, even though it is less than 1.5 in. (4cm) long.

▽ *Surrounded by vicious spines, a fully inflated porcupine fish is a meal few animals would want to tackle. Once it is inflated, the fish can hardly move.*

PARTNERS AND PARASITES

TEAMING UP WITH ANOTHER SPECIES IS OFTEN A RECIPE FOR SUCCESS. IN MANY ANIMAL PARTNERSHIPS BOTH SPECIES BENEFIT, BUT PARASITIC PARTNERS TAKE WHAT THEY CAN AND GIVE NOTHING IN RETURN.

W hen ants meet aphids, a strange ritual takes place. Instead of attacking the aphids, the ants tap them with their antennae, and the aphids respond by producing droplets of sugary fluid called honeydew. For the aphids life is much safer with the ants acting as guards. In return they give the ants a useful supply of food. Partnerships like this are common in the animal kingdom, but ones involving parasites are even more widespread.

◁ *Ants are aggressive toward most insects, but they look after aphids in return for food. Some ants even build mud shelters to protect these sap-sucking insects.*

EQUAL SHARES

The clear waters above coral reefs are the setting for one of the most remarkable partnerships in the world. Here fish line up and wait to be cleaned. The cleaners are often brightly colored shrimps that pick their way carefully over the scales of the fish. Cleaner shrimps feed on dead scales and encrusting animals, and they sometimes venture right inside their clients' mouths. Once a fish has been cleaned it swims off, and another one takes its place.

Animals cannot plan ahead, so their partnerships do not involve

△ *Most shrimps are well camouflaged, but cleaner shrimps have bright colors to attract clients. Fish remember where they live and return regularly to be cleaned.*

agreements like they would in the human world. Instead each animal behaves in ways that make its partner respond. For example cleaner shrimps "advertise" themselves by having bright colors and by sitting

△ *Before a female tick can lay her eggs, she needs a meal of blood—the only time she eats during her adult life. By the time she finishes feeding, her abdomen has swollen up like a balloon.*

in a prominent place. Client fish keep still while they are being cleaned, and they resist the temptation to swallow the cleaner while it is busy at work.

TAKING ADVANTAGE
Shrimps are not the only animals that make their living by cleaning. Some fish do and so do oxpeckers on land. These African birds scurry over buffalo, rhinos, and other large

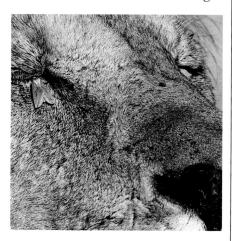

△ *Perched on a lion's face, a moth sips tears from its eye. In warm parts of the world several types of moths feed on tears, and some even try their luck on humans.*

mammals, removing insects and other pests. But oxpeckers do something else as well—they peck at wounds and feed on their host's blood. As well as helping their host, oxpeckers also harm them, so they

are not exactly the perfect partners they seem to be. With parasites things are even more unequal because a parasite does nothing to help its partner, or host. Instead it uses it as a source of food and often as a place to live. Parasites are extremely common in the animal kingdom, and they include thousands of species of invertebrates such as worms, fleas, flies, lice, and ticks. In the wild almost all animals harbor some type of parasite, and despite modern medicine many people have to put up with them too.

MOVING ON
Fleas live on the outside of animals, so it is not too difficult for them to spread from host to host. The adults scatter their eggs in nests and in bedding, and the eggs hatch into tiny, white, legless grubs. When the grubs are around two weeks old, they seal themselves in a cocoon and turn into adults. But a flea cocoon does not open as soon as an adult flea is ready to emerge. Instead it waits for weeks or months until an animal—or person—walks close by. Alerted by the vibration the cocoon pops open, and the newly emerged flea jumps onto its host.

Ticks have a different way of finding a host. They climb to the

▷ *Lampreys are among the few parasitic vertebrates (animals with backbones). Using its suckerlike mouth, this one has attached itself to a trout so that it can feed on its blood.*

ends of twigs and blades of grass and wait patiently for animals to walk by. If they feel warmth from a moving body, they quickly climb on board. Like fleas, ticks can carry disease, so walking in grassy places can be hazardous if ticks are around.

INTERNAL PARASITES
Parasites that live inside animals have more complicated life cycles because it is harder for them to spread from host to host. Human tapeworms alternate between two hosts—humans

△ *This caterpillar is surrounded by cocoons made by tiny parasitic wasp grubs. The grubs grew inside the caterpillar and fed on it while it was still alive.*

and pigs—while some parasites even have three. But because the chances of reaching a new host are so small, these parasites often produce incredible numbers of eggs. Tapeworms release up to half a million every day, and they can continue producing eggs for several years. This makes them the most prolific egg layers on the planet.

ANIMAL REPRODUCTION

BREEDING TAKES TIME AND ENERGY, BUT IT IS THE MOST IMPORTANT TASK IN AN ANIMAL'S LIFE. SOME ANIMALS CAN BREED ON THEIR OWN, BUT FOR MOST BECOMING A PARENT MEANS FINDING A MATE.

△ *Most insects have to mate before the female lays her eggs. Here a male grasshopper is using his hooked feet to cling to the female while mating.*

Compared to humans, many animals start breeding at a very young age. Lemmings can get pregnant at the age of two weeks, but some insects grow up even faster, becoming parents at the age of eight days. But successful reproduction is not only a matter of speed. Future parents often have to compete to win a partner. They also have to avoid being spotted by predators during this dangerous but crucial moment in their lives.

△ *Tugging in different directions, two halves of a sea anemone are about to become separate animals. This way of reproducing is common among microorganisms, but it is much rarer in the animal kingdom.*

SINGLE PARENTS
When sea anemones are fully grown, they can reproduce by tearing themselves in half. This drastic step is the simplest way of reproducing because only one parent is involved. But it only works for very simple animals. Most species, including ourselves, cannot work if we are divided in two.

This does not mean that lone parents are rare however. Many small insects can also reproduce on their own, although they do it in a different way. The females produce egg cells, and these develop into young without the mother having to mate. This is called parthenogenesis, or "virgin birth." In the spring female aphids use it to produce enormous families without any help from male aphids.

BEING DIFFERENT
In the animal world one-parent families have a big drawback—the young are all identical. They share exactly the same genes, which means that they share the same features—both good and bad. Normally this is not a problem. But if food runs short or if disease breaks out, the young are equally at risk, and entire families can die.

Sexual reproduction makes this type of calamity less likely. That is because it involves two parents.

The parents' genes are shuffled like a deck of cards, and a different combination is passed on to each of their young. Because the young are all slightly different, there is a better chance that at least some will survive. This advantage explains why sexual reproduction is so common.

△ *Most animals are either male or female, but parrot fish often start out as females and change to males later on. This photograph shows a male (left) and a female (right).*

GETTING TOGETHER

For sexual reproduction to work, two partners have to get together so that a male's sperm cells can fertilize the female's eggs. It can be a dangerous job—

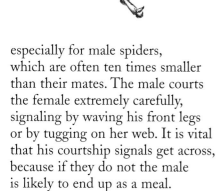

especially for male spiders, which are often ten times smaller than their mates. The male courts the female extremely carefully, signaling by waving his front legs or by tugging on her web. It is vital that his courtship signals get across, because if they do not the male is likely to end up as a meal.

Not many animals run this type of risk, but in every species partners have to track each other down. Often the males court the females—either with their colors and patterns or by the way they behave. Birds and frogs often use sound as a signal and so do many insects. But fireflies use their own light, and every type flashes on and off for a different length of time. Their message is a simple one: "I'm here, I belong to your species, and I would make an ideal mate."

THE RIVALS

In most species the female gets to choose a partner from the available males. As a result males often compete with each other like rivals in a talent contest. Male birds sometimes compete by singing or by parading their plumage, but weaverbirds show off a different skill. Each male builds an elaborate nest and then shows it off whenever a female flies past. If a female is impressed, she will move in, mate, and lay her eggs. But if the nest

△ *Male elephant seals battle ferociously for control of a stretch of beach. The winner assembles a group of females together and chases any rival males away.*

does not attract attention, the male eventually abandons it and starts another one nearby. For male weaverbirds this type of contest creates a lot of work, but rival males very rarely fight one another.

△ *With its throat swollen up like a balloon, a frog broadcasts a call that will attract any females nearby.*

But with mammals the breeding season involves serious combat. Male deer charge at each other with their antlers, while male elephant seals rip into their rivals with their teeth. The winner mates with many females, while the loser backs off—biding its time until the following year.

◁ *Male fireflies use light to signal to females waiting on the ground. Each species has its own sequence of flashes, creating different patterns as the males fly through the sky. Four sequences are shown here.*

STARTING LIFE

WHEN SNAKES LAY EGGS THEY USUALLY ABANDON THEM,
AND THEIR YOUNG HAVE TO FEND FOR THEMSELVES.
BUT MANY ANIMALS CARE FOR THEIR OFFSPRING
UNTIL THEY ARE READY TO LIVE ON THEIR OWN.

Parental care is an essential part of human life, as we take an exceptionally long time to grow up. Other mammals also care for their young, protecting them and feeding them milk. But in the rest of the animal world family styles vary enormously from one species to another. Birds often feed their young, but Komodo dragons do exactly the opposite. These giant lizards are cannibals, and they eat any young that make the mistake of coming too close.

◁ *When the coast is clear, a male mouthbreeder fish lets his young swim out to feed. They dart back into his mouth at the first sign of danger.*

△ *After tearing open its egg, a green mamba takes its first look at the outside world. It will be fully independent from the moment it slithers out of its shell.*

EGGS AND EMBRYOS
Practically all of the world's animals—including ourselves— start life as eggs. In all mammals, except for platypuses and echidnas, the eggs stay inside of the mother's body. Here they develop into embryos, and the mother eventually gives birth to living young. With birds the start of life is very different. Birds lay their eggs, and the embryos develop as soon as the mother sits on them. This is called incubation,

▽ *Young shrews follow their mother by forming a line and gripping each other with their teeth. But shrews have poor eyesight, and these ones have latched on to a toy instead.*

and it keeps the developing embryos warm. Laying eggs makes good sense for birds because it would be hard for them to fly with young on board. But in other groups in the animal kingdom things are not as clear cut. For example pythons lay eggs and then incubate them, but many other snakes keep their eggs inside of their bodies until the moment they are ready to hatch. These eggs often tear open as they are laid, making the snakes look as though they are giving birth.

Most fish also lay eggs, but some sharks—including the great white— give birth to live young. In some species life gets off to a gruesome start, as the largest embryos eat the smallest ones before they are even born.

PARENTS ON GUARD
Ocean sunfish can lay over 100 million eggs every time they spawn.

△ *With its head deep inside of its parent's throat, a young pelican enjoys a fishy meal. Fish-eating birds often regurgitate food instead of carrying it back to the nest in their beaks.*

The eggs drift away in the water, and only a tiny number of them survive for more than a few days. Sunfish make no attempt to look after their eggs—it would be an impossible task with such a gigantic brood.

Animals like the sunfish put all of their energy into mass production. At the other extreme animals that produce much smaller families often devote an immense amount of energy into looking after their eggs and young. Male sea horses collect the female's eggs and carry them in a pouch, while mouthbreeding fish hold their eggs and hatchlings in their mouths. Albatross spend up to ten weeks sitting on their eggs, but female octopuses are even more devoted. They watch over their eggs for several months, cleaning them and keeping guard. During this time the octopus eats nothing, and when the eggs hatch she dies.

FAMILY LIFE
Once an animal's eggs have hatched, life can become even busier. Young snakes and lizards find their own food, but newly hatched birds often

▷ *Young dolphins often stay with their mothers for over one year. As they grow up they learn to recognize other dolphins by their calls.*

depend on their parents to bring them what they need. Adult blue tits have up to 12 nestlings. The young are blind and helpless when they hatch, and it takes them almost three weeks before they are ready to fly. Until then the two parents search for food, making over one thousand trips back to the nest every day.

Because young birds are so vulnerable, the parents are always on the lookout for danger. This is especially important for wading birds, such as lapwings and killdeer, because they nest on the ground.

△ *Earwigs are among the few insects that take care of their eggs. The female periodically cleans them to prevent them from being attacked by mold.*

If a predator heads toward the nest, the female stages a special display to steer it off the trail. She moves out into the open and then walks away, pretending to drag a broken wing. Hopefully the predator follows her. Once she has lured it far enough from the nest, she flies up and away.

MAMMAL FAMILIES
Because mammals feed their young milk, the bond between the mother and her baby is very strong. Most mammals recognize their own young by their scent, and they take care of them with great attention. At this time of life adult males can be a threat, so many female mammals bring up their offspring on their own. Young mammals often cling to their mothers, but young marsupials are even better protected because they travel in their mother's pouch.

During their time together young mammals watch how their parents feed. This is a vital part of growing up because it teaches the young how to behave. Predatory mammals watch how their parents hunt, while the brainiest mammals—such as dolphins and chimps—learn sounds and gestures that enable them to communicate with their own species. For humans this is even more important because language allows us to exchange skills and ideas.

GROWING UP

WHEN ANIMALS START LIFE, THEY SOMETIMES LOOK VERY DIFFERENT FROM THEIR PARENTS. MANY CHANGE COLOR AS THEY GROW UP. BUT SOME ANIMALS CHANGE MUCH MORE DRAMATICALLY WHEN THEIR BODIES ARE COMPLETELY REBUILT.

Young mammals look very similar to their parents, even though their bodies are not yet fully developed. But with some animals it is hard to see any resemblance at all. Caterpillars look nothing like butterflies, while young lobsters are transparent and do not have any claws. Young animals like these are known as larvae. They live in different ways to their parents, but once their "childhood" comes to an end they develop an adult shape and an adult way of life.

◁ *Like most crustaceans, lobsters begin life as larvae that live in the plankton. This four-week-old larva has a transparent body case, which makes it harder for predators to spot.*

LARVAL LIFE

Insects often have larvae, but the best place to find them is in watery habitats—especially the sea. Here thousands of types of animals begin life as larvae that hatch from eggs. They are produced by some fish and also by a huge range of invertebrates—from lobsters and barnacles to clams, sea urchins, and starfish. Most of these larvae look nothing like their parents, and in the past scientists sometimes mistook them for completely separate species.

Unlike young mammals or young birds, larval animals are fully independent, and they have

important tasks to carry out. For caterpillars that task is feeding— something that they do around the clock. By feeding up, caterpillars collect all the raw materials that are needed to build an adult butterfly. For marine larvae the mission is very different. These larvae are often produced by slow-moving animals or ones that spend their adult lives attached to one place. They usually drift in the plankton, traveling far and wide and helping their species spread.

Tadpoles are larvae and so is the axolotl—a pink amphibian from Mexico that is sometimes

kept as a pet. This remarkable animal can breed while it is still a larva, but for most larvae breeding cannot begin until they are adults.

METAMORPHOSIS

The change from a young shape to an adult shape is known as metamorphosis. In the sea most larvae metamorphose gradually so that their bodies alter step by step. A larval lobster changes slightly every time it sheds its skin. By its fourth molt it has well-developed legs and antennae and small but

▽ Emperor angelfish change colors and patterns as they grow up. This photograph shows an adult fish (top) with a young fish below it.

effective claws. At this stage the young lobster is less than 0.8 in. (2cm) long, but its life in the plankton is already nearing its end.

Tadpoles also change gradually. Their gills shrink, their legs appear, and their tails are slowly absorbed. During metamorphosis their diet changes. Newly hatched tadpoles normally eat plants, but they slowly switch to a diet that includes animal food. By the time they are adult frogs or toads, they are entirely carnivorous and never touch plant food again.

SLOW CHANGE

Many insects change in stages as well. Just like young lobsters, young grasshoppers become more like their parents every time they molt. A newly hatched grasshopper has a large head, short body, and stubby legs. It cannot fly because it has no wings. But as it grows and molts, wing buds start to appear on the sides of its body. By its sixth and final molt the adult grasshopper is fully developed, and once its wings have hardened it can fly away.

This type of development is called incomplete metamorphosis because the changes are limited. Many other insects, including dragonflies, beetles, and bugs, also develop in this way. But for butterflies and moths—as well as flies, bees, and wasps— metamorphosis is much more drastic. Instead of changing slowly, these insects change suddenly when their larval life comes to an end.

BUILDING A BUTTERFLY

The first sign of this change comes when a caterpillar loses interest in its food because it now has other priorities instead. It builds a protective case, called a chrysalis, which is sometimes surrounded by a silk cocoon. To do this moth caterpillars often climb down from their food plants so that they can build their chrysalis underground. Butterflies usually make theirs in the open, hanging from leaves or stems.

Once the chrysalis is complete, remarkable events start to take place. The caterpillar's body is slowly dismantled into a soup of living cells. If the chrysalis is opened at this stage, there is no sign of anything living inside. But within days major reconstruction work is under way as the body of an adult moth or butterfly is assembled. When the adult insect is complete, it breaks out of its protective case. A brand-new moth or butterfly emerges. This type of change is known as complete metamorphosis because the caterpillar's body is totally transformed.

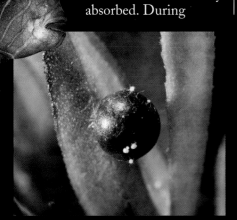

△ *Swallowtail butterflies begin life as eggs laid singly on food plants. The egg darkens when the caterpillar inside is about to hatch.*

△ *The caterpillar feeds, doubling in size every four or five days. At this stage in life its main enemies are insect-eating birds.*

△ *After feeding for around one month, the caterpillar spins a chrysalis. The chrysalis splits open when the butterfly is complete.*

INSTINCT AND LEARNING

SPIDERS CANNOT DESIGN OR PLAN, BUT THEY STILL MANAGE TO BUILD COMPLICATED WEBS. UNLIKE OUR BEHAVIOR, THEIRS IS CONTROLLED BY INSTINCT—A BUILT-IN PROGRAM THAT IS HANDED DOWN FROM PARENTS TO THEIR YOUNG.

△ *When a spider spins a web, it does not have any idea how it should look. The spider simply carries out instinctive actions, and the web gradually takes shape.*

Instinct is the invisible guide that keeps the animal world running smoothly. With simple animals like spiders and insects, it controls everything that the animal does and usually the way that it does it. Instinct allows these animals to carry out some amazingly complicated tasks, even though they have tiny brains. Animals with bigger brains also have instincts, but their behavior is more flexible. This is because they are able to learn through experience.

WHAT IS INSTINCT?

An animal's instincts make it behave in fixed ways in everyday situations. Young birds instinctively beg for food when their parents arrive at the nest, while young mammals instinctively suckle milk. Later in life instincts control all types of behavior—from courtship and migration to web building and nestmaking. Because instinctive behavior does not have to be learned, an animal can carry out all of these tasks without ever having done them before and without having to understand any of the steps that are involved.

Sometimes instinctive behavior is so impressive that animals really seem to know what they are doing. For example beavers construct amazingly elaborate dams and channels (see page 150), while termites build large and complex nests. But unlike human builders, these animals cannot come up with new designs. They simply carry out the instructions that are held in their genes.

MAKING THE RIGHT RESPONSE

Instinctive behavior is always sparked off by some type of trigger. For example toads instinctively lunge at prey that is moving, but they will ignore the same animal if it is still. Fish in a school bunch together if they are threatened and then fan out again when the danger has passed. Behavior can also be sparked off by environmental factors such as the change of seasons or the shifting tides. Fiddler crabs, for example, have a built-in "clock" that is set by

▽ *When threatened by a snake, a fire-bellied toad instinctively arches its back. This reveals bright markings, warning the snake that the toad's skin is poisonous.*

the tide. They come out to feed at low tide, even if they are moved far from the shore. Instincts like these are very important because they help animals survive. But sometimes instincts can go wrong. Moths navigate by using the Moon, for example, but this instinct also makes them spiral toward lights after dark. This is one of the big disadvantages of instinctive behavior—it cannot adjust to anything new.

LEARNING FROM EXPERIENCE

Humans have some instincts, but most of our behavior is learned.

△ *Squirrels bury surplus acorns in the fall. They do not understand the seasons, but this instinctive behavior provides them with food for the winter ahead.*

We learn not only from our own experience but also from other people's, and we are so good at it that we pick up new skills all the time. In the rest of the animal world animals often carry out tasks by instinct, but learning can sometimes make them better.

▷ *These young chimpanzees are using grass stems to fish termites out of their nest. They have learned how to do this by watching adults and copying the way they behave. This type of learning is unusual in wild animals, but humans use it all the time.*

▷ *This female goose will be followed by her goslings wherever she goes. The goslings recognize their mother by a type of learning called imprinting.*

Nest building is a good example of how these two types of behavior blend together. When a bird makes its first nest, it follows an instinctive plan. The nest may not be perfect, but it will be the right size and shape. But if the bird lives long enough, it will become a better builder. It will learn where the best materials can be found and discover which places are good for building nests. This experience will often make it better at attracting mates.

ANIMAL INTELLIGENCE

It is very difficult to compare animals' intelligence with ours. Many animals are capable of using simple tools, but very few actually make them for themselves. Some birds can count up to five or six, but numbers seem to play no part in their daily lives. Octopuses are even "brainier." In experiments they have figured out how to take the lids off of bottles to reach the food inside. But our closest relatives are even brighter. Orangutans have learned how to operate machinery, while chimps communicate using a language that has more than 30 separate "words."

△ *Egyptian vultures use stones to break open ostrich eggs. Although they look intelligent, they sometimes throw the stone beside the egg instead of against its shell.*

Life in a lion pride is usually peaceful, but fighting can break out when one pride meets another one. Here in Kenya's Masai Mara National Park lionesses from one pride are defending their territory against some intruders. These fights look dangerous, but most of the aggression is just for show—serious injuries are rare.

LIVING IN A GROUP

SCHOOLS, SWARMS, FLOCKS, AND HERDS ARE A FEATURE OF THE ANIMAL WORLD. BUT WHY DO SOME ANIMALS GATHER TOGETHER, WHILE OTHERS SPEND THEIR LIVES ON THEIR OWN?

Animals do not live together just because they enjoy each other's company. Instead they do it because group life improves their chances of survival. Some gather together for a specific reason and then go their separate ways. At the other extreme social animals—such as ants and termites—depend on life in a group and cannot survive alone.

△ *During the day striped grunts live in tightly packed schools. At night the school splits up as the fish feed on the seabed.*

TEMPORARY GROUPS

On warm spring evenings clouds of midges often dance in the air. Each cloud contains hundreds of male midges that gather together to attract female partners. When a female approaches the swarm, the males rush toward her, and one of them usually succeeds in luring her away to mate. The other males return to their dance, but for the happy couple group life is at an end.

Midge swarms are temporary groups—the type that usually happen at particular times of the year. Spring is the season when frogs and toads gather at their breeding pools and when some birds gather at traditional courtship grounds called leks. Animals also get together in the winter, when they take refuge against bad weather. Ladybugs cluster together under bark, while wrens crowd together in nest boxes and tree holes. But these animals do not become permanent companions. As soon as the days lengthen they disperse and sometimes never meet again.

△ *Ladybugs often gather together when they hibernate. Their bright colors serve as a warning that they taste bad—a clearer message with many packed together.*

△ *Kookaburras live in extended families. Instead of leaving the nest when they can fly, the young stay behind and help their parents raise other broods.*

LIFE IN A HERD

An antelope herd is a very different type of group because animals stay in it for life. Antelope live in herds to protect themselves because there is less of a chance of them being attacked if they stick together than if they live alone. The same is true with many fish, as predators often find it difficult to pick out prey from these fast-moving schools. In these groups animals really do behave like "one of the herd," often doing the same thing at the same time.

But just because animals live together does not mean that they help each other. In fact if an antelope is attacked by a predator, the other members of the herd often seem unconcerned. The reason for this is that animals put their relatives first. If a calf is attacked its mother will defend it fiercely, but she will not do anything to protect a calf belonging to another animal.

EXTENDED FAMILIES

Life in an elephant herd could hardly be more different, as the group is held together by very close family ties. The herd is led by an old female called a matriarch, and most of the other females in the herd are her daughters or some type of relative. The matriarch has many years' experience of the best places to find water and food, and as the younger elephants grow up they visit these places themselves. By the time the matriarch dies another female is ready to take her place.

Unlike antelope, elephants bond with all of the other members of their herd. If an elephant is sick the herd slows down, and healthy herd members may protect it from being attacked. When a female is about to give birth older females—known as "aunts"—stay close by and make sure that the calf does not stray.

And when a herd member dies, all the elephants seem to be distressed and upset. Compared to antelope elephants seem much more like us.

GIANT COLONIES

Group living reaches its peak among social insects, which include ants and termites as well as many types of bees and wasps. These animals live in giant families called colonies that can be over two million insects strong. In a colony only one member breeds. She is known as the queen, and she devotes her entire life to laying eggs. The rest of the colony consists of workers. They build and defend the nest, collect food, and raise the young.

For a colony to operate the workers have to carry out exactly the right tasks at the right time. Their "orders" come in the form of chemical scents, called pheromones, that are issued by the queen.

As long as she produces these chemicals, the workers continue with their daily routines. Workers can also give off some pheromones themselves—if they are attacked, for example. When a worker releases "attack pheromone," others quickly gather around to fight off the threat.

△ *A queen termite can lay 30,000 eggs in one day. Her sausage-shaped body is so large that she is unable to feed herself—instead workers bring food to her.*

Colonial life is extremely successful, but sometimes intruders manage to break in. Certain types of ants invade other colonies and capture their workers, while some caterpillars feed inside of ants' nests. The caterpillars feel and smell just like ants—a trick that fools the ants into thinking they are friend rather than foe.

▽ *Meerkats live in groups that contain two or three families. These sociable animals always stick together and take turns watching out for danger. If they spot any trouble, they let out a loud call.*

ANIMAL ARCHITECTS

LONG BEFORE HUMANS LEARNED HOW
TO MAKE BRICKS AND CONCRETE, ANIMALS
WERE BUILDING HOMES OF THEIR OWN. SOME
OF THEIR HOMES WOULD FIT IN AN EGGCUP,
BUT OTHERS WEIGH OVER ONE TON.

Animals are well adapted to outdoor life, so most of them
do not need homes for themselves. But animals often build
homes to protect their young. Nests keep young animals
dry and warm, and they also conceal them from predators looking
for an easy meal. Animals build other structures as well. These
include traps for catching food and also bizarre structures
called bowers, which some birds use to attract their mates.

THE DAM BUILDERS

The largest structures made by
animals are coral reefs. They can
be hundreds of miles long, but they
are not built in an organized way.
Beaver dams, on the other hand, are
built intentionally, and they are the
largest pieces of engineering in the
animal world. The longest one on
record was 2,300 ft. (700m) from
end to end. It was strong enough to
support human sightseers and
people on horseback.

△ *A female hummingbird attaches
her nest to a twig using strands of spiders'
silk. Like many female birds, she is the
builder—the male gives her no help at all.*

Beavers make dams to create
somewhere safe to live. Water
builds up behind the dam, forming
a freshwater lake. In the deepest
part of the lake the beavers construct
a mound called a lodge, which has
their living quarters hidden away
inside. The walls of the lodge can be
over 3 ft. (1m) thick, so even during
the winter the central chamber stays
warm. The only way of getting into
the lodge is through underwater
tunnels—a security feature that
keeps most predators at bay.

To make their dams beavers
gnaw through young trees and then
float the wood into place. As the
wooden framework builds up they

▽ *Using their sharp front teeth, beavers can
gnaw through trees 12 in. (30cm) thick. Like
other animal architects they instinctively
know what building materials to use and
how to fit them together.*

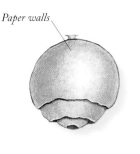

Paper walls *Cells*

1 **2** **3** **4**

△ *Common wasps make their nests by chewing wood fibers and spreading them into papery layers. Figures 1 and 2 show a new nest that has been started by a queen wasp. Figures 3 and 4 show the same nest three months later. It has been expanded by the workers, who have added many extra "floors." These floors contain cells that hold developing grubs.*

add vegetation and mud to make it watertight. Once the dam is complete, these natural engineers keep on the lookout for leaks and make repairs. A well-built dam can last for decades, so generations of beavers use the lodge as a home.

MAKING AN ENTRANCE
Birds are famous for their building skills, and unlike beavers many of them start afresh each year. Hummingbirds make their nests out of mosses and lichens, holding them together with spiders' webs. The result is warm and surprisingly strong—a perfect nursery for the smallest nestlings in the world. Larger birds often build with twigs and sticks, but some specialize in using mud. Swallows often make mud nests shaped like cups, but the rufous ovenbird from South America makes one that looks like a large balloon. It has a side entrance that leads into a curving passage, making it hard for predators to reach the eggs or chicks. Weaverbirds and oropendolas have a different way of keeping out unwanted visitors.

Their nests are made of woven leaves, and they have tubular entrances. These hang down like trunks and can be almost 3 ft. (1m) long.

△ *This termite's nest has overlapping roofs that keep it dry. It is built on the ground, but many termites nest in trees, using chewed-up wood as their building material.*

HAND-ME-DOWNS
Nests like these take a long time to build, but even still many of them are used only once. The reason for this is that nests get dirty, and they can harbor parasites such as ticks and fleas. But birds of prey do not seem to care about these hygiene problems because they often use

▷ *In Australia and New Guinea male bowerbirds build amazingly elaborate structures to attract females. The owner of this bower is decorating it with red berries to increase its appeal.*

the same nest year after year. Sometimes a nest is passed on down the generations, and each new pair of owners makes it even bigger.

The largest tree nests are built by bald eagles using branches as thick as a person's arm. Their nests may be over 20 ft. (6m) deep and weigh twice as much as a car. Despite these vast constructions bald eagles lay just two eggs every time they breed.

INSECT NESTS
The insect world contains some exceptional builders as well. Potter wasps make miniature mud flasks to house their grubs, while some caddis flies fish for food by spinning underwater nets. But the most impressive insect nests are made by social species, including ants, bees, wasps, and termites. The pharaoh ant makes nests smaller than golf balls, but some termites make mounds up to 30 ft. (9m) high. Built of mud, these insect fortresses bake rock hard in the tropical sunlight.

ECOLOGY

LIVING THINGS ARE LIKE PIECES
IN A GIANT, EVER-CHANGING JIGSAW
PUZZLE. ECOLOGISTS INVESTIGATE
HOW THE PIECES FIT TOGETHER—
WITH EACH OTHER AND THE WORLD AROUND THEM.

△▽ *Grasslands are one of over a dozen ecosystems that exist on land. Most ecosystems do not have clear-cut boundaries—instead they merge into one another. Together they make up the biosphere, which is home to all life on Earth.*

T he natural world is full of connections. For example owls eat mice, and bumblebees use old mouse nests, so the fewer owls there are the more chances bumblebees have of finding a home. Zebras eat grass, but because they also nibble away at other plants they actually help grass spread. Connections like these are what make nature work.

△ *Africa's grasslands and its wildlife form one of the most distinctive ecosystems on Earth. This ecosystem is famous for its large herds of grazing mammals.*

WHAT IS ECOLOGY?
When scientists first started studying nature, they concentrated on individual living things. They traveled the world sending specimens back to museums so that they could be cataloged and identified. Today this work still goes on, but scientists also study the way living things interact. This research is especially important because it helps us understand how the changes humans bring—such as pollution and deforestation—can affect the living world.

Ecology is the study of these connections. It involves living things themselves and the raw materials and nutrients that they use. Energy is also important in ecology because it is the driving force that keeps living things alive.

STICKING TOGETHER
When researchers investigate wild animals, they sometimes get to know them extremely well. Experienced researchers can identify chimps by their faces and humpback whales by the patterns on their tails. Individuals can be fascinating to follow, but ecologists are more interested in how life works on a bigger scale.

Moving up from individuals, the first important level is a population. This is a group of living things belonging to the same species that live in the same area at the same time. Some populations contain just a handful of members, while others have thousands, and they also change in different ways. A population of elephants or oak trees changes slowly because these species take a long time to breed and live for many years. But a population of grasshoppers changes very quickly because insects have much shorter and faster lives.

In some populations individuals are spread out randomly, but more often they live in scattered groups. This can be a problem for scientists trying to monitor wildlife because it makes populations difficult to count. Things get even trickier with animals that are always on the move such as tigers and whales.

COMMUNITY LIFE

After populations the next level up is called a community. This contains populations of several different species mixed together, like neighbors in the same part of town. In nature community life is always busy, but it is not always as peaceful as it sounds. That is because the species have very different lifestyles. Some get along extremely well, but others use their neighbors as prey.

Living communities vary hugely from region to region. In the tropics they often contain thousands of species that fit together in extremely complex ways. But in the world's most hostile habitats, the list of species does not even fill a page. For example deep-sea vents teem with bacteria, but there is no plant life at all because there is no light. In these difficult conditions fewer than one dozen types of animals make vents their permanent home.

HABITATS AND ECOSYSTEMS

A community is a collection of living things and nothing else. But the next step up—called an ecosystem—includes their home, or habitat, as well. Ecosystems include all types of habitats and their wildlife— from coniferous forests and tundra to coral reefs and caves.

Ecosystems need energy to work, and this usually comes from the Sun. Plants collect sunlight on land, while algae collect it in the surface layers of the sea. Once they have gathered this all-important energy, they use it to grow, and this makes food that other living things can use. Each time something gets eaten, this energy passes from one species to another. Deep-sea vents are among the few places where life is fueled in a different way. Here bacteria collect energy from minerals dissolved in the water, and they create the food that keeps animals alive.

Added together the world's ecosystems make up the biosphere, which is the largest ecological level of all. This incredibly varied stage— with all of its teeming inhabitants— includes every place on Earth where living things can be found.

△ Together with different plants and animals, zebras form a community —a living mixture of different species that live in the same area and use each other for survival. Zebras need grass for food, but they help it spread by nibbling away other plants.

◁▽ All the zebras in an area make up a population. They mix with each other all the time, so they interbreed. In a zebra population all the individual animals have slightly different patterns, but it takes an expert eye to tell one individual from another.

HOMES AND HABITATS

BECAUSE OF MODERN TECHNOLOGY, HUMANS CAN SURVIVE ALMOST ANYWHERE ON EARTH. COMPARED TO US, EARTH'S WILD PLANTS AND ANIMALS ARE MUCH MORE SELECTIVE ABOUT WHERE THEY LIVE.

In nature every species has its own habitat, or home. A habitat provides it with somewhere to live and also with everything else that it needs. Most species have a single habitat, but some animals can use two or three at different times in their lives. Species fit into their habitats because they have adapted to them over thousands or millions of years. If their habitat changes or disappears, they can have difficulty surviving.

▷ *The leopard can survive in many different habitats, which is one of the reasons for its success. It often eats and sleeps in trees.*

△ *The leopard's range extends across a large part of Africa and southern Asia. Because it is widespread, it has a better chance of surviving in today's changing world.*

A SPACE TO LIVE

Habitats are like addresses because they show where something lives. For example giant pandas live in the mountains of central China where they feed almost entirely on bamboo. But they would not survive for long in most other parts of the world

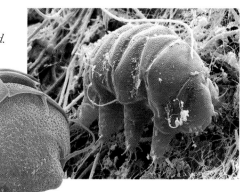

▽▷ *Water bears, or tardigrades, live in damp "microhabitats" throughout the world. If their home dries up, they pull in their legs and dry out as well. Once they are dormant they can survive for years— until it turns wet once more.*

because pandas depend on bamboo. Without it they cannot feed.

Compared to the giant panda, the leopard is much more flexible about what it eats and where it makes its home. It can survive on open grassland and in tropical forests and even in farmland close to towns. This helps explain why the leopard is the most successful big cat alive today. But some of the world's most widespread animals live in habitats that most people do not even realize are there. Microscopic creatures called water bears live in pools, puddles, and gutters and even in the thin film of water between

▽ *The coco-de-mer palm is a unique tree that grows the largest seeds in the world. It can only live where the ground is fertile and where the temperature is warm throughout the year.*

individual particles of soil. Habitats like these can be found all over the world, which is why water bears live worldwide as well.

SPECIAL HOMES

Long ago our ancestors headed north out of Africa—a journey that eventually carried them all over the globe. But in nature some species evolve in one place and never manage to spread anywhere else. This is often because they are isolated on remote islands or in valleys high up in the mountains.

Species like these are called "endemics." They include thousands of unusual plants, such as the coco-de-mer, and also a large collection of extraordinary animals—from the lemurs of Madagascar to the famous giant tortoises of the Galapagos Islands. The kiwi, from New

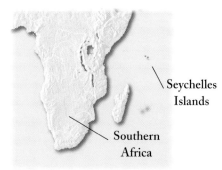

△ *The coco-de-mer has a tiny range compared to most other trees. In the wild it grows in a few valleys in the Seychelles Islands in the Indian Ocean and nowhere else in the world.*

Zealand, is an endemic species, and so are almost all of Hawaii's native birds and snails.

Endemic species are often rare because their natural home is usually small. This makes them very vulnerable. If their habitat changes or if humans bring in new species from outside, they can disappear in a remarkably short period of time. Many endemic species have already become extinct. In places such as New Zealand and Hawaii conservationists are trying hard to protect the ones that still remain.

△ *These plants have moved into a brand-new habitat—a field of lava produced by a volcanic eruption. As time goes by soil will start to form and more plants will grow.*

NEW HABITATS

Most of the world's habitats are fully stocked with wildlife, but sometimes completely new habitats open up. If a river changes course or a wildfire breaks out, plants and animals waste no time moving into newly vacant ground. Sometimes big disasters create opportunities on a much larger scale. In southwest Washington, for example, Mount Saint Helens erupted in 1980. The eruption flattened thousands of trees and coated the ground with a deep layer of ash. But just three years later the ash was covered with flowers and insects, and today the forestland is rapidly returning.

LIVING TOGETHER

WHEN LIONS SHARE THE SAME HABITAT WITH ZEBRAS, IT IS EASY TO GUESS WHAT HAPPENS. BUT SPECIES LIVE TOGETHER IN MANY WAYS—SOMETIMES THEY HELP EACH OTHER SURVIVE.

◁ *Bats eat many insects, but insects breed much faster than bats. This is one of the reasons why prey species survive despite being hunted.*

Habitats provide living things with a home, but they do not guarantee them an easy time. In each habitat food and space is limited, so each species has to work hard to get its share. In this struggle some species compete head-on, some join forces, and some do not affect each other at all. The result is a complicated world where things are not always what they seem.

△ *Chased by a lioness, this zebra is in serious danger. But for zebras as a whole being hunted is much less of a problem than running out of food.*

HUNTERS AND HUNTED

For zebras in Africa's grasslands being hunted is a fact of life. A single adult lion needs to eat up to 20 large animals a year, and zebras often feature on their menu. As well as coping with lions, zebras have to put up with other predators. These include leopards and hyenas on land and crocodiles that lurk in rivers and water holes, waiting for animals to come within their range.

With all of these enemies an individual zebra's life can be cut short at any time. But for an entire species—such as zebras—predators are not a major threat. Most predators target young animals or ones that are injured or ill. While these stragglers are picked off, the healthiest animals survive. Far from endangering their prey, predators help keep the species in good condition by ensuring that the healthiest animals breed. Predators actually need animals to escape, because if they did not they would run out of food.

JOINING FORCES

In every habitat some species form partnerships that help them survive. This is called symbiosis, and it can be a temporary arrangement or something that works full-time. In Africa's grasslands one of the strangest short-term partnerships involves a mammal called the ratel, or honey badger, and a bird called the honeyguide. The honeyguide feeds on insects, and it is good at finding beehives, but it cannot break them open. Instead it looks for help. The honeyguide attracts a ratel by flying toward it and making a clicking sound. Once the ratel becomes interested, the bird leads it to the nest. When the ratel has broken into the nest and eaten its fill, the bird feeds on the insects, honey, and wax that is left behind.

Honeyguides and ratels can survive well without one another. But full-time partners are very different. They often completely depend on one another and cannot survive on their own. Figs and fig wasps are partners like this (see page 91). So are yuccas and yucca moths, which live in deserts in the Southwest. Yuccas grow creamy-white flowers, and these provide food and shelter for the yucca moth's caterpillars, which develop hidden inside of them. In return the adult moths pollinate yucca flowers.

Yuccas are often grown in gardens in other parts of the world, but without their moths they hardly ever produce seeds.

BATTLES FOR SURVIVAL

If different species compete head-on, a battle breaks out. This is what happened around three million years ago when North and South America joined together after millions of years of being apart. Once the two continents were linked, a two-way traffic of species began as animals

△ *These butterflies have gathered on a tropical riverbank to collect nutrients in the mud. They look like an easy target for birds, but there are so many of them that most will manage to escape if they are attacked.*

moved north and south. In the tough competition that followed North America's grassland mammals proved to be a big success. They spread so far and so fast that many of South America's homegrown species died out. But some of South America's forest mammals managed to make a home in the north. Marsupials were among them, which explains why North America still has a few marsupial mammals today.

▷ *In the coniferous forests of the Northwest Douglas firs are home to many different types of birds. By living at different levels and eating different foods, the birds share the same habitat without competing head-on.*

MAKING ROOM

Extinction is perfectly natural, but it does not always happen when two species find themselves in a head-on clash. That is because species can adjust to one another. Instead of eating the same food or using the same homes, they slowly change as time goes by. As a result they end up being able to live side by side.

This is exactly what researchers find in long-established habitats where species have had plenty of time to adjust to their neighbors. For example in forests birds often live in the same trees and seem to feed on the same food. But a closer look usually shows that each species lives at a different level and has a slightly different diet.

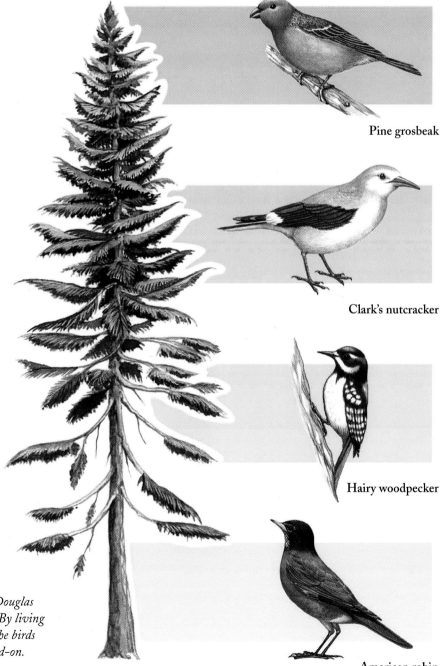

Pine grosbeak

Clark's nutcracker

Hairy woodpecker

American robin

FOOD CHAINS AND WEBS

IN NATURE FOOD IS ALWAYS ON THE MOVE.
WHEN A BUTTERFLY FEEDS ON A FLOWER
OR WHEN A SNAKE SWALLOWS A FROG, FOOD
MOVES ONE MORE STEP ALONG A FOOD CHAIN.
SO DOES THE ENERGY THAT IT CONTAINS.

Food chains are not something that you can pick up or touch, but they are an essential part of the living world. That is because food is passed on whenever one thing eats another. Eaters often end up being eaten themselves, and when this happens food is passed on again. The result is a food chain. Most living things play a part in several different chains. Added together the food chains make up food webs—networks that can involve hundreds or even thousands of different species.

△ *A glass frog is species number four in the chain. It lives in trees and feeds on many different animals—some are plant eaters, but many are predators like itself.*

HOW FOOD CHAINS WORK

On these two pages you can trace your way through a tropical food chain. Like almost all food chains on land, it starts with a plant. Plants collect energy directly from sunlight,

△ *The photographs on these pages show a food chain in the rain forest of Central America, beginning with a flower. A heliconid butterfly becomes species two in the chain when it feeds on the flower. The butterfly is the first food eater in the chain.*

so they do not need to eat. But plants do make food, and this is passed on when they are eaten by herbivores, or plant-eating animals.

Many herbivores feed on roots, leaves, or seeds. But in this food chain the herbivore is a butterfly, which settles on the plant's flowers to drink nectar. Nectar is rich in energy, so it makes an ideal fuel. Unfortunately for the butterfly, it is preyed upon by a green lynx spider—the third species to join the chain. Like all spiders, this one is strictly carnivorous, and it is an expert at catching insects. But to hunt butterflies, the spider has to risk moving around during the day. Its movements attract the attention of a glass frog, which swallows the spider, becoming species number four. Glass frogs have many enemies, and one of them is the eyelash pit viper— a small but highly poisonous snake that often lurks near flowers.

When it eats the frog, it becomes species number five. But the snake is also vulnerable, and its life is cut short when it is spotted by a rare harpy eagle, which joins the chain as species number six. The harpy eagle has no natural enemies, so the food chain comes to an end.

FOOD CHAINS AND ENERGY

Six species may not sound like very many, especially in a habitat that is brimming with life. But it is actually above average—many food chains have just three or four. So why do

△ *A green lynx spider catches the butterfly and collects food energy from its prey. The spider is species number three in the food chain, but it is the first predator so far.*

△ An eyelash pit viper spends most of its life off of the ground, and it catches animals feeding near flowers. It is species number five and the third predator in the chain.

the most common animals are tadpoles and water beetles. Further up the chain, predatory fish are less common, and fish-eating birds are even rarer. The same type of pyramid works for most habitats—from grasslands to Arctic tundra. It explains why "top predators," such as herons, lions, and harpy eagles—need a lot of space to survive.

WORLDWIDE WEBS

Food webs are more complicated than food chains because they involve many different species. As well as prey and their predators, they also include species that live by breaking down dead remains. In a food web some species have only a few connections. Others have dozens because they eat many types of food.

Elaborate food webs are often a sign of a healthy environment because

△ A harpy eagle is the last species in the chain. Nothing hunts it, but when the eagle dies its remains will enter a separate food chain, where they will be broken down by decomposers.

they show that many species are living side by side. If a habitat is damaged—by pollution or deforestation for example—food webs can be disrupted because some of their species disappear.

food chains run out so soon? The reason is to do with energy.

When animals eat food, they use its energy in two different ways. Some is built into their bodies, but most of it is used to make their bodies work. Built-in energy can be handed on, but working energy is lost once it has been used up. With active animals, such as birds and mammals, working energy makes up around 90 percent of the total, so only ten percent is left as potential food. By the time a food chain reaches its fourth or fifth species, not much energy is left. When it reaches the sixth, there is hardly any at all.

PYRAMIDS OF LIFE

This rapid drop in energy explains another feature of food chains—in most there are many more species near the bottom of the chain than toward the top. If the chain is arranged in layers, the result is a "pyramid of numbers," like the one shown on the right.

This particular pyramid shows a single food chain in a freshwater habitat. Working up from the bottom,

A food chain pyramid in a freshwater habitat

Gray herons hunt alone. Standing still in shallow water, they watch patiently for movement and strike with a quick lunge of their daggerlike bill.

Perch are predatory fish. They eat a wide range of prey, including water insects, frogs, and other fish.

Great diving beetles hunt tadpoles, seizing them with their front legs before slicing them up in their jaws.

Tadpoles feed on water plants when they are young. They switch to a meat-eating diet as they grow older.

Floating water plants form the bottom of the pyramid. They create food that can be passed up a food chain.

A boat heads downriver in Bowling Green Bay National Park, a wetland habitat in northeast Australia. In this part of the world there is a long dry season every year, so trees can only survive if they grow close to the riverbank. Crocodiles lurk in the murky water, and the narrow strip of forest teems with birds.

PART 3
WILDLIFE HABITATS

BIOMES OF THE WORLD

THE HUMAN WORLD IS SPLIT UP INTO NATIONS, BUT THE NATURAL WORLD IS ORGANIZED IN A VERY DIFFERENT WAY. ITS "COUNTRIES" ARE CALLED BIOMES, AND EACH ONE HAS A DISTINCTIVE MIX OF LIVING THINGS.

From the air biomes are easy to locate. Deserts are dry and brown, while tropical forests look like dark-green carpets. Tundra is open, bleak, and bare, while wetlands are often full of waterlogged vegetation. In everyday language biomes are often known as habitats—a word also used to mean the exact surroundings that a species uses as its home.

THE BIOME MAP
On land there are ten major biomes. They are mainly shaped by climate because that affects the type of plants that can grow. For example tropical rain forests are found in places that are always warm and wet, while deserts form where it is too dry for trees to survive. Each biome is found in several different parts of the world, wherever the climate is the same. The plants in each biome vary from place to place, but because they grow in the same conditions, they often have the same shape and even the same type of leaves.

Animal life depends on plants, so it is divided into biomes too. Most of the world's grazing mammals live in grasslands, and a huge slice of the insect life is found in tropical and temperate forests. Deserts are one of the most important biomes for snakes and lizards, although scrublands are good places for them too. A big portion of the world's fish live in coral reefs—the closest thing to a biome in the sea.

BIOMES ON THE MOVE
Because biomes are shaped mainly by the climate, they often do not have clear-cut frontiers. Instead

A R C T I C

Lincoln Sea

Beaufort Sea

Baffin Bay

Arctic Circle

Hudson Bay

Gulf of Alaska

Labrador Sea

NORTH AMERICA

A T L A N T I

O C E A N

Tropic of Cancer

Gulf of Mexico

Caribbean Sea

Equator

P A C I F I C

O C E A N

SOUTH AMERICA

Tropic of Capricorn

Key
- Polar (The Arctic/Antarctica)
- Arctic tundra
- Mountains
- Coniferous forests
- Temperate forests
- Grasslands and savanna
- Scrublands
- Deserts
- Wetlands
- Tropical forests
- Coral reefs

Antarctic Circle

neighboring biomes usually merge. In the far north coniferous forests gradually give way to tundra, while in the tropics, scrublands give way to deserts. In places the boundary zones between two biomes can be hundreds of miles wide.

Climate patterns slowly shift, so biomes shift too. Deserts expand when the climate turns drier and contract again when wetter times return. The further back in time you go, the bigger these changes become.

At the height of the last ice age tundra covered large parts of North America, Europe, and Asia. Tropical rain forests shrank because the climate was cool and dry, and with the forest on the retreat rain forest animals had to retreat as well.

PEOPLE AND BIOMES

The map below shows where the world's biomes are today. What it does not show are the changes that have been caused by human beings.

Ever since we learned how to farm, around 10,000 years ago, we have had a growing impact on the world's biomes. Forests have been cut down, grasslands plowed up, and wetlands drained. In some parts of the world desert conditions have spread, as farmland soil has been washed or blown away. If none of this had happened—or if it somehow went into reverse—the world's biomes would look exactly as they are shown here.

ARCTIC AND TUNDRA

IN THE FAR NORTH OF THE PLANET
TEMPERATURES CAN GO AS LOW AS −58°F
(−50°C), AND WINTER DAYS ARE JUST A FEW
HOURS LONG. FOR THE PLANTS AND ANIMALS
THAT LIVE THERE THE ARCTIC IS A LAND OF
OPPORTUNITY, BUT IT TAKES REAL TOUGHNESS
TO SURVIVE IN THIS SEA OF ICE AND SNOW.

The heart of the Arctic is a frozen ocean—one that
is almost completely surrounded by land. This
ocean is the world's smallest, and most of it
is covered by a layer of floating ice that is constantly
on the move. The land around the Arctic Ocean—
known as the tundra—is bleak and treeless and is
frozen for much of the year. But for a few months
during the spring and summer the surface thaws,
and the tundra suddenly explodes into life.

◁ Jellyfish are an
important part of the
Arctic Ocean's wildlife.
This type swims, but some
jellyfish spend most of their
time upside down on the seabed.

LIFE IN THE ARCTIC OCEAN
For humans the Arctic Ocean
is dangerously cold. Even in the
summer the temperature is close
to freezing, and anyone falling in
needs to be rescued right away. In
the winter sea ice stretches as far
south as the tip of Greenland,
sealing the ocean like
a crystalline lid. Icebergs
become trapped in the winter
ice, but when the ice melts, they can
drift south for thousands of miles.
In 1912 the *Titanic* hit an iceberg
as far south as Spain, and in 1926
an iceberg was seen off of Bermuda.

▽ *Three young polar bears follow their
mother across the ice. Females look after
their cubs until they are around two years
old—after that they are on their own.*

△ *Every spring the edge of the Arctic sea ice begins to break up, forming ice floes that drift with the currents. Here, off the coast of Greeland, floes are beginning to break away from the main ice sheet.*

Compared to air, water is very good at draining away warmth, which is why people cannot last long if they fall into the icy waves. But despite the intense cold, the Arctic Ocean is one of the busiest wildlife habitats on Earth. It teems with microscopic plankton, with jellyfish, brittle stars, and burrowing worms, and also with fish, seals, and whales. How do they manage to survive?

For most Arctic Ocean animals the cold is simply not a problem because they do not have any body heat to lose. These "cold-blooded" animals feel at home in the icy water, as long as it does not actually freeze over. Many live on the seabed where the temperature stays at a steady 39°F (4°C) all year-round. In this dimly lit and not-quite-frozen world the cold-blooded animals move slowly, but they have no trouble staying alive.

DEEP HEAT

For the mammals in the Arctic Ocean the cold is more of a threat. Seals and whales are warm-blooded, and their body temperatures are hardly any different from ours. If they become chilled—even by a few degrees— they risk dying of hypothermia.

Arctic mammals get around this problem by having a wraparound layer of fat called blubber between their internal organs and their skin. Fat is an extremely good insulator, and it makes it hard for body heat to escape. In Arctic seals this layer is usually around 4 in. (10cm) thick, but in bowhead whales it can be 20 in. (50cm) thick with a total weight of several tons. When these whales were hunted—as long ago as the 1600s—their blubber was highly prized, and it was often cut up into blocks and floated back to shore.

Blubber alone is enough to keep whales warm, but most seals also have a short coat of dense fur. One Arctic Ocean animal— the polar bear—has much shaggier fur that is good for keeping warm in the air but not nearly as effective in the water. However, because of its blubber the polar bear has no fear of the cold. It is a true seagoing animal, sometimes swimming dozens of miles from the nearest ice or land.

△ *Soaking up the summer sunshine, tundra plants bloom among rocks near the Arctic coast. There are hundreds of different flowering plants in the Arctic, but most of them are just a couple of inches tall.*

▽ *Watched by its mother, a harp seal pup enjoys a meal. Unlike polar bears, female harp seals abandon their young when they are 12 days old. The pup has to molt its silky coat before it can start eating at sea.*

◁ *Like passengers waiting for a bus, male narwhals line up in a "lead," or crack, in the sea ice. Narwhals sometimes live in family groups, but all these narwhals have long tusks, proving they are adult males.*

moving prey. However walrus actually eat seabed clams, sucking them up from the chilly mud like gigantic vacuum cleaners.

Polynyas are also a favorite home of two of the Arctic's smallest whales—the white whale, or beluga, and the narwhal—an extraordinary animal with a single tusk that points forward.

GAPS IN THE ICE

Near the North Pole the Arctic Ocean's surface is almost always frozen, making it difficult for air-breathing seals and whales to survive. But in most parts of the Arctic strong winds and currents jostle the sea ice, opening up cracks of water in some places, crunching

▽ *Walrus often lounge on ice floes between feeding sessions. Their tusks are mainly just a sign of rank, but they also come in handy when a walrus needs to haul itself out of the water and onto the ice.*

the ice together in others. Small stretches of open water called leads can appear almost anywhere, but they rarely last for long. Much larger expanses, known by a Russian name—polynya—can last for years or even decades. Today one of the biggest Arctic polynyas is at the northern end of Baffin Bay. It is almost as big as Switzerland, making it easily visible from space.

For Arctic wildlife polynyas are like oases in a frozen desert. They are some of the best places to see seals, including the walrus—the biggest Arctic species of all. Weighing up to 2,650 lbs (1,200kg) and equipped with impressive tusks, this wrinkly skinned animal looks as if it is designed to attack large, fast-

Species Profile

Arctic fox: *Alopex lagopus*

This dainty and inquisitive predator lives right across the Arctic region. In the summer it stays on land, but in the winter it may wander hundreds of miles onto the sea ice. Most Arctic foxes have a brown summer coat and a white winter coat for camouflage against the snow. However in some Arctic foxes the winter coat is bluish-gray. These foxes are not picky eaters, and they eat anything they can catch or scavenge—from nesting birds to the remains of polar bear kills such as seals.

◁ *Polar sunshine does not have much strength, but in the summer it never stops. This photograph shows the Sun at midnight in northern Norway at the height of the northern summer. At the North Pole the Sun shines constantly between late March and late September, but then it vanishes below the horizon for the next six months.*

hope of escape. This is bad news for the whales but good news for the Arctic's native inhabitants, who use narwhal meat as a winter food.

TUNDRA TIMES

In the Arctic winter is a season of darkness, while the summer is full of light. On the Arctic Circle the Sun dips down to the horizon on a summer's day but starts rising again before it actually sets. Farther north the summer is even more strange.

Narwhal tusks look like the horns of legendary unicorns and in the past were often sold for their supposedly magical powers. Even today narwhal tusks are mysterious. Found only in males, they are highly specialized teeth up to 10 ft. (3m) long. Males sometimes use them in ritual fights, but their function is still not fully understood.

TRAPPED

Giant polynyas like the one in Baffin Bay make a permanent home for animals that need open water. But with smaller ice-free areas, changing weather and shifting currents can turn a refuge into a prison. As the sea begins to freeze over in the late summer polynyas begin to shrink. Sometimes they completely close up.

For seabirds this is only a slight inconvenience because many species are already heading south to spend the winter in milder climes. But for seals and whales the ice can cause real problems if they linger too long. A fully grown walrus can smash its way up through ice 10 in. (25cm) thick, but as the fall moves into winter and the ice keeps growing, keeping a breathing hole open becomes a really tough task.

Sometimes things go very wrong. Narwhals live farther north than any other Arctic whales, which means that they are especially in danger from the late-summer freeze. Occasionally hundreds of narwhals find themselves trapped in shrinking pools of water with little

△ *In the winter the snowy owl's plumage is perfect camouflage. But in the summer, when this picture was taken, this Arctic hunter is much easier to see.*

In the world's northernmost town—Ny Ålesund in Spitsbergen—the Sun lifts clear off of the horizon in early June and then does not set again until late July. For almost eight weeks there is nonstop daylight, making it difficult to know when to get up and when to go to bed.

Arctic animals have no trouble adapting to these conditions and are out and about around the clock. Ducks and geese feed at midnight on the tundra or along the shore, while snowy owls hunt in broad daylight, relying on surprise to catch their prey. Arctic foxes (see page 166) are also on the prowl, patrolling nesting sites and coastal rocks in the hope of finding

△ *Shown about twice its actual size, this is a single catkin from the world's shortest "tree," the Arctic willow. These tough tundra plants are often pollinated by bumblebees, which visit them in the early spring.*

undefended eggs or chicks. Unlike other foxes, these thickly furred animals breed in underground dens handed down from one generation to the next. The largest can have one dozen entrances and be over one hundred years old.

THE TUNDRA IN BLOOM

For the plants of the Arctic the lengthening daylight triggers a race to reproduce. As the snow clears bright-green mounds of sphagnum moss emerge on the waterlogged peat, and bog cotton sprouts around the tundra's jet-black pools. Stony ground is often covered by lichens—

Species Profile

Reindeer moss: *Cladonia rangiferina*

Despite its name, reindeer moss is not a moss but a lichen—a living partnership between an alga and a fungus. It grows throughout the tundra and is an important food for reindeer, particularly during the harsh winter months when other food can be hard to find in the icy, snow-covered landscape. Reindeer moss is gray in color, but it grows bright-red tips that make its spores.

particularly types that look like gray-green bushes just barely one inch tall. These are among the toughest plants in the Arctic, and they are an important food for reindeer, which use their hooves to scrape the plants clear of snow. The tundra is also home to the Arctic willow, which grows no more than ankle height. By sticking close to the ground this polar "tree" keeps safely out of the wind—an important survival technique in a habitat where the windchill can kill.

Because the Arctic summer is so short, tundra plants work to a very tight schedule to make their seeds.

▽ *Spread out across the snow, reindeer make their way toward their winter quarters. The largest herds, in the Canadian Arctic, can be up to half a million animals strong, and they migrate hundreds of miles each year.*

Arctic willow grows yellow or rust-colored catkins and then keeps them "on hold" until the ground is clear of snow. As soon as the air temperature reaches around 50°F (10°C) they open up, ready to attract any insects that are active. A brightly colored plant called purple saxifrage is even more eager to start. Its flowers sometimes open up while the snow is still melting above them.

ARCTIC INSECTS

For the Arctic's human inhabitants the summer can be a difficult time. This is because the sunshine melts the surface of the soil, turning the tundra soft and boggy so that it is difficult to move around. To make matters worse, this is the far north's mosquito season. In countless lakes and ponds across the Arctic billions of immature mosquitoes turn into adults and take to the air on their brand-new wings. Male mosquitoes are harmless because they feed on flowers, but the females need to

drink blood before they can lay their eggs. They normally attack wild animals, but they also cluster over clothing, shoes, and even camera lenses, searching for the smallest patch of exposed human skin.

△ *For Arctic mosquitoes humans are an irresistible attraction. The Arctic has some of the largest mosquitoes in the world with an equally large appetite for blood. Unlike tropical mosquitoes, they rarely carry diseases.*

△ *By flying in a V formation, geese reduce the amount of energy they use during their long migration flights. Each bird is helped by the slipstream from the one in front, and they take turns leading the flock.*

The Arctic is also home to blackflies —tiny humpbacked bloodsuckers with an extremely itchy bite. These troublesome insects can be as little as 0.08 in. (2mm) long, but they can attack in clouds that send animals (and people) rushing to escape.

Fortunately not all tundra insects are as unpleasant as these. Arctic bumblebees perform an essential task by pollinating the tundra's flowers, while damselflies eat bloodsucking insects, catching them in midair. And on warm days when the air is calm, butterflies take to the skies. Some of them are homegrown residents of the tundra, but others are long-distance migrants that arrive when the long days of summer begin. Their journey north can sometimes be more than a massive 1,240 mi. (2,000km) long.

FLYING MIGRANTS

It may seem strange that butterflies travel to such a cold and remote part of the world, but in the summer the Arctic's plants are an almost endless source of food. And butterflies are not the only animals that make the journey. Even before the snows have fully melted, flocks of geese arrive from warm lands to the south, ready to raise their young. Each species has its winter and summer living quarters. Snow geese spend the winter in the southern and western U.S. and nest mainly in the Canadian Arctic, while the much rarer red-breasted goose

△ *Guillemots are fish-eating birds that use their stubby wings to race underwater after their prey. These birds are the Arctic's equivalent of penguins, although unlike real penguins they are still able to fly.*

Species Profile

Arctic bumblebee: *Bombus polaris*

One of the northernmost insects in the world, the Arctic bumblebee is often buzzing around when other insects are grounded by the cold. Like all bumblebees, it is covered with furlike scales that help it keep its flight muscles warm as it races from flower to flower. Because the Arctic summer is short, Arctic bumblebees have to work fast to breed. When the fall approaches, the queen bees hibernate until the freezing weather begins to turn warmer, but all the worker bees die.

spends its winters near the Black Sea and nests in the Taymyr Peninsula in northern Siberia.

Although geese are good swimmers, they do not eat in the water. Instead they eat grass and other land plants, tearing it off with a sharp tug of their beaks. Throughout the summer the adults and goslings eat and fatten up, preparing for the long journey south.

▽▷ Musk oxen are the largest full-time land mammals in the Arctic. Their shaggy coats protect them from the cold—especially when they stand with their backs to the wind like the snow-caked bull below.

HERDS ON THE MOVE

The Arctic's largest grazing animals also travel with the seasons, but their journeys are on the ground. Herds of reindeer move south until they reach the great northern forest, marching across the snow on their unusually broad hooves and swimming across any rivers or sea inlets in their way.

In Scandinavia the Sami people once lived as nomadic reindeer herders, following their animals between tundra and forest and keeping wolves and other predators at bay. Today some of the Sami still do this, although these modern reindeer herders often have motorized sleds and comfortable houses at the journey's end.

As the summer slips into fall the Arctic's musk oxen carry out a different kind of migration, moving from low-lying tundra to higher ground. These massively horned animals develop an extra-long winter coat, so they are almost unaffected by the cold. But winter snow can be a real problem because it makes it hard to get at food. In their homes in Greenland and northern Canada moving uphill takes the musk oxen to places where the wind clears the snow off of the ground.

HOMES BENEATH THE SNOW

During the Arctic winter one of the warmest places to be is under the snow. This explains why Arctic plants grow best in snowy areas and why lemmings prefer them too. There are 12 types of lemmings in the Arctic, and all are fast breeders, producing young when they are as little as two weeks' old. One of them, the Norway lemming, is famous for its population explosions about every four years. During a "lemming year," lemmings use up their own food supply, and millions of them set off to search for something to eat.

Legend has it that migrating lemmings commit suicide by jumping off of cliffs into the sea. Lemmings are actually good swimmers, but occasionally disaster strikes, and huge numbers drown.

△ Even when it is −22°F (−30°C) outside, the tunnels lemmings make are relatively warm. When the snow melts in the spring, trails of plant remains often show where they have been feeding and hiding away.

These two photographs show Blomstrandbreen glacier on Svalbard Island, almost 370 mi. (600km) north of Norway. The main photograph shows the glacier in 1918, while the smaller picture shows it in 2002. Like most of the world's glaciers, Blomstrandbreen is shrinking fast—a change brought on by global warming. In years to come global warming will have a far-reaching effect on wildlife—especially in the polar regions.

ANTARCTICA

HUMANS ARE LATECOMERS TO ANTARCTICA—
THE COLDEST AND MOST REMOTE OF ALL THE
CONTINENTS ON EARTH. FOR MILLIONS OF
YEARS LIFE HAS FLOURISHED IN THIS FROZEN
WORLD, NOURISHED BY THE INCREDIBLE
RICHNESS OF THE SURROUNDING SEA.

Unlike the Arctic, Antarctica is a giant landmass almost entirely covered by ice. At its deepest point the Antarctic ice cap is more than 2.5 mi. (4km) thick, and its immense weight squashes the bedrock far beneath. Aside from scientists hardly anything lives on the ice cap itself, but Antarctica's coastline—and the stormy Southern Ocean—abounds with life.

△ *Photographed by a satellite, a huge iceberg drifts off the coast of Antarctica. It is early fall, and the sea is already freezing over. The iceberg is surrounded by sea ice and will soon be trapped until the spring.*

▽ *Waves crash against a grounded iceberg off Laurie Island, 370 mi. (600km) north of the Antarctic Circle. Laurie Island is covered by glaciers and is far too cold and desolate to have any full-time human inhabitants. Storm-force winds and jagged rocks make it dangerous to even approach the shore.*

THE DEEP SOUTH

Few maps show Antarctica's real frontier with the rest of the world. It is not the ice-covered coast or the Antarctic Circle but an invisible boundary far out at sea. Called the Antarctic Convergence, it is the point where cold water flowing north from Antarctica meets much warmer water heading south. The Convergence is always on the move, shifting slightly from year to year, but it marks the point where the temperate world stops and the polar world begins.

At this latitude a ship can sail around the Southern Ocean without ever running into land. Because there is no land there is nothing to block the hurricane-force winds that blow clockwise around the Pole. South of the Convergence lies one of the stormiest regions in the world, with mountainous waves and dark, ragged skies. From onboard a ship it looks like one of the most hostile habitats on Earth, but nothing could be further from the truth.

COMING UP

In the ocean around Antarctica the currents behave in complicated ways. As well as carrying water from west to east, they also lift it up from below. With this "upwelling" water comes a rich mixture of seabed nutrients—exactly what planktonic algae need to grow. Because of this endless source of natural fertilizer, the Southern Ocean is one of the richest marine habitats in the world.

Every spring these planktonic plants develop at a rapid rate, just like grassland turning green on land.

In the ocean there are no herds of grazing mammals to eat the plants, but there are unimaginably vast swarms of krill. These small shrimplike crustaceans are only the size of a finger, but a single swarm of them can weigh more than 10 million tons. During the spring and summer krill filter out planktonic algae and turn them into protein-packed food. In the fall and winter as the algae die out the krill sink to deeper waters where they survive on leftovers that drift down from the waters above.

THE FILTER FEEDERS

For Antarctica's marine life krill swarms are an almost inexhaustible source of food. Small fish, squid, and penguins catch krill one by one, but larger hunters operate on a much bigger scale. One of these larger hunters is the crabeater seal. Despite its name the crabeater survives almost entirely on krill, sucking up large mouthfuls and then straining them out with its serrated teeth. In a single feeding

△ *Krill usually swim in the same direction, just like fish in a school. These krill were photographed in a tank at an Antarctic research station. Confused by captivity, they are trying to find their way out.*

session one crabeater can swallow up to 18 lbs (8kg) of krill—around five times as much food as most people eat in an entire day. Altogether crabeaters are believed to gulp down at least 60 million tons of krill a year, making them the leading krill eaters in the Southern Ocean.

Species Profile

Antarctic cod: *Trematomus pennelli*

This fish, like its close relatives, is specifically adapted to survive in cold water. Its blood contains a chemical antifreeze, and this allows it to live at temperatures close to the freezing point of seawater, which is 28°F (–1.9°C). It is so well adjusted to these chilly conditions that it dies if the temperature rises by even 10 degrees. It lives near the seabed and eats smaller fish and animal leftovers, including seal droppings.

Krill are also a favorite food of leopard seals, ferocious and fast-swimming hunters that attack penguins as well. A leopard seal's back teeth have three sharp points, and they can either work like daggers or can close to make a krill-trapping sieve. But for individual krill consumption nothing beats the Southern Ocean's rorqual whale. Rorquals include the world's largest whales, and they all have deep grooves running lengthwise down their throats. When a rorqual hits a swarm of krill, it swims through it with its mouth open, and the grooves expand so that its throat swells up like a balloon. The whale closes its mouth and strains out the krill, swallowing up to one ton of them at a time.

Until the 1900s blue whales and other rorquals consumed a huge share of the Southern Ocean's krill each year. But when whale stocks began dwindling in the Northern Hemisphere, more and more whaling boats began operating in Antarctic waters. Their catch was processed either on remote islands like South Georgia or on special factory ships designed to spend months at sea. Rorquals were the main whales to be targeted and caught—29,000 blue whales were killed in one year alone. Today the entire Southern Ocean is a whale sanctuary, but because whales breed slowly it will be many years before their numbers reach anything like the level they were at before.

▽ *Leopard seals can swallow small penguins whole, but with large penguins they have to shake their prey until it falls apart. This seal has caught an Adélie penguin—one of the few types that breed on ice.*

△ *Whales migrate south to Antarctica in the southern spring when the shrinking sea ice makes it easier for them to get at food. These humpbacks, shown here off Australia, cover 125 mi. (200km) a day.*

A DANGEROUS COAST

Antarctica's coastline is unlike any other on Earth. Only around five percent of it is bare rock—the rest consists of immense ice shelves that inch their way slowly out to sea. These shelves are fed by glaciers that contain ice thousands of years old. As the ice is pushed out to sea entire sheets up to 656 ft. (200m) high begin to float. Eventually giant slabs of the ice split away from the front of the sheet, creating flat-topped islands that are by far the biggest icebergs in the world.

From the early fall Antarctica is also surrounded by an expanding belt of floating sea ice that grows northward at up to 2.5 mi. (4km) per day. Because sea ice forms in the water itself, it never gets more than ten feet thick. However, by late winter it covers an area that is three times bigger than Australia before it shrinks again in the warmth of the Antarctic spring.

For some of Antarctica's animals floating ice makes a useful place to perch or rest. But for shore animals ice can be dangerous, particularly when it is on the move. Sea ice shifts and settles with each tide, scraping animals off of shallow rocks and gouging deep grooves into the seabed mud. Icebergs cause even more havoc, especially when winds or currents drive them back toward the shore. To avoid being scraped or squashed, limpets and other shore animals often move to deeper water in the fall, creeping back to the shallows in the spring.

ABSENT PARENTS

More than 40 species of birds live around Antarctica, but very few of them breed on Antarctica itself. Instead most nest on the Southern Ocean's islands, which include the remotest pieces of land on Earth. Bouvet Island, or Bouvetøya, is the loneliest of all—the closest land to it is the coast of eastern Antarctica, around 1,000 mi. (1,600km) away.

These storm-lashed islands receive few human visitors and landing on them is hazardous because of storms and gusting winds. But with so much sea and so little land, they are vital nesting sites for albatross—the world's largest seabirds.

△ *Off the coast of Antarctica animals often grow slowly, but they can live a long time. These feathery sea anemones survive well into their twenties, but some Antarctic limpets can live for over one hundred years.*

▽ *Four fifths of Antarctica's icebergs come from ice shelves that slowly feed into the sea. Known as tabular bergs, they have flat tops and sides that look like cliffs. As they drift north, cracks start opening up in the ice until they finally break apart.*

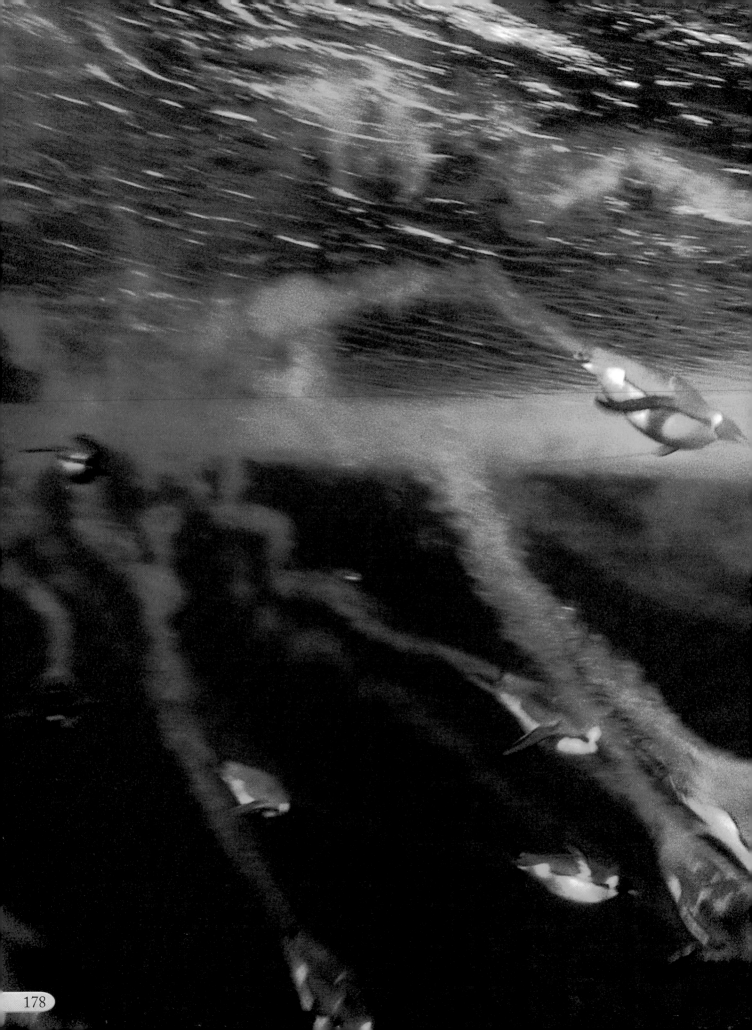

Penguins often look clumsy on land, but they are graceful swimmers, speeding along by flicking their "wings." These emperor penguins reach a top speed of 19 mph (30km/h). They can dive more than 820 ft. (250m) deep and can stay underwater for almost 20 minutes. Like all penguins, emperors have a bulletlike shape that helps them race through the sea.

Albatross look like giant gulls, but they feed far out at sea, gliding effortlessly for days at a time and snatching jellyfish from the surface of the waves. They can live to an old age, but compared to most other birds they are very slow at breeding. Parent albatross raise just one chick at a time, and they can wander more than 1,860 mi. (3,000km) from their nest before returning with food. Amazingly their chick waits for them, and the parents never seem to lose their way home.

BREEDING ON THE ICE

Antarctica's islands are much too windy for trees—instead their tallest plant is a kind of grass that grows in sturdy clumps that sometimes reach waist level. These clumps of hairgrass shelter spiders, insects, and also rats that have escaped from ships. On some islands, such as Kerguelen, rats

▷ *Six types of albatross breed near Antarctica. This is the black-browed albatross— a species that sometimes wanders as far north as Australia. It snatches food from the sea without having to land on the water.*

Species Profile

Antarctic skua: *Catharacta antarctica*

Wherever penguins breed, Antarctic skuas are rarely far away. These aggressive birds steal penguin eggs and eat newly hatched penguin chicks. They also feed on dead remains, using their hooked beaks to tear open the bodies of seals and even whales. Antarctic skuas often breed close to penguin colonies and will attack anything that gets too close to their nests. They spend the winter throughout the southern seas, returning to Antarctica in the spring.

have become a real conservation problem because they eat eggs and attack nestlings. Scientists are trying to devise ways of reducing the numbers of these intruders so that birds have a better chance of raising their young. Hairgrass also grows in the Antarctic Peninsula, a part of Antarctica that points toward South America. The tip of the peninsula is like an Antarctic version of Florida because conditions here are much milder than farther south.

This is where many of Antarctica's scientists are based, and it is also where almost all of Antarctica's land-based animals are found. But compared to the Antarctic's seagoing animals, its land-based animals are extremely small. The largest land predator— a carnivorous mite—is less than one inch long.

PETRELS AND PENGUINS

On the Antarctic mainland two small seabirds share the record as the most southerly breeding birds in the world. Petrels normally feed on the coast, but the snowy petrel and the Antarctic petrel have been found nesting in cliff crevices up to 155 mi. (250km) inland. These hideouts protect the petrels' eggs and chicks from the bitter Antarctic wind, but they still have to be exceptionally cold-proof in order to survive.

In complete contrast Antarctica's largest birds breed on the windswept ice without any shelter at all. They are emperor penguins, and they are the animal world's unrivaled experts at keeping warm. Throughout the dark winter male emperors remain on the ice while their partners are away feeding at sea. By huddling together they survive temperatures as low as −58°F (−50°C). When the windchill is added, this is colder than in any other natural habitat on Earth. It is an amazing feat of endurance, but male emperors have more to worry about than just themselves. All winter long each male protects and incubates its partner's egg, using its feet as a "nest" and a fold of skin as a warm and feathery pouch.

Most birds lay their eggs in the spring, but with emperors things are the other way around. The females lay their eggs in the fall, just before they set out to sea. This might seem like a case of extremely bad timing, but emperor eggs take two months to hatch, and their chicks then need four months to grow up. By laying their eggs in the fall, the females make sure that their young will be leaving home at the best time of year—at the height of the Antarctic spring.

◁ *For emperor penguins huddling together in a large group is the best way of surviving the bitter cold. The chicks take turns at being on the inside, where they get the best protection from the bitter winds.*

▽ *Young albatross can take up to nine months to leave the nest—a record for any bird. They are brooded for the first few weeks; after that they sit in the nest alone.*

DESERTS

DESERTS COVER ALMOST ONE THIRD OF
THE WORLD'S SURFACE AREA, MAKING THEM
THE MOST EXTENSIVE LAND HABITAT ON EARTH.
DESERT WILDLIFE IS OFTEN THINLY SPREAD OUT,
BUT IT IS GOOD AT COPING WITH TEMPERATURE
EXTREMES AND HARSH CONDITIONS.

Most of the world's deserts are in the subtropics, where giant swirls of dry air called anticyclones sit for months at a time. Deserts also exist in other places that moisture cannot reach—either because they are so far inland or because mountains shield them from rain-bearing winds. Although most deserts are warm and dry, some can be cold, and rare storms sometimes drench them with rain.

▽ These giant sand dunes in Africa's Namib Desert are some of the tallest in the world. In the Namib Desert the coastal wind keeps the sand on the move, and the dunes creep inland like slow-motion waves.

A FICKLE CLIMATE
In June of 1991 one of these storms hit the Chilean port of Antofagasta, where it washed away houses and roads. This storm was even more remarkable because Antofagasta is in the Atacama Desert, which is normally the driest place on Earth. In this strip of land sandwiched between the Pacific Ocean and the Andes Mountains the average rainfall can be as low as 0.1mm per year. Filling a coffee mug with rain here would take about one century, and every drop of drinking water has to come in through pipes or by road.

These desert downpours are known as flash floods, and they are one of the reasons why deserts are difficult homes for living things. In deserts drought is a daily fact

◁ *In deserts exposed rocks are often carved into strange shapes by the wind. It sweeps up pieces of grit and sand and hurls them against anything that stands in the way.*

of life, but when it does rain the results can be dramatic as well as dangerous. Another problem is the wind, which can fling sharp-edged grit horizontally across the ground or blow clouds of sand up into the sky. Add boiling-hot sunshine and chilly nights to the equation and the result is a habitat where almost everything is extreme.

LIVING RESERVOIRS

Parts of the Atacama Desert are so dry that nothing grows there at all. But in most deserts there is enough moisture to allow some plants to take hold. Two inches (5cm) of rain per year is enough for a number of low, drought-resistant plants to grow, while 6 in. (15cm) allows a few taller shrubs as well. By the time rainfall hits 10 in. (25cm) per year, desert becomes shrubland (see page 204)—a habitat where many more types of plants live.

Plants are the key to desert life because without them there is no food for animals to eat. Desert plants are extremely varied, but none can rival cacti for their drought-resisting power. The largest cacti—saguaros and cardóns— can be more than 33 ft. (10m) tall, and their fluted stems work like expandable reservoirs, holding enough water to fill many bathtubs. Like all plants, these giant cacti "breathe" through microscopic pores, but they do it during the cool desert night, preventing too much water from escaping in the outside air.

Some desert trees and shrubs have incredibly long roots that search out water deep underground. In Arizona, for example, miners have discovered the roots of mesquite trees over 164 ft. (50m) underground. But cactus roots are different. Most of them fan out just beneath the surface where they can intercept the rain as soon as it falls.

△ *Seen from a plane, water pours over Australia's Simpson Desert after a heavy storm. These sudden downpours can flood huge areas of land, but the water is shallow and quickly evaporates.*

◁ *In the Mojave Desert in southern California a spectacular flower show follows the spring rain. A few weeks later all these flowers will have disappeared, and the plants that grew them will be dead.*

△ *The boojum tree grows in the heart of northwest Mexico and nowhere else in the world. It has pencil-sized twigs and a trunk that looks like it belongs on an elephant rather than on a plant.*

Because cacti soak up moisture so quickly, they are often surrounded by a "no-man's-land" where it is difficult for other plants to set up home. This is a good hunting ground for many animals, especially the roadrunner, a bird that sprints around desert rocks and plants catching all types of small animals—from scorpions to snakes.

BIZARRE BOTANY

Throughout the world's deserts many plants use the survival technique of cacti and store water in their stems. These plants include some of the strangest shrubs, such as the Mexican boojum tree or cirio, which looks like a prickly telephone pole. On the island of Socotra, just off the Horn of Africa, the sack-of-potatoes tree is another strangely shaped desert speciality. It has a small cluster of fleshy branches that sprout out of a lumpy, baglike trunk.

Africa's deserts are home to many botanical oddities, including baseball plants (see page 48) and living stones. The baseball plant's stems are green and round and are about the size of a baseball. They contain a lot of water and several mouthfuls of thick, milky white sap. This sap has a fiery taste—much hotter than the strongest chili pepper—and this helps keep hungry animals at bay. Living stones (see page 106) have a different type of defense. Their tiny, flat-topped stems look just like pebbles, except once a year when the "pebbles" suddenly bloom.

But Africa's strangest desert plant, from the Namib Desert, is even more curious. Named welwitschia after a German botanist, it is a distant relative of coniferous trees. It is around 3 ft. (1m) tall and has just two straplike leaves that keep growing for hundreds of years. The leaves are as tough as wood and become frayed as they age.

CHEATING THE HEAT

Welwitschias grow extremely slowly and can live to be more than 1,000 years old. But desert plants also include species that grow, flower, drop their seeds, and die in a minute fraction of that time. These plants are known as ephemerals, and they appear only after it has rained.

In California's Death Valley ephemeral plants often appear after

Species Profile

Welwitschia: *Welwitschia mirabilis*

The *welwitschia* plant only grows in one place: the gravelly plains at the heart of the Namib Desert. It has a stubby, flat-topped trunk and just two leaves that split and curl as they grow. The plant does not have flowers and reproduces by growing cones instead. It grows extremely slowly, but it is one of the world's toughest plants and can live for up to 2,000 years.

▷ *Within hours of it raining, this spadefoot toad has made its way to the surface and is calling to attract a mate. Toads are common in deserts, but they spend most of their lives underground.*

making seeds. When the summer comes, the plants themselves have been dead for awhile, but their seeds are scattered across the ground in their millions, waiting for the next burst of life-giving rain.

EPHEMERAL ANIMALS

Plants are not the only things that have evolved this fast-forward lifestyle—some desert animals have as well. Most of these breed in the water, which means that they depend on rare downpours to survive.

In Australia's Simpson Desert this type of rain falls roughly one year out of every five. This desert is one of the world's flattest, so the floodwater drains away very slowly. Shallow pools and lakes spread out in all directions, and within a few days the water begins stirring with life. Among the first animals to appear are tadpole shrimps, which hatch from eggs that were laying dormant in the ground.

the rains of early spring. For a few weeks patches of the valley floor turn green and then yellow as the plants blossom. But the ephemerals have to work against the clock, because as each day passes the sun rises higher into the sky. By the time the summer arrives the air temperature can hit 130°F (55°C), turning Death Valley into one of the hottest places on Earth. And the ground temperature can be even higher. In one part of the valley called Furnace

▷ *Tadpole shrimp are prehistoric-looking crustaceans that breed in desert pools. The adults have to breed quickly before their home dries up.*

Creek it once reached 190°F (88°C)—22° degrees below boiling point.

With this type of heat just a few months away, there is no time to grow large and bushy or send out long-running roots. Instead each plant soaks up the moisture around it and puts all of its energy into

Species Profile

Namaqua sandgrouse: *Pterocles namaqua*

There are 16 species of sandgrouse, all specialists in desert life. They can fly long distances to find seeds, and their speckled plumage helps camouflage them when they are feeding on the ground. They also carry water in their feathers—a remarkable skill that helps their nestlings survive. The Namaqua sandgrouse is a typical species; it lives in the deserts of southern Africa.

Like ephemeral plants, the shrimps immediately begin reproducing as if they know that their watery surroundings will not last for long.

Heavy rains also bring frogs and toads scrambling to the surface, ending a deep sleep underground.

During their long wait they are wrapped in waterproof cocoons made from thin layers of molted skin. When rain seeps through the soil, this protective jacket softens, and its owner gulps it down before heading up toward the light. Soon the shrimps, frogs, and toads are joined by black swans and even pelicans, creating one of the most unlikely-looking collections of desert animals in the world.

WATER MISERS

Burrowing amphibians live in many of the world's deserts, although their part-time lifestyle makes them hard to find. But many desert animals are active throughout the year, which means that they need water all the time. These animals manage their water resources as carefully as an accountant manages money in the bank. They collect water whenever and wherever they can and make sure that very little goes to waste.

Some desert animals perform an apparently impossible feat—they survive without drinking at all.

WATER MAKERS

Among these animals are kangaroo rats, seed-eating rodents from the deserts of North America. Kangaroo rats are easy to raise in captivity, so scientists have been able to discover the secret behind their survival—they take in some moisture along with their food. This is enough to supply around one tenth of the water that they need. The remaining nine tenths comes to them in a different way. Kangaroo rats actually "manufacture" it through chemical reactions as they digest and break down their food. Called metabolic water, it is something that many animals allow to go to waste. But kangaroo rats use up almost all of it, which explains how they thrive in places where other animals would die of thirst.

WATER STORERS

In deserts animals get hold of water in some ingenious ways. Desert elephants locate water in dried-up rivers, probably by smell, and dig down many feet to reach it. Sandgrouse fly to distant water holes and ferry water back to their chicks. They wade in until they are up to their chests and use their breast feathers to soak up water like a sponge. In the Namib and parts of the Atacama deserts some insects and lizards survive by drinking fog. They use their bodies to gather droplets of water that form on them like dew.

When desert animals do find water, many of them store it up so that they can survive through dry times.

△ *A kangaroo rat can go through life without drinking a single drop of water. Kangaroo rats need water—just like all other animals—but they can get all they need from their food.*

This is not actually that unusual—wood-boring beetles do it all the time. But in deserts nondrinkers also include mammals, which usually need plenty of fluids to stay alive.

◁ *There are more than 2,000 different types of cacti, and the saguaro is the largest as well as one of the longest living of them all. The water that is held inside a saguaro's stem can weigh more than one ton.*

These living water storers include desert antelopes, such as the gemsbok, and the two types of camels. The Arabian or one-humped camel can drink 16 gallons (60L) of water at one time, while the Bactrian or two-humped camel can swallow 29 gallons (110L) in a single drinking session. That is enough to fill two gasoline tanks in an average family car.

△ *In North Africa, the Middle East, and central Asia camels have been used for milk, meat, and muscle power for at least 4,000 years.*

NIGHT LIFE

In the days when camels were the only type of desert transportation people often traveled at night. It made sense because in deserts the nights are usually more comfortable than the days. Once the sun sets the ground quickly loses its warmth, and the air cools under the cloudless sky. Desert animals also take advantage of this temperature change, and many are active at night rather than during the day. These nocturnal animals include almost all small- and medium-sized mammals, from gerbils to jackrabbits, and also many predators such as coyotes and the dainty fennec fox. The fennec fox finds its prey mainly by listening with its giant ears, while coyotes track down food by having good eyesight, a sharp sense of hearing, and an acute sense of smell.

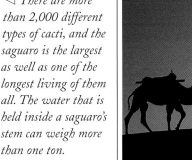

△ *A fennec fox's ears are so sensitive that they can hear a beetle walking many feet away. Fennec foxes are the smallest members of the dog family, and insects make up an important part of their diet.*

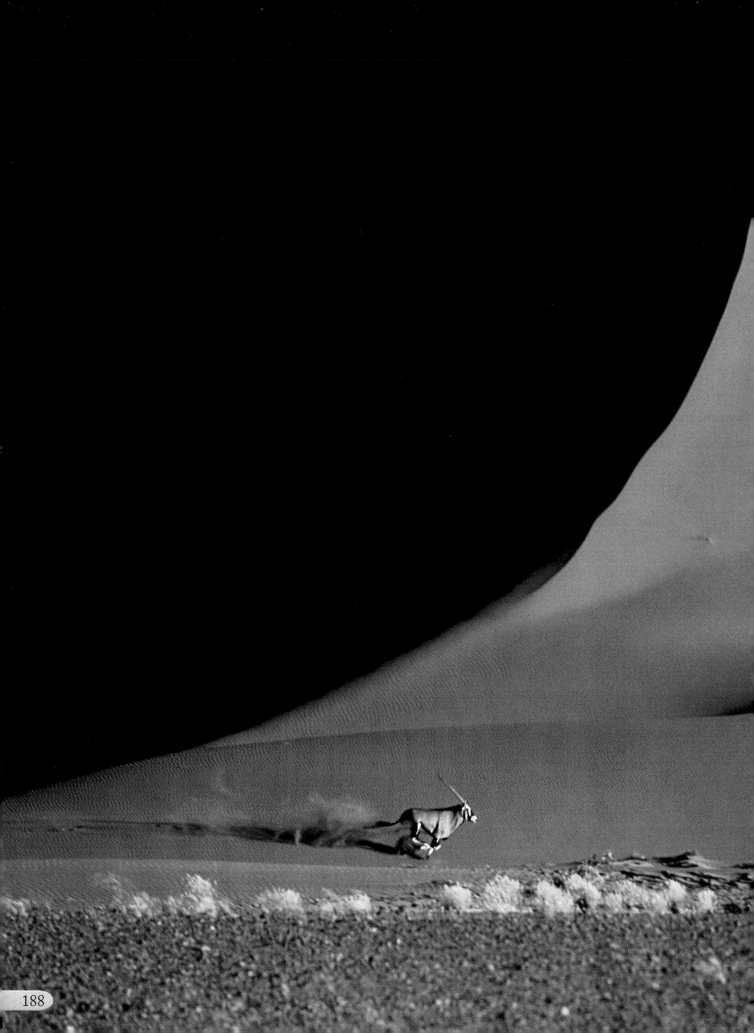

Dwarfed by a sand dune, a gemsbok gallops off to rejoin the rest of its herd. Like many desert animals, gemsboks spend most of their lives on the move, searching out places where rain allows plants to grow. In dry times these African antelope get water by eating gourds—small fruits that look like melons.

△ *For snakes with built-in heat sensors, night is the best time to hunt. Under clear desert skies the ground quickly cools down. As a result, warm-blooded prey can be sensed more clearly than during the day.*

Deserts are also the home of rattlesnakes and other pit vipers that find their food by sensing body heat. These snakes have a heat-detecting pit between each eye and nostril, and they use these to "see" anything that is warmer than its surroundings (see page 127). The pits can detect a temperature difference of just 0.2°, so to these snakes, warm-blooded birds or mammals must stand out like beacons in the dark.

Because they have a pair of heat detectors, snakes can pinpoint their prey and tell exactly where to strike. If a pit viper is blindfolded, it will even lunge at a glass of warm water—a clear demonstration of how heat guides it toward its prey.

DESERTS IN THE WINTER

Only a few of the world's deserts are hot all year-round. Many have a cool season, but in some the winter can be bitterly cold. In the Gobi Desert in central Asia winter temperatures can be as low as −22°F (−30°C), although there is not much snow because this is the driest time of year. Icy winds make it dangerous to go outside, and the intense cold means that water is almost impossible to find. The Great Basin Desert in the U.S. can get just as cold, and even Death Valley has frosts—the lowest temperature recorded is 16°F (−9°C).

For cold-blooded animals, such as tortoises, lizards, and snakes, winter is no time to be on the move. Instead these animals hide away, often in burrows underground.

▷ *For the Gobi Desert's Bactrian camels molting is a serious business. The camel on the left still has some of its winter coat, but its partner is ready for the spring.*

△ *In cold deserts some of the year's moisture falls as winter snow. But if the air is dry, the snow can evaporate without melting, so very little moisture finds its way into the ground.*

Their temperatures drop so low that their bodies are barely ticking over, and they can survive for months without food. Insects behave in the same way, although many of them spend the winter not as adults but as cold-resistant eggs. Some desert mammals go into hibernation, while others spend their time underground eating food that they have stored up. In the Gobi gerbils are experts at this—a single family can hide away more than 110 lbs (50kg) of roots and seeds. Staying above ground calls for different tactics such as growing warm winter coats. When the spring arrives, a Bactrian camel's coat comes off in patches, making the camel look as if it is falling apart.

Desert birds often migrate to warmer places, but one North American species—the common poorwill—has a unique survival technique. It sometimes crawls into rocky crevices where it goes dormant for weeks at a time. Because dormant poorwills hide so carefully, the first one was not discovered until 1946. Only a handful more have been found since, and they are still the only known hibernators in the entire bird world.

Species Profile

Web-footed gecko: *Palmatogecko rangei*

Geckos are skillful climbers. Some can climb up windows, and many can run along ceilings upside down. But this gecko lives on desert dunes. Its toes are joined by webs, and they work like miniature snowshoes to keep it from sinking into the sand. Web-footed geckos live in southwest Africa and mainly eat insects and other small animals.

GRASSLANDS AND SAVANNA

WITH THEIR OPEN HORIZONS, SCATTERED TREES, AND ISOLATED WATER HOLES, GRASSLANDS AND SAVANNA ARE CLASSIC WILDLIFE TERRITORIES. THEY ARE ALSO THE HABITATS WHERE HUMAN LIFE BEGAN.

The world's grasslands and savanna are in places that have "in-between" climates—ones that are too dry for forests but too wet for deserts. Grasslands grow in some cool parts of the world, but tree-studded savanna is found mainly in the tropics. Both of these habitats are rich in plant-eating animals—from termites and grasshoppers to the largest land mammals in the world.

SECRET OF SUCCESS
Grasses may not be very eye-catching, but they are some of the most indestructible plants on Earth. They can survive being nibbled, chewed, and trampled flat, and they even grow back if they are burned. This explains why grasses make good lawns and football fields

◁ *Spinifex grass is a common sight in the bone-dry landscape of Australia's Red Center. As each plant grows out the innermost part dies, creating a grassy ring.*

Most plants have growth zones just at the tips of their stems, which means that they stop growing if the tips are eaten away. But grasses are different because they can regrow even if they are eaten right down to the ground. As well as growing upward, grass plants spread outward too.

GRASSES AND GRAZERS

Scientists do not know exactly when the world's first grasses appeared. Fossil pollen shows that it was at least 60 million years ago, which makes it possible that the earliest grasses existed when dinosaurs still roamed the planet. In those distant times there were no grasslands. Instead grasses probably lived on the edges of tropical forests, where they were scattered among other plants.

and why they cover the entire landscape in some parts of the world.

The secret of this amazing toughness lies in the way grasses grow. Unlike most plants, grasses branch close to the ground. Their stems are hollow, and they have knobbly joints spaced out from top to bottom. At each joint there is a single leaf and a growth zone where cells rapidly divide.

△ *Impalas are the most widespread grazing antelope in Africa. They are also one of the fastest—running at full speed they can clear 30 ft. (9m) in a single jump.*

△ *Grass flowers are pollinated by the wind. Their feathery flower heads open up to release pollen into the air.*

△ *Surrounded by a sea of grass, a herd of wildebeest moves across the open plains on the border between Tanzania and Kenya. It is soon after the rainy season, and the grass is still green.*

◁ *Giraffes nibble on scattered trees, but the males and females feed in different ways. Male giraffes reach up into the treetops, but the females bend their necks to eat leaves closer to the ground.*

But after the dinosaurs became extinct grasses slowly became more widespread until they were some of the most successful plants on Earth. This remarkable change happened partly because Earth's climate became drier. But a more important reason was that large, plant-eating mammals evolved at the same time.

These animals had specialized teeth for chewing their food and hard hooves that flattened soft-stemmed plants. Many plants could not survive this type of treatment, but grasses could. Because of these grazers, grasses spread out from the tropics, creating the grasslands that exist today.

GRASSLANDS OF THE WORLD
Until 200 years ago huge stretches of grasslands existed in every continent except Antarctica. Each one had its own grazing mammals. In North America the prairie grassland was grazed by American bison and by antelope called pronghorns, while South America's pampas teemed with grazing rodents and herds of deer. European and Asian grasslands, known as steppes,

---

Species Profile

American bison: *Bison bison*

Until 200 years ago American bison were the most common large animals in the grasslands of North America. There were almost 100 million of these grazers, and Plains Indians depended on them for their survival. But with the arrival of European hunters and farms, their numbers collapsed—today only around 5,000 are left. Most of these survivors live in Yellowstone National Park.

▷ *Nothing can run faster than a cheetah, but speed does not always guarantee success. Gazelles can turn sharply when they are on the run, and a cheetah has trouble following in their tracks.*

were grazed by wild horses that originally came from this part of the world. Australia was unusual because its grasslands were grazed not by hoofed mammals but by wallabies and kangaroos.

But the grasslands of Africa were—and still are—home to the largest herds of grazers in the world. In 1888 settlers in South Africa encountered a record-breaking herd of springbok migrating across the treeless grassland, or veld. It contained at least ten million animals—all of them fueled by a diet of grass.

MAMMALS ON THE MOVE

Since those times the world's grasslands have changed a great deal. During the 1800s and early 1900s buffalo and springbok were hunted so heavily that they almost disappeared. (Fortunately hunting stopped before they actually became extinct.) In many grasslands wild mammals were squeezed out by cattle and sheep, and in others the land was plowed up so that it could be used to grow grain. But despite these changes natural grasslands still exist, and they are the setting for some of the greatest wildlife spectacles on Earth.

One of the most impressive can be seen in East Africa's Serengeti and Masai Mara National Parks. Here, on the edge of the Great Rift Valley, a huge mixed herd of grassland mammals carries out a year-round migration in search of fresh food. These animals include over one million wildebeest, around one fourth of a million gazelles, and 200,000 zebras, all moving along with the seasons. They travel into open grassland at the beginning of the rainy season and then into wooded savanna as the dry season begins. In this part of the world no fences stand in their way, so they can go where they like—just as all grassland animals did until a few hundred years ago.

STAYING TOGETHER

For grazers grassland is an ideal place to live because food is all around. But it has one serious negative point—there is almost nowhere to hide. Predators can spot grazers from a long way off, and the only sure defense is to run away. Over millions of years grazing mammals have developed powerful legs, giving them a good chance to make an escape. They have also developed a lifestyle based around herds because these make good early warning systems. In a herd many eyes and ears are on the alert, and a few animals are always watching the horizon while the others feed. If one of these spots possible danger, the entire herd gets ready to run.

If grazers actually ran off at the first sign of trouble, they would die of exhaustion in only a few days.

◁ *At the end of the rainy season, zebras have no trouble finding food. Life will get harder for them later in the year, when the grass turns brown and dry.*

Instead they adjust their behavior according to the danger they face. For example gazelles will often let a lion come within 656 ft. (200m), which looks like a careless way to behave. But instinctively gazelles know that lions hunt by stealth,

△ *Most people would prefer to see rhino horns and elephant tusks where they belong —on living animals. Sadly not everyone agrees. These horns and tusks were seized from poachers before they could be sold.*

so if a lion is out in the open it is probably scouting instead of preparing to attack. Cheetahs, on the other hand, are much more dangerous because they hunt by speed rather than surprise. If gazelles see one of these, they will break into a run when it is still 1,640 ft. (500m) away— the minimum for a good head start.

ENDANGERED HEAVYWEIGHTS
Giant grazers, such as rhinos and elephants, behave in a different way. They normally move away from danger, but sometimes they stand their ground or even charge. A charge may be just a warning or the start of a genuine attack. It can be difficult to tell the difference, which

▷ *A mother wildebeest looks unconcerned as her calf is born. Compared to many young mammals, wildebeest calves are extremely well developed at birth.*

is why experienced guides always treat these animals with respect.

Elephants and rhinos are shortsighted creatures and detect danger mainly with their sharp sense of smell. Unfortunately for them this is not a good defense against their most serious enemy— humans armed with guns. Over the last 30 years enormous numbers of African elephants and rhinos have been illegally slaughtered for their ivory or their horns.

Today Africa's white rhinos are making a gradual recovery due to a successful breeding program in South Africa's national parks. The black rhino, however, is in serious danger and may be heading for extinction in the wild. With Africa's elephants the situation is more complicated. Although there are still thousands of them, their numbers have plunged, and their habitat is shrinking year by year. Some conservationists think that the best method of protecting elephants is to crack down even harder on poachers. Others believe that the ivory trade should be legalized so that elephants pay their way.

QUICK START
With fast-running predators on the lookout for an easy meal, grasslands are risky places to give birth and even more dangerous places to be born. In Africa's grasslands many antelope improve their chances by moving to the safety of thickets, where they can give birth unseen. After giving birth the mother leaves her calf hidden away. She visits it up to four times a day, but between meals the calf remains curled up and completely still. Its scent glands

are switched off, making it more difficult for predators to sniff it out, and it will not move even if a person walks just a few yards away.

For wildebeest life begins in a very different way. Instead of wandering off on their own, female wildebeest give birth in the open, and they do it in record time. The calf is often on its feet within three minutes, and it follows the first moving thing that

△ *A young gazelle's hiding place has to stay secret if it is to survive. When the mother arrives to feed her calf, she stops several yards off to avoid giving it away.*

it sees, which is normally its mother. In less than an hour mother and calf can be trotting along with the rest of the herd. This express delivery means that the herd can keep moving and

feeding—the ultimate adaptation to life in the open plains.

However it is a high-risk strategy because the mothers and calves are in full view of any predators nearby. To reduce the risk thousands of females give birth within a two-week period, making it harder for any one of them to be singled out. Amazingly if a female is threatened while she is in labor, she can put the birth "on hold."

▽ *While their parents feed, young prairie dogs take the chance to play. For prairie dogs "kissing" is a way of identifying close relatives—an important part of life in prairie dog towns.*

SAFETY UNDERGROUND

Although there are no hiding places on the surface of grassland, there are plenty underground. This is the safe haven used by burrowing animals— ones that use their claws or teeth to dig a home for themselves. Grassland is a good habitat for burrowing because grass roots hold the soil together, making sure that burrows do not collapse.

Before the world's grasslands were farmed, some of these burrowers worked on an incredibly large scale. In western Texas a single prairie dog town contained around 400 million animals scattered over an area almost twice the size of Switzerland. Over countless generations these industrious rodents dug over 62 million mi. (1 billion km) of tunnels, complete with grass-lined nesting chambers and volcano-shaped entrance mounds. The town's inhabitants were divided up into neighborhoods, and they lived in small groups called coteries, with each keeping a section of burrows to themselves. On the whole neighbors maintained good relations—unless an animal strayed into a neighbor's burrow instead of its own.

With the spread of farming, North America's prairie dogs went into a steep decline. Prairie dog towns still do exist, although none are on this gigantic scale. In some places prairie dogs are still being shot as pests,

but in others conservationists are trying to help them survive. They believe that prairie dogs are actually good for grasslands because their feeding and burrowing helps fertilize the grass.

One fact is not in doubt— prairie dog burrows are home to many animals besides prairie dogs themselves. They include burrowing owls, snakes, and spiders, as well as the black-footed ferret—one of North America's rarest predators, only found in prairie dog towns.

Once considered to be a pest, this animal is now being reintroduced into places where it has died out.

Species Profile

Burrowing owl: *Athene cunicularia*

Most of the world's owls nest in trees, but the burrowing owl lives in grassy habitats where trees are few and far between. It sets up home inside burrows left by other animals, and if it cannot find one it digs a burrow itself. Burrowing owls spend a lot of their time at their burrow entrances, where they look like sentries standing guard.

THE INSECT EATERS

Prairie dog burrows are around 6 in. (15cm) wide, so only slim-bodied hunters can slip inside. But in Africa one of the biggest grassland burrowers makes tunnels up to 3.3 ft. (1m) across. Holes this size are big enough for people to crawl into, and they are a serious hazard for tractors and safari jeeps.

During the dry season in Africa's grasslands water holes are magnets for wildlife. Elephants can drink in safety, but antelope have to be on the lookout, as water holes make perfect places for predators to launch surprise attacks. Faced with this danger, antelope drink and leave as quickly as they can.

The animal that digs out these subterranean homes is the aardvark—one of a select band of large grassland mammals that eats termites and ants. This piglike creature feeds at night and rips its way into termite mounds with its scoop-shaped claws. It is one of the world's fastest diggers and can work faster than a team of people equipped with shovels. In South America the giant anteater is another powerful excavator, although it does not tunnel underground. Its front claws work like pickaxes, hacking open ants' nests made out of sunbaked dirt.

Both of these animals are too large to survive by eating their prey one by one. Instead they sweep them up with their amazingly long, sticky tongues. Using this gathering device, a giant anteater can eat 30,000 ants and termites in one day.

△ Alarmed by a sudden noise, a flock of budgerigars takes to the air. In the wild budgerigars are just as wary as other birds, and they stay far away from people.

Species Profile

Potter wasp: *Sceliphron* and other species

Potter wasps are common in grasslands and dry places, where they hunt for caterpillars. When one of these wasps finds a caterpillar, it paralyzes it with its stinger and then drags it back to its pot-shaped nest. It puts the caterpillar inside and then lays an egg on it before closing the pot. Once the wasp grub hatches, it uses the caterpillar as its food.

GRASSLAND NOMADS

Grass is easy to find, but it is low in nutrients and difficult to digest. As a result grazing animals must spend a lot of time eating to stay well fed. Grass seeds, on the other hand, are packed full of protein and energy-rich starch and are much easier to break down. This is why humans eat cultivated grass seeds—or cereals—and why many animals feed on grass seeds in the wild.

In the Australian outback budgerigars specialize in exactly this type of diet. As cage birds, parakeets

▽ *In Australia compass termites make flat-sided nests that are always lined up north-to-south. The nests' flat sides soak up the warm sunlight at dawn and dusk but stay cool in the afternoon.*

▷ *Caught by a remote-controlled flashgun, an aardvark takes its own photo as it leaves its burrow to feed.*

or "budgies" are often kept on their own, but wild budgerigars (which are always green and yellow) live in flocks of hundreds or thousands of birds. They have adapted to life in dry grasslands, where good places to feed may be hundreds of miles apart. To survive in these conditions they are nomadic. Once they have finished most of the seeds in a certain area, they soon move on. Budgerigars nest in tree holes, but they do not have a set breeding season—instead they lay their eggs only after it has rained.

In Africa a small finch called the quelea lives in a similar way. However its flocks can contain one million birds, and they wheel over grasslands like clouds of gray smoke. Queleas sometimes descend on farmland, which is bad news for

Baobab: *Adansonia digitata*

With its massive trunk and elephant-gray bark, the baobab is one of Africa's most distinctive trees. It grows in dry savanna, and its trunk works as a water store to enable it to survive droughts. This water sometimes attracts elephants, which gouge into the trunk with their tusks. Baobabs that escape this damage can live to be over one thousand years old.

farmers because a million-bird flock can swallow 60 tons of grain in a single day.

LIFE ON THE GROUND

Budgerigars and queleas are small and fast-flying, which helps explain their success. But grasslands are also home to much larger birds that never leave the ground. They include two species of rheas from South America—the Australian emu and the African ostrich, which is the largest of all flightless birds. Like grazing mammals, these birds depend on their sharp senses and speedy legs to survive. Their main food is seeds, but they sometimes eat insects and other small animals as well.

△ *When rheas breed, the male takes on the job of incubating the eggs and taking care of the young. In Africa's grasslands male ostriches behave in exactly the same way.*

These giants of the bird world have had mixed fortunes over the last 100 years. Rheas and ostriches are not as common as they once were, and their range is smaller than it was before. But the emu is thriving and is probably more common now than it was before farming in grasslands began. During the 1930s emus became so numerous in Western Australia that the army was called in. Despite soldiers being armed with machine guns they could not keep the emus out, and today emu-proof fences are used instead.

A SHIFTING BALANCE

Even without humans grassland wildlife would have to adapt to change. Whenever the climate turns slightly wetter, trees get a foothold and turn grassland into savanna, but if it turns drier fires burn away the trees and give grass a chance to spread. The result is like a slow-running contest between two

△ *Sometimes it takes an extraspecial effort to get to your favorite food. Standing on its back legs, this bull elephant can reach up almost as high as a giraffe.*

closely related habitats, with each one trying to get the upper hand.

In Africa elephants play a part in this contest by knocking down trees as they feed. They use their heads like living bulldozers so that they can reach the highest and juiciest leaves. After a herd has moved on, the savanna looks as if it has been vandalized, and with the trees gone the grass soon moves in.

But this is only part of the story because elephants help spread trees as well. They do this by swallowing the trees' seeds and then scattering them in piles of dung. These fertile seedbeds give trees the best start in life, and they help the savanna woodlands spread. Together elephants and trees form an ever-shifting balance—one of several thousand that shapes the grassland and savanna world.

▽ *Emus stride through the Australian bush. They can run almost as fast as ostriches, and they are also good swimmers—an unusual talent for birds that live in grasslands and deserts.*

SCRUBLANDS

SMALLER THAN TREES BUT JUST AS TOUGH, SCRUBS MAKE UP A DRYLAND HABITAT THAT IS SCATTERED ACROSS THE GLOBE. IN SCRUBLANDS LIFE HAS TO SURVIVE LONG SUMMER DROUGHTS AND THE CONSTANT THREAT OF FIRE.

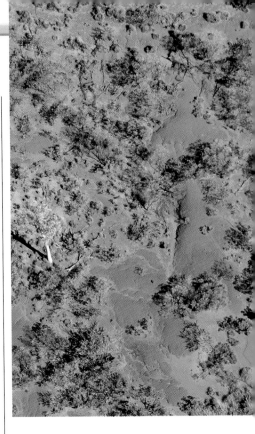

When the world's land habitats are listed, scrublands often get left out. That is because humans often think of scrublands as wasteland, where it is difficult to move around and hard to get anything useful to grow. But for wildlife scrublands provide many places to hide and plenty of food.

WHAT IS A SCRUB?

Trees are easy to recognize because they usually have a single trunk. Scrubs are different because they do not have trunks, and their branches start on or near the ground. Some scrubs can be taller than a one-story house, but the smallest of them are only ankle high. They often grow in dense, spiky thickets, which can make traveling through scrublands hard work.

In South America's Gran Chaco conditions are so uninviting that few people venture far off the tracks and into the scrubland itself. Here, to the south of the Amazon rain forest, the winters are warm and dry, but the summers are extremely hot and humid with storms that can turn the ground into a sea of mud. This thorny wilderness is hard going for humans, but it is a perfect habitat for animal life. Among its natural

▽ *In California chaparral scrubland is home to cacti, sagebrush, and to prickly-leaved oaks. For early settlers on horseback, crossing it could have been an uncomfortable experience.*

◁ In Kalbarri National Park in Western Australia low-growing scrubs provide cover for rock wallabies and gray kangaroos, as well as over 170 types of birds.

in southern California many cities are surrounded by a type of scrubland called chaparral.

SCRUBLAND CLIMATE

Most of the world's scrublands are found in places where it is dry for several months of the year. This type of climate makes life difficult for trees, but it allows smaller woody plants to thrive. In fact the scrubland climate seems to encourage plants to evolve, so an astonishing number of different plants may end up living side by side.

For sheer plant variety one type of scrubland breaks all records for a habitat of its size. This is South Africa's fynbos (pronounced "fine boss"), which grows on mountains

around the Cape of Good Hope. Fynbos is like an evergreen carpet across the ground. Although the fynbos region is less than 310 mi. (500km) across, it contains 8,500 species of scrubs and other plants—

△ South Africa's fynbos starts flowering in August—the start of the southern spring. By December most of the flowers are over as the summertime heat sets in.

residents are colorful birds and biting insects and also some of the most poisonous snakes in the world.

But not all scrublands are this inhospitable or this little known. In southern Europe, for example, scrubland grows along the coast of the Mediterranean Sea, while almost as many as in all of the countries of Europe combined.

Thousands of miles to the east, across the Indian Ocean, the scrublands of Western Australia are another of the biological hot spots of the world. Unlike South Africa this region is almost flat, and scrubland grows on a deep layer of peaty sand. But despite this poor ground Western Australia has over 7,000 different types of plants, and it is famous for its incredibly varied spring flowers. This part of Australia is surrounded by desert, so it is like a biological island in the corner of a continent. In some places over four fifths of its plants are ones that live nowhere else in the world.

SCRUBS AND POLLINATORS

Most flowers are pollinated by insects or by the wind, but in scrublands birds often visit flowers as well. In South Africa and Australia some of these birds have become very close partners with scrubs—without them they would find it difficult to survive.

In the fynbos the Cape sugarbird visits scrubs called proteas and uses their nectar as food. Proteas grow in scrublands throughout southern

◁ *With its long tail feathers fluttering in the breeze, a male Cape sugarbird looks out from its perch on a protea bush. At the beginning of the breeding season the males call loudly from their own private patch of flowers.*

Africa, but the fynbos is their most important home. The largest ones grow into head-high bushes, and they have red or yellow flower heads packed with dozens or hundreds of blossoms. Each flower head is shaped like an ice-cream cone, and it produces nectar for weeks at a time.

Sugarbirds often feed on insects, but they switch to nectar when the proteas start to bloom. Their slender bills are ideally shaped for probing deep into the flowers, which is important as they may visit up to 250 in a day. As the birds feed they collect pollen on their foreheads

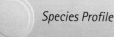

Species Profile

Honey possum: *Tarsipes rostratus*

This tiny Western Australian marsupial is not much bigger than a mouse. It is active at night, when it climbs up banksias and other scrubs, feeding on nectar and pollen from their flowers. It finds the flowers using its sharp sense of smell, and it pollinates them as it feeds. Honey possums have feet that are good at gripping and nonslip pads on their toes.

△ *Australian blackboy trees have spires of flowers that look like poles pointing toward the sky. These plants almost always bloom after there has been a fire.*

and carry it from plant to plant, which enables the proteas to form their seeds. Later in the season the birds collect some of the seeds because their fluffy down makes a snug lining for sugarbird nests.

MAMMALS THAT FEED ON FLOWERS

Bird-pollinated scrubs are not hard to recognize, even when birds themselves are not around. Their flowers are often bright red, orange, or yellow, and they grow on long stalks, making it easier for birds to come and go. The flowers are also extratough because birds can do much more damage than insects as they go about finding a meal. But in the fynbos one type of protea has dull-colored flower heads that open at night and are hidden away near the ground. Flowers like this do not attract birds at all—small mammals visit them instead. These mammalian visitors include at least two types of rodents and an elephant shrew (*Elephantulus edwardii*) from

Africa. All of these animals are nocturnal, and all of them track down protea flowers by smell rather than by sight. The flowers have a musky scent, and they produce an extrasyrupy nectar that suits mammals best. The nectar is a useful food, especially as it is produced during the winter, which can be a hungry time of year.

Australia also has mammalian pollinators, although these are small marsupials. They include several species that feed high up in eucalyptus trees and glide between them using flaps of skin as wings. But one nongliding species—the honey possum—depends entirely on scrubland flowers. This mouse-sized marsupial lives in the scrublands of Western Australia, and it gives birth to the

△ *The pygmy glider lives in eastern Australia in forests and scrublands. It feeds at night, jumping fearlessly into the dark so that it can glide from tree to tree.*

tiniest young mammals on Earth. Each one weighs around 0.0002 oz. (0.005g)—less than a postage stamp.

FIRE!

Fires are a normal part of scrubland life, especially after weeks or months without rain. Dead leaves and wood are easily set alight, and within a few hours thousands of acres of scrubland can go up in flames. These fires are a threat to

Fanned by strong winds, a wildfire sweeps through Joshua trees on the edge of the Mojave Desert in southern California. In this dry scrubland dead vegetation burns away quickly, but living plants are much tougher. The Joshua trees will lose some of their leaves, but otherwise the fire will cause them little harm.

▷ *Although it is not venomous, the California king snake uses its speed and strength to attack poisonous rattlesnakes.*

people and their homes, but for scrubs themselves they are not as harmful as they seem.

In California these summer fires often hit the headlines because of the speed at which they spread. But once a fire has burned out, nature soon starts carrying out repairs. Within a few weeks many of the scrubs are sprouting leaves, and within two or three years the

△ *Two months after a heathland fire a pine seedling sprouts a tuft of brand-new leaves. The ash on the ground contains minerals that will help it grow.*

burned chaparral starts to look like it did before.

Chaparral can recover like this because many of its scrubs have developed their own fire defenses. For example one common scrub called chamise, or greasewood, has tough woody stems and roots that run deep underground. Fire often burns away its smaller branches, but usually the core of the plant is left alive. Once the damage has been done chamise produces new buds, and then a new set of branches starts to grow.

SCRUBS AND FIRE

After a plant has been pollinated, it sets out making and scattering its seeds. But in scrublands, plants like proteas and chamise behave in an unusual way. Instead of shedding their seeds as soon as they are ripe, they can hold on to them for years, waiting for a fire to come their way. When a fire does sweep past, their seed cases open up, and the seeds inside drop to the ground. Some conifers behave in a similar way because the heat from a fire opens

up their cones to release the seeds.

Scrubs do this because the days after a fire are the ideal planting time. The ground is covered in fertile ash, and all of the dead leaves have been cleared away. This gives the seedlings a good start in life, and it also makes sure that they will have

---

Species Profile

California quail: *Lophortyx californica*

This attractive ground-feeding bird sometimes lives in fields, but its natural home is scrubland on mountains and hills. California quails live in flocks called coveys—in the winter these can contain as many as 200 birds. They feed mainly on seeds, and they only take to the sky if they are alarmed. Like many ground-feeding birds they spend the night roosting in trees.

several years to grow before they have to face a fire themselves.

GROUND PATROL

In scrublands wildlife can be difficult to spot, but sounds often give animals away. The snapping of twigs may be a sign that antelope or deer are feeding, while a rustle of dry leaves followed by silence often signals that lizards are on the move. For lizards scrubland is close to an ideal habitat. There is plenty of cover, but there are also patches of open ground that allow them to warm themselves in the sunlight.

For most scrubland lizards insects top the menu—especially the fat-bodied crickets and katydids that feed among the leaves. Lizards hunt insects mainly by sight, and they

△ *Trap-door spiders are common in scrublands. They live in silk-lined burrows that have a hinged lid, or trapdoor. If anything edible comes close by, the spider rushes out and grabs it with its fangs.*

are easily tricked by camouflage. The moment an insect moves, however, it risks being spotted and then snapped up by the quick-moving jaws of a predator. But the insect eaters themselves also have to stay alert because many birds and snakes like to feed on lizard flesh. Even worse many lizards like to as well.

For reptiles this type of behavior is not at all unusual. Large lizards often eat smaller species, and some types have a cannibalistic streak, even attacking their own young.

△ *Shrikes catch insects and lizards, spearing any surplus food onto thorns. They use this "pantry" if food becomes hard to find.*

As a result young lizards have to be very wary of adults if they are to avoid ending up as their prey.

SNAKES THAT EAT SNAKES

Just as lizards eat other lizards, some scrubland snakes use other snakes as food. For snakes this makes good sense because a smaller snake makes a perfectly shaped meal. Once the unfortunate victim has been swallowed and digested, it can provide the predator with enough food

▷ *Madagascar's Spiny Forest is one of the strangest habitats in the world. Here scrubs and trees have adapted to the harsh climate by developing bizarre shapes, sharp spines, and tiny leaves.*

for several weeks. Surprisingly poisonous snakes are often eaten by ones that have no venom at all. For example in Mediterranean scrubland nonpoisonous whipsnakes sometimes eat venomous adders, while in the Californian chaparral, nonpoisonous king snakes feed on highly poisonous rattlesnakes. In both cases the hunter relies on the fact that its prey is comparatively slow. It makes a lightning-fast lunge, grips its prey's neck with its teeth, and then coils itself tightly around it. Once the victim is dead it can then be swallowed—a task that may take over an hour.

TEMPERATE FORESTS

MANY HABITATS CHANGE WITH THE SEASONS, BUT IN TEMPERATE FORESTS THESE CHANGES ARE MORE IMPRESSIVE AND MORE COLORFUL THAN ANYWHERE ELSE ON EARTH.

Temperate forests originally covered large parts of Europe and North America. Despite hundreds of years of clearance, a lot of these forests still remain. In this habitat animal life has to cope with very different seasons and some wild shifts in the forest's food supply. There is plenty to eat in the summer, but in the winter food can be much more difficult to find.

TREES AT THE END OF THE WORLD
Because the continents are unevenly spread out, the world's temperate forests are uneven too. The Southern Hemisphere has by far the smallest share, concentrated mainly in New Zealand and the tip of South America. In both of these places the most important trees are southern beeches. Some of these trees are evergreen, but one South American species, called the nire or Antarctic beech, turns a brilliant shade of red every fall just before losing its leaves. The nire grows on the stormy coast around Cape Horn, which is closer to Antarctica than any other type of tree in the world.

◁ In midwinter the bare branches of this ancient oak snake up into the sky. The tree's shape shows that it was coppiced—cut down to ground level—long ago.

and lives in forest streams. Its breeding system is unique— the male guards the eggs until they hatch and quickly swallows them. Instead of ending up in his stomach, the tadpoles lodge in a pouch in his throat, where they stay for several weeks. When the tadpoles have turned into froglets, the male coughs them up, and they swim off.

WORKING WOODLANDS

In South America and New Zealand some parts of the beech forest are very similar to how they were before humans arrived on the scene. But in Europe and North America temperate forests have had a very different history. Here many forests have been managed for their timber, while others have been cleared to make way for farms. As a result the original forest has

become a patchwork of woodland, scattered among fields and towns.

In these woodlands old trees often have a story to tell. For example, in England it is not unusual to find ancient trees that have been cut down to ground level long ago.

△ With its bright-green skin and sharply pointed nose, Darwin's frog looks like a freshly fallen leaf. This male is guarding one of his froglets.

▽ In Chile's Huerquehue National Park southern beech trees show off their beautiful fall colors. Southern beeches grow in South America and also in New Zealand and Australia.

These southern forests are home to some unusual animals, including the world's southernmost parrots and one of its strangest amphibians. Called Darwin's frog, this South American oddity has a sharply pointed snout

◁ *In English woodlands bluebells turn the ground into a carpet of blue in the spring. Bluebells finish flowering by the time the trees are fully in leaf.*

This operation, called coppicing, created many fast-growing shoots that could be used to make charcoal and many different useful objects—from fence poles to wooden clogs. The shoots were harvested every few years, and after each cut another batch would grow in their place. Today coppicing is not as common, but old coppiced trees are still easy to identify. That is because they have many trunks growing from a massive stump only an inch or so tall.

Coppicing sounds drastic, but it can actually lengthen a tree's life. In English woodlands some coppiced hazel trees are believed to be 1,500 years old—ten times the age that they normally reach in the wild.

THE FOREST YEAR

On a cold day in late winter temperate forestland can seem like a habitat where the wildlife has disappeared. There are no leaves on the trees, no flowers, no insects, and only a few mammals and birds on the move. The forest floor is silent—especially when it is covered in snow. Looking at a scene like this, it is hard to imagine how quickly it can change. But by the time spring arrives this type of forest is completely transformed. With the lengthening days and increasing warmth, woodland wildflowers quickly come into bloom. Soon after buds burst overhead as the trees start growing. For three hectic months some of these trees can outgrow ones in the tropics, as their branches lengthen and their leaves soak up the strengthening sunshine. At the same time animal life also takes off. The air is full of flying insects, and newly hatched caterpillars nibble through the fresh young leaves. Migratory birds flood in to eat them, and their songs resonate throughout the treetops, showing that spring is fully under way.

CLOSING DOWN

This burst of growth is so fast that it cannot continue for long. And by the time midsummer is over, life shifts gears. Animals are still everywhere, although the forest birds are much quieter now that their breeding season is nearing its end. But by now most of the trees have finished growing and are concentrating on producing seeds. Their leaves have lost their brand-new look, and some have even started to brown—an early hint of some major changes that are on their way.

By the time the clock has ticked on another three months, the fall is well underway. The forest's animals are preparing for harder times up ahead, and most of the migratory birds have headed to warmer areas. But the biggest difference

△ Lady's slippers are woodland orchids that grow across the Northern Hemisphere. In many places they have become rare because their flowers are often picked.

is overhead, where the deep greens of summer have given way to a rainbow of fall hues. After a working life of just six months, billions of leaves are starting to drop, marking the end of the forest year.

WHY LEAVES CHANGE COLOR
This annual blizzard of leaves is one of the most beautiful spectacles in the natural world. It happens in places as far apart as Europe and Japan, but nowhere quite matches the display in the northeastern corner of the U.S. In New England the forest's birches, maples, and beeches blaze with color after the first sharp frosts strike and before their leaves slowly melt away.

Leaves suffer a lot of wear and tear, which means that they have to be shed and replaced. Evergreen trees do this all the time, so their branches are never left bare. But in the temperate world most broad-leaved trees shed all of their leaves at once and grow a whole new set the following spring.

Species Profile

White trillium: *Trillium grandiflorum*

Trilliums are common forest floor plants across North America. This species—also known as the wake robin—is often one of the first flowers to appear in the spring. Like many woodland wildflowers, trilliums store food in underground stems so they can start growing as soon as the spring arrives. Trillium seeds have a stick-on package of food that attracts ants. The ants take the seeds, eat the food package, and drop the seeds on the ground.

◁ Eurasian badgers spend most of the winter sleeping. As soon as the spring starts they become much more lively, emerging from their burrows every evening to look for food.

△ *Wood lice eat all types of plant remains, including rotting wood and fallen leaves. They have to stay damp to survive—if they dry out they cannot breathe.*

▷ *Pseudoscorpions have pear-shaped bodies and tiny mouths. They are often less than .08 in. (2mm) long.*

millions of microscopic fungi, and several billion bacteria. For all of them leaf litter is a complete habitat, just as mud and ooze is for animals that live at the bottom of the sea.

Most of the inhabitants in this hidden world live by breaking down dead remains. These natural recyclers include wood lice and millipedes, as well as much smaller animals that can barely be seen with the naked eye. With the help of the leaf-litter microbes, they process every scrap of dead matter, using up its energy and returning its nutrients to the soil. Like all habitats, leaf litter contains predators too. They include centipedes armed with poisonous claws and minute animals called pseudoscorpions, which look like miniature versions of real scorpions, with poisonous pincers instead of a stinger. Pseudoscorpions use their pincers to paralyze prey and also to communicate with their own kind.

This stop-start lifestyle means that broad-leaved trees do not need leaves that can cope with the winter. But throwing away an entire set of leaves is still an expensive business, so the trees recycle any useful substances that they contain. One of these is chlorophyll—the green chemical that plants use to grow. The tree breaks this down and removes it, and the leaf's green color slowly fades. This often reveals other colored chemicals in the leaf, which are broken down in time. Many leaves turn brown, but some become orange, scarlet, or several shades at once. The warmer the summer has been, the more colorful the display.

Once everything useful has been extracted, the tree shuts off the leaf stalk. This disconnects the leaf's water supply, and a few days later it flutters to the ground.

LIFE IN LEAF LITTER
In the steamy climate of tropical rain forests fallen leaves rot away within a few weeks. But in the broad-leaved forests of the temperate world, leaves take much longer to break down. As a result the forest floor is covered in leaf litter—a fertile layer of leafy remains that gives the forest its earthy smell. A teaspoonful of leaf litter can contain hundreds of tiny animals,

△ *For a fire salamander an earthworm makes a filling meal. Like many salamanders, this European species has bright colors to warn predators that its skin is poisonous.*

▷ *A nutcracker fluffs out its feathers to keep warm. Nutcrackers live in Europe and Siberia.*

They live in forests all over the world, but because they are so small few people ever see them.

With so much life underfoot, other predators also search the leaf litter for food. Shrews push their way through it like miniature moles, rustling the leaves as they sniff out their prey. Although shrews are tiny, they are always hungry because their high-speed lifestyle uses up energy at a rapid rate. Toads and salamanders are very different—they move slowly and can survive for several weeks between meals. They hide under logs and leaves during dry weather but come out to feed when the forest floor has been dampened by rain.

OAKS AND ACORNS

In broad-leaved forests animals often need particular trees to make them feel at home. For example the common dormouse is often found in hazel woods because hazelnuts are one of its favorite foods. But of all deciduous trees, oaks hold the record for animal life. Oak leaves and acorns provide food for dozens of mammals and birds and hundreds of species of insects—from moths to tiny flies. Some of these animals are occasional visitors, but many live on or near oak trees for their entire lives.

For the Eurasian jay a bountiful acorn crop makes the winter a much easier time. Unlike many birds, jays stay in deciduous forests all year round, and their diet changes as the seasons pass. In the spring and summer they eat insects, and they also search out other birds' eggs and young. But in the fall, when these are off the menu, acorns are their most important food.

Jays do not only eat the acorns—they also bury them in the ground. They have an amazing memory for these food stores, and in the winter they dig up the acorns and eat them. A few always get overlooked, and these take root, helping oak trees spread.

SECRET STORES

This food-storing behavior is called "caching" from a French word that means "to hide." Eurasian jays cache food on their own, and so do nutcrackers, which live in coniferous woodlands and bury seeds from pine trees. But in North America acorn woodpeckers work in family groups. They store acorns in the trunks of dead trees, wedging each one into a prepecked hole. A single storage tree can contain up to 50,000

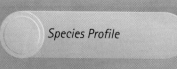

Eurasian jay: *Garrulus glandarius*

This noisy bird lives in woodlands from Western Europe to Japan. Like other jays, it belongs to the crow family, but it has brightly colored plumage. During late summer and fall Eurasian jays are busy collecting acorns. They can only carry one at a time, so they have to make frequent flights between oak trees and the places where they bury their food.

acorns, enough to keep a group of woodpeckers well fed until spring. This food hoard often attracts other birds, so the woodpeckers keep watch like a team of security guards.

Foxes and squirrels keep food stores as well. None of these animals can actually plan ahead, and none of them knows that winter is a difficult time. Instead their behavior is controlled by instinct, enabling them to survive.

◁ *Some squirrels nest in trees, but chipmunks make their nests in underground burrows.*

DIGGING FOR FOOD

During the Middle Ages many of Europe's forests were owned by feudal landlords, who kept them as land to hunt wild boars and deer. A hunting forest was a status symbol, designed to impress visitors just as much as to provide food. Most of these private forests disappeared long ago, but wild boars and deer still thrive, even in woodlands close to cities and towns. The success of these animals is mainly due to their wariness—they steer clear of people, and in busy areas they feed only after dark.

Wild boars are the original ancestors of domestic pigs, and they have the same powerful jaws and flat-ended snouts designed for shoveling through the ground.

The tip of the snout can swivel up, quickly turning it from a bulldozer into a shovel. Using this tool a wild boar can dig through the ground to reach nutritious roots, or it can unearth moles and earthworms. In fact there are very few things that these animals will not eat— they prefer fresh food (including crops), but they also dine on dead remains. Wild boars find most of their food by using their sense of smell. It is so sharp that a boar can tell the difference between types of potatoes when they are still underground.

Like many of their relatives in the pig family, wild boars have striped young, and they give birth to litters of up to ten piglets in a leafy "nest" on the forest floor. Females, or sows,

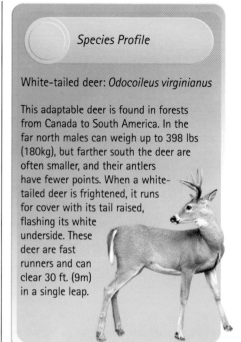

Species Profile

White-tailed deer: *Odocoileus virginianus*

This adaptable deer is found in forests from Canada to South America. In the far north males can weigh up to 398 lbs (180kg), but farther south the deer are often smaller, and their antlers have fewer points. When a white-tailed deer is frightened, it runs for cover with its tail raised, flashing its white underside. These deer are fast runners and can clear 30 ft. (9m) in a single leap.

FEEDING ON BARK

Wild boars live in Europe and Asia, but deer live in almost all of the broad-leaved forests of the world.

White-tailed deer live only in the Americas, but the red deer is found across the Northern Hemisphere— from Canada to China. It has also been introduced in other parts of the world, including Argentina, Australia, and New Zealand, where it arrived in 1851. Here red deer have become so common that they are now a problem for New Zealand's own wildlife.

For most of the year deer mainly feed on the leaves of forest floor plants and trees. But when the leaves disappear in the fall, they have to switch to tougher food. They bite the tops off of small saplings, and they also feed on bark. During the winter a tree's bark is firmly connected to its wood, so deer can only gouge out small pieces at a time. But in the early spring, when a tree's sap starts to rise, the

△ *Moving as quietly as a cat, the red fox is good at pinpointing small animals beneath the snow. Like a cat, it catches them with a well-aimed pounce.*

have strong nest-building instincts, which is the reason why thoughtful farmers give their domestic pigs nesting materials.

▷ Wild boar piglets start life with a striped coat that is very different from their mother's bristly fur. Their markings help camouflage them on the sun-dappled forest floor.

outer wood turns slippery, which loosens the bark. When a deer bites on the bark and pulls, it comes away in long strips, sometimes killing the tree.

These eating habits do not cause too much harm in a natural forest, but they can wreak havoc on plantations. That is why young trees are protected by fences or have plastic guards around their trunks.

Unlike wild boars, most deer give birth to only one young, called a fawn. At first the fawn stays curled up in the undergrowth, and its mother returns every few hours to give it a meal of milk. Red deer fawns follow their mother after around three or four days, but young white-tailed deer can stay in hiding for one month. Fawns look as if they have been abandoned, and they are sometimes taken to animal rescue centers by people trying to help them. But they do not need a hand from humans because their mothers are never far away.

ANTLERS
Most animals look their best during the breeding season. Some birds grow extracolorful plumage, while woodland butterflies show off their brightly patterned wings. But male deer grow antlers—some of the biggest and most eye-catching

▷ The size of a deer's antlers depends partly on its age and partly on its food. This red deer has six points on each of its antlers, but some of the biggest red deer stags can have twelve.

accessories in the animal world. Unlike horns, a deer's antlers are made of solid bone. Red deer antlers can be 27 in. (70cm) long and weigh up to 7 lbs (3kg). Moose antlers are even larger—theirs can weigh 66 lbs (30kg) and may measure 6.6 ft. (2m) from end to end.

Antlers grow from the top of a deer's forehead, and at first they are covered by a layer of velvety skin. They often branch out as they grow, and after 15 to 20 weeks the new antlers are complete. Once they have finished growing the velvety skin dries up and starts falling off.

This is an uncomfortable time for the deer, and they scrape their antlers against trees and scrubs to wipe off the remaining skin.

In the fall the rutting season begins, and rival males use their antlers in the annual contest for the right to mate. Sometimes two males simply show off to each other until one decides it is safer to retreat. If neither backs down, the contestants clash head-on, and serious injuries can occur. The winners attract a group of females, while the losers nurse their bruises and save their energy for the following year.

Why do deer go to all the trouble of growing new antlers every year? The answer is probably that it helps them impress females just as much as males. Large antlers are a sign that a deer is strong and well fed, and these are features that he is likely to pass on to his young. When females decide which males to mate with, antlers help them make their choice.

PREDATORY FUNGI
For broad-leaved trees deer are a problem, but much more serious enemies are all around. These are fungi, an ever-present and sometimes deadly feature of forest life. For fungi every tree—no matter how young or old—is a potential source of food. With their microscopic feeding threads, they grow through leaf litter and wood, digesting living matter and dead remains.

Some woodland fungi behave like roving predators, spreading unseen through the forest floor. One of these is the voracious honey fungus, which lives throughout the northern world. Honey fungus grows average-sized toadstools, but its underground threads can reach incredible lengths. One network, found in an oak forest in Michigan, covered 37 acres (15 hectares) and may have weighed ten tons. The clump was probably started by a single spore, and it had been feeding in the forest for over one thousand years. Some fungal networks can be even bigger—they include the largest living things ever found by scientists (see page 75).

When honey fungus finds a suitable victim, it grows up from underneath a tree's bark, stealing nutrients from its new wood. During the first stage of the attack the tree still looks healthy, but as time goes by the damage begins to show. Its leaves turn yellow, its growth slows down, and whole branches start to sicken. By the time honey-colored toadstools sprout around its trunk, the tree's fate is sealed.

STAYING ALIVE
Unlike animals, trees can take many years to die. English oaks are especially stubborn, and they can be "on their last leg" for over 200 years. Even when the inside of its trunk has rotted away, a tree can keep going. In the 1800s one famous hollow oak in Bowthorpe, England, was carved out even more to make a large room. The local squire and up to 20 guests were able to dine inside of it. Over the last one hundred years in California, several giant redwoods were hollowed out so that cars could drive through them. The tallest of these living "drive-thrus" is doing well and is over 295 ft. (90m) high. Trees can also recover after being struck by lightning or after

△ *Unlike other woodland birds, woodpeckers usually feed with their bodies upright. They cling on with their claws, and their strong tail feathers work like a ledge, stabilizing them while they peck into the wood.*

STARTING AGAIN
Antlers take a lot of time and energy to grow, but once the rutting season is at an end they begin to weaken at the point where they grow out of the skull. For several weeks each antler stays in place like a dead branch on a tree. Finally a sudden movement by the deer makes the antler snap off and drop to the ground.

having their trunks snapped in two by storms. Some types, including oaks, sweet chestnuts, and hazels, can even survive being coppiced (see page 214)—not just once but many times over hundreds of years.

Trees can put up with all of this because the only wood that really matters is the living layer just beneath the bark. As long as enough of this is left, it can carry out the vital task of carrying water and sap. But if a tree is attacked by fungi, the sapwood finds it harder to do its work. Eventually its pipelines become blocked, and the tree slowly dies.

◁ Honey fungus toadstools grow in clumps around dying trees. This fungus is dreaded by gardeners because it attacks many types of trees and is very hard to get rid of.

△ *The greater mouse-eared bat hunts in fields, gardens, and woodlands. Compared to other small mammals, bats live a long time—the record for this species is 28 years.*

AT HOME IN DEADWOOD
Once a tree is dead, its useful existence is far from over. Dead tree trunks make high-rise homes for woodpeckers and birds that nest in these holes after their original owners have moved on. These hole nesters include dozens of different woodland species—from tits and chickadees to predators such as owls. Woodpeckers and owls lay

their eggs on the bare floor of their homes, but many smaller birds make their nest holes cozy by lining them with moss and leaves.

In some woodlands—especially ones that are managed for timber—dead trees are few and far between. Here there is strong competition for homes, and if a bird is lucky enough to find a hole, it may have to fight off others that want it for themselves. Nuthatches have an ingenious way of stopping larger birds from moving into their nests. They plaster mud around the entrance until there is only enough room for a nuthatch to squeeze inside. If a bigger bird examines the hole, it mistakes the mud for wood and decides that there is not enough room to move in.

▷ *Burying beetles search for dead animals and then bury them under loose ground. These beetles have found a dead mouse—once it is underground they will use it as food for their grubs.*

Hollow trees are also favorite roosting places for bats because they shelter them from the weather and hide them from prying eyes. In temperate woodlands most bats are insect-eating species that catch their prey in midair. But woodland bats are very varied, and not all of them behave in this way. One of the exceptions is the greater mouse-eared bat, which lives in Western Europe. It emerges late at night and grabs beetles and spiders on the ground, as well as hunting in the air. It does not use its sonar to do this—instead it simply listens for the sounds of moving insects as they crawl across the ground. But the short-tailed bat from New Zealand is the real expert at this way of life. It folds its wings up tightly and catches food by scurrying across the forest floor or even up the trunks of trees. Short-tailed bats feed mainly on insects, but they also eat fruit, as well as nectar and pollen from flowers.

For a few weeks every fall the woodlands in New England attract admiring visitors from all over the world. In this part of North America fall colors are especially vivid—a result of the sudden drop in temperature as cold air sweeps down from the north. This woodland walk is flanked by maple and birch trees. Soon all the trees will have lost their leaves, and the forest will be quiet and bare until springtime.

CONIFEROUS FORESTS

CONIFERS ARE SUPERBLY PROTECTED AGAINST DROUGHT, WIND, AND COLD, AND THEY THRIVE IN PLACES WHERE OTHER TREES STRUGGLE TO SURVIVE.

Coniferous trees are experts at coping with extreme conditions. Because of their needlelike leaves they can grow high up in mountains and on dry, rocky hillsides. Some conifers also grow in tropical forests and waterlogged swamps, although they are greatly outnumbered by broad-leaved trees. But the real stronghold of conifers is in the far north. Here they form the boreal forest— a vast and often remote habitat that almost encircles the planet.

CROSSING CONTINENTS
The boreal forest is often known as the taiga, which is its Russian name. In Russia itself the taiga stretches across 11 time zones and in some places is over 930 mi. (1,500km) wide. By train, traveling right across it can take over a week,

◁ With their straight trunks and sloping branches, coniferous trees are good at coping with the snow. Frost is more of a problem, as it can kill buds when they start growing.

figure is not much higher. By comparison tropical forests can have hundreds of different trees in an area as small as a football field.

For wildlife fewer species mean fewer opportunities to find food. But there is a flip side to the coin. If an animal can make a living here, its home is the largest land habitat on Earth.

WINTER FUR

For animals in boreal forests surviving the winter is the most serious challenge in life. Where Canada's forest meets the tundra, winter temperatures can often drop to –40°F (–40°C), but in eastern Siberia the climate is even more severe. Here a temperature of –90°F (–68°C) was recorded in the mining

town of Verkhoyansk, making this region even colder than the North Pole. During the winter the ground freezes solid for months on end, making liquid water hard to find.

△ Tits and chickadees are common birds in coniferous forests. This is the crested tit, a European species that lives in forests containing mature trees.

▽ Reindeer run through the forest near Oymyakon in eastern Siberia. The open spaces between the trees are a sign of the cold winter climate.

but it is a journey with very few changes in the outer appearance of the forest. Sameness is a trademark of boreal forests because of the remarkably small variety of trees. In the entire Russian taiga, for example, the forest is dominated by only ten different types of trees, while in North America's boreal forest the

Protected by its thick winter coat, a Siberian tiger looks completely at home in a winter landscape. Weighing up to 663 lbs (300kg), Siberian tigers live in the Russian Far East—a part of the world where the summers are warm but the winters are cold, with plenty of snow. One of five surviving subspecies of tigers, they are among the largest and the rarest, with only a few hundred animals left.

One way to deal with the cold is to leave it behind—a solution used by the forest's migratory birds. Mammals do not have this option, however, because they cannot travel

△ *The Russian sable has a foxlike face, but it is a close relative of the American mink. It lives alone, except in the breeding season, and it fiercely defends its territory against any rivals on the lookout for food.*

as far. Instead they rely on one of the natural world's best insulators— a coat of fur. The outer part of the coat is made of long guard hairs, while the inner part consists of fluffier underfur. The underfur becomes thicker in the fall, adding extra warmth for the winter ahead.

Many of the boreal forest's carnivorous mammals are renowned for their luxurious coats. One of the best known is the American mink, an agile and aggressive hunter that normally feeds in or near the water. Another is the fisher—an animal that looks a lot like the mink but that actually hunts in trees.

▷ *Gray wolves live in a wide variety of habitats—from coniferous forests to Arctic tundra. In each pack all of the adults hunt, but only the senior male and female breed.*

But as a furbearer the most famous by far is the Russian sable, a fox-sized animal that lives in eastern Siberia, where it has to face the record-breaking cold. The sable eats small animals and fruit, and due to its thick fur it keeps active even in temperatures of −58°F (−50°C).

Unfortunately for all of these mammals, humans value their fur, and they have been trapped and hunted for hundreds of years. Many of them are now raised in captivity —sometimes in cruel conditions— but each year hundreds of thousands are still caught in the wild.

THE VANISHING WOLF

In folklore the coniferous forest is a threatening place, full of dangers for the unwary. Most of these dangers are make-believe, but at one time people did have reason to fear the forest's wolves. Until around 400 years ago the gray wolf was widespread across the entire northern world, and the forest was where it was most at home.

There are very few records of wolves attacking people, but they can be a major threat to farm

animals—especially if their natural prey starts to disappear. As a result wolves have been widely persecuted. Over hundreds of years they have been driven back to uninhabited regions or wiped out altogether. In the British Isles, for example, the last wild wolf died in around 1770. There are still plenty of wolves in Russia, Canada, and Alaska, but in the rest of the U.S. wild wolves have almost disappeared.

MAKING A COMEBACK

America's wolves could have vanished entirely if not for

◁ The American mink hunts mainly at night, stalking animals on riverbanks and in the water. Like the Russian sable, it usually kills its victims with a bite to the back of the neck.

human help. During the 1990s conservationists began a program of wolf reintroductions, with the aim of putting wolves back in territory that was once their own. Canadian

Species Profile

Fly agaric: *Amanita muscaria*

Many fungi grow in coniferous forests because they thrive in dim, damp conditions on the forest floor. Fly agaric is one of the easiest to recognize because its toadstools are so brightly colored. It almost always grows near spruce or birch trees, and its toadstools appear in late summer and early fall after it has rained. Fly agaric is very poisonous to humans, but some forest animals eat it.

wolves were flown to mountains in Montana, Idaho, and Wyoming, and they were gradually released. These reintroductions were very successful, and there are now over two dozen wolf packs in this part of the U.S. alone.

Not everyone is happy about the wolf's return, however. Most ranchers think that the wolves will attack their cattle, and in some places suspect wolves have been caught and killed. For this reason the introduced wolves are being carefully monitored and controlled in the hope that people and wolves will be able to live side by side.

THE LONG SLEEP

Wolves may not deserve their dangerous reputation, but there is no doubt at all about the brown bear. After the polar bear brown bears are the world's largest land-dwelling carnivores, and their strength is both awesome and legendary. They eat an amazing variety of food—from roots and insects to fish and deer—and they are capable of dragging an adult moose or horse hundreds of yards in their jaws. For these shortsighted but immensely powerful animals a human can be a threat and occasionally a meal.

Like wolves, brown bears once lived right across the Northern Hemisphere, and they have seen the same steep decline in their natural range. But brown bears have a very different way of coping with the ups and downs of life in the forest habitat. Instead of constantly moving throughout the year, they hibernate for up to six months—a survival technique that saves energy when food is hard to find. Their winter quarters are usually dug into a north-facing slope, and they are lined with branches and leaves. The den is usually not more than 5 ft. (1.5m) wide, making it a tight fit for an animal that can weigh half a ton.

In the fall up to one half of a bear's weight consists of fat—its equivalent of winter fuel. Fat is the richest source of energy in an animal's body, and a bear builds this up by eating

△ Despite their huge size, brown bears—or grizzlies—are good runners and climbers. They can easily overtake a human running at top speed and have been known to chase people up trees.

whatever food it can find. When the bear enters hibernation, its body temperature drops by around 41°F (5°C), its heartbeat slows down, and the fat is used up to keep it alive.

◁ These pine shoots are just starting their burst of growth. The yellow objects are male cones that will soon scatter pollen into the air. The female cones are bigger—their woody scales protect developing seeds.

tent that they spin at the tip of a branch. The silk is strong but elastic, making it hard for animals to rip apart and difficult to cut even with a knife. From the nest, silk trails lead down the tree toward other shoots with fresh leaves. At night the caterpillars file out to feed in a single line—a feature that gives them their name.

LIVING IN WOOD

For some coniferous forest insects wood is much more appetizing than leaves. In boreal forests one of the most impressive of these animals

But compared to many other hibernators, such as marmots (see page 263), bears sleep lightly, and their temperature drop is relatively small. They remain dimly aware of their surroundings, and they can wake up instantly if they are disturbed. This rapid response means that even in the depths of winter, bears' dens are not good places to explore.

◁ Pine sawfly grubs can kill trees by eating their leaves. The adults look like small wasps—females can live for several weeks, but the males often die a few hours after they have mated.

THE LEAF EATERS

Bears will eat almost anything, but even they avoid conifer leaves. Compared to most leaves these ones are tough and waxy, and they contain strong-smelling resins that make them hard to digest. They are left to the forest's professional leaf eaters: moth caterpillars and sawfly grubs. The pine beauty moth is one European species that grows up on this unpromising food. The adult moth is brown and gray, but the caterpillars have green and white stripes that exactly match a pine needle's waxy shine. They feed voraciously on young pine needles, staying stretched out on their food, making them even harder to see. A single adult female can lay hundreds of eggs, so moths like these can spread quickly.

Pine beauty caterpillars feed around the clock, but another species—the pine processionary moth— organizes its time in a different way. During the day processionary moth caterpillars live in a silk

Species Profile

Black woodpecker: *Dryocopus martius*

This woodpecker lives in coniferous forests from western Europe through Siberia to the Far East. It feeds on insect grubs, hacking out wood chips up to 8 in. (20cm) long as it digs out prey. It also eats the chicks of hole-nesting birds by smashing into their nests. Woodpeckers usually dig nest holes in rotting wood, but this species uses healthy tree trunks too.

is the horntail, or giant wood wasp, which buzzes noisily among the trees. The adults are black and yellow, and the females are equipped with what looks like a menacing stinger. This "stinger" is harmless, however,

◁ *Using her ovipositor, a female horntail drills deep into wood to lay her eggs. When not in use her ovipositor is stowed inside a yellow sheath—seen here on the left.*

because it is actually an egg-laying tube, or ovipositor, which is designed to drill through wood.

Female horntails search for weakened or fallen trees, and they inject their eggs one by one into the wood just beneath the bark. When the grubs hatch they spend up to three years burrowing through their home. But instead of eating the wood, they are believed to feed on a fungus that grows on the inside of their tunnels. Fungi are good at breaking down the tough substances in wood, and horntails turn this to their own advantage by "farming" the fungus and helping it spread.

ATTACK FROM OUTSIDE
Unfortunately for horntail grubs, their homes are not as safe as they seem. That is because another insect, the giant ichneumon wasp, uses horntail grubs as food for its young. Using its incredibly acute sense of smell, the wasp can detect horntail grubs feeding in the wood. It drills down toward them with its own ovipositor and lays a single egg next to each grub. When the egg hatches, the ichneumon feeds on the horntail grub, eating it alive.

If a grub escapes this fate, another type of danger can strike at any time. Woodpeckers hammer their way into trees and flick their tongues up and down any tunnels that they find. Their tongues have barbed tips to haul out the grubs.

THE CONE CUTTERS
Conifers do not grow flowers or fruit, but they do produce nutritious seeds tucked away inside of cones. Most cones are small enough to fit in your hand, but the ones grown by North American sugar pines can be 20 in. (50cm) long. The heaviest cones are produced by the Australian bunya pine. Shaped like a prickly melon, they are hard and weigh up to 11 lbs (5kg).

Bunya pinecones break up when they are ripe, making it easy for animals to reach their seeds. But most other cones stay in one piece and release their seeds before they drop onto the forest floor. Jays and nutcrackers collect the seeds once they have fluttered to the ground, but some birds intercept them even before they have left the tree. In the boreal forest the first to reach the seeds are crossbills—finches with beaks that cross over at their tips. Using this device, a crossbill pulls apart the scales and removes the seeds with its tongue.

Crossbills rely on the seed crop, and their numbers boom if the harvest is good. But if a bad year follows a good one, many birds find that they have too little to eat. When this happens, crossbills fly far south of their usual range, turning up in places far away from the boreal forest zone. This type of migration, called an irruption, happens with other seed-eating finches as well.

FLYING PREDATORS
With long winter nights and dense cover, coniferous forests seem to be especially made for owls. Some of the world's largest species live here, including the northern eagle owl from Europe and Asia.

◁ *When crossbills hatch, they have normal beaks. But as they grow up, the ends of the beaks slowly cross over.*

This owl is large enough to attack young deer, and its call is so deep and powerful that it can be heard over 0.6 mi. (1km) away.

Eagle owls need room to maneuver, which is why they hunt in places where the trees are spaced out. The great gray owl, on the other hand, is equally at home in the dense forest or more open country. This imposing bird lives across the far

△ *The great gray owl's round face works like a feathery satellite dish. It funnels sound toward its ears, which are hidden beneath its plumage. Using sound alone, this owl can find rodents under the snow.*

north, where it perches in living trees and on dead trunks, looking at the world through glaring yellow eyes. Despite its great size it almost entirely eats small rodents, using its hearing to pinpoint them beneath the winter snow. In coniferous forests most birds steer clear

of humans, but the great gray owl does not hesitate to attack if its nest is under threat. With a wingspan of 5 ft. (1.5m), it can scare off even the most determined intruder.

UNEQUAL PARTNERS

During the daytime most owls roost in trees, but birds of prey come out to hunt. Eagles and buzzards find it hard to steer between the trees, but the northern goshawk is built especially for this type of terrain. Using its tail and wings like a rudder and a brake, it twists and swerves through the forest, attacking prey in trees and on the ground. This high-speed hunter mostly eats other birds, but it also snatches up squirrels or young porcupines from branches where they are easy to grab.

With mammals males are often larger than females, but with birds of prey things are often the other way around. The female northern

◁ *Swooping down with its talons outstretched, an eagle owl moves in for the kill. This giant owl has no natural enemies, and it is large enough to attack goshawks and other birds of prey.*

goshawk can weigh nearly one third more than her mate, and she often catches heavier prey. But to make up for this the male is more agile. As he skims through the maze of tree trunks and branches, he can grab birds as small as blue tits and chickadees. With another forest hunter, the sparrow hawk, the difference between male and female is even greater—female sparrow hawks sometimes weigh twice as much as their mates.

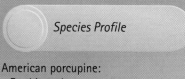

Species Profile

American porcupine:
Erethizon dorsatum

Porcupines are common in the tropics, but this is the only species that lives in the northern coniferous forest. If the porcupine is attacked, its sharp quills come loose and work their way into its enemy's skin. American porcupines eat leaves, bark, and buds. They gnaw at wooden tools and even window locks because they like the salty taste of human sweat.

CHANGING FORESTS

Wild animals are not alone in finding coniferous forests useful. For hundreds of years people have harvested conifers for their timber because it is often very straight and easy to work with. During the 1800s millions of conifers were used for making sleepers for railroads, and millions more ended up as pit props in mines. Today conifer wood is used in construction and to make paper, and conifer resin is used to make all types of products—from ink and solvents to glue.

Despite this the world's coniferous forests are not shrinking, so they are in no danger of dying out. But they are changing. Every year large areas of forest are cut down for their

▷ *After coniferous forests have been cut they are often replanted with saplings grown in nurseries. Unlike wild trees, the saplings are bred to grow rapidly and to produce straight-grained wood.*

timber, and they are then replanted or allowed to regrow. These planted forests are different from natural ones because they often only contain one type of tree. All of the trees are the same age, and the forest is often cut down long before the trees mature. For most animals these planted forests are difficult places to make a living.

PRESERVING OLD FORESTS

Alarmed by the spread of plantations, conservationists have been working hard to protect the remaining truly wild forests. One of the most important battlefronts has been in the Pacific Northwest, straddling the border between the U.S. and Canada. This region is one of the world's leading producers of timber, and most of the "old-growth" forest has already been cut down.

On the American side the Olympic National Park in Washington State protects one of the world's few coniferous rain forests—an extraordinary habitat where ancient trees grow over 328 ft. (100m) high. Farther north, in Canada's Clayoquot Sound, a new biosphere reserve has been set up to safeguard ancient forestland on Vancouver Island. Compared to the forest that has already been cut down, these reserves are small, but they show that ancient forests can be saved.

◁ *Running as straight as a ruler, a boundary line marks the edge of a recently cut block of forest. This photograph was taken in the Cascade Mountains, which extend across Oregon and Washington.*

TROPICAL FORESTS

TROPICAL FORESTS ARE FILLED WITH WILDLIFE—
FROM APES AND MONKEYS TO THE WORLD'S
LARGEST INSECTS. BUT A LOT OF THIS WILDLIFE
IS THREATENED BECAUSE TROPICAL FORESTS
ARE DISAPPEARING FAST.

There are two main types of forests in the tropics. The type that most people have heard of—called tropical rain forest—grows near the equator, where the climate is wet and warm all year round. These steamy conditions can be really uncomfortable for humans, but they are perfect for trees and other plants. The other type—called seasonal or monsoon forest—grows near the edges of the tropics. Here there is a long dry season every year. In this habitat plants and animals have to cope with torrential rain followed by months of drought.

A SEESAW CLIMATE
In seasonal forests the rainy season begins in a spectacular way, when electric storms light up the night sky. At first these storms are dry, but a few days later the rain begins to fall. As the heavy clouds roll in, grape-sized raindrops crash their

△ Asia's tropical forests are home to three fourths of the world's tigers—some of the most endangered predators in the world.

▽ Early morning mist snakes over the forest-covered hillsides of central Africa. These forests are the habitat of the rare mountain gorilla.

way through the foliage and pound the forest floor. The forest often floods, but trees need this water because this is the time when they start growing.

Six months later, during the height of the dry season, the forest looks completely different. The floods have been replaced by drought, and most of the trees have shed their leaves. The air shimmers in the heat, and fallen leaves crunch underfoot. With so many bare branches the forest looks like a winter landscape, but not all of the trees are asleep. Instead some of them choose this time of year to bloom. One of the most famous of these dry-season flowerers is the jacaranda, which is covered with lilac blossoms. This colorful tree has been planted in parks and gardens and along roadsides all over the tropical world.

TOP CATS
Seasonal forests grow right across the tropics, from Central and South

△ Jacaranda trees grow wild in the forests of Bolivia and northern Argentina.

America to Southeast Asia and northern Australia. In Asia they are home to rhinos and elephants, as well as three of the world's biggest cats. The tiger is the largest and also the one that is causing the most concern to conservationists. One hundred years ago tigers were widespread across southern Asia. Today they are dwindling fast, almost entirely because of hunting.

Tigers are dangerous animals, so it is not surprising that people do not want them living too close to home.

Reaching out with its arm, a baby orangutan plays with its older sister while its mother chews some food. Young orangutans stay close to their mother until they are four years old, and after that they keep in touch by visiting her regularly. These gentle plant eaters live in the forests of Southeast Asia—a part of the world that has been badly affected by deforestation in recent years.

But safety is not the main reason why tigers are killed—a more important factor is money. Tiger body parts are sold for use in traditional eastern medicine, and they sell for astronomical prices. A leg bone, for example, can be sold for around $5,000. It is illegal to sell tiger body parts, but with such huge profits at stake the trade still goes on.

The second of the big three cats—the Asiatic lion—is a close relative to the lions that live in Africa. Asiatic lions once ranged across the Indian subcontinent, but today they live only in the Gir Forest Sanctuary in northeast India. There are only around 400 of these lions left, but their forest refuge is carefully guarded, so their future seems secure. From a distance Asiatic lions look very similar to their African cousins, but two features tell them apart—their manes are smaller, and they have an unusual fold of skin

▽ *The jaguar is the largest cat in Central and South America. It looks a lot like a leopard, but it behaves more like a tiger, hunting in thick forests and swamps. Jaguars like water and are good swimmers.*

running along their undersides.

Compared to tigers and lions, leopards have proven to be surprisingly good at coping with humans and habitat change. Like most cats they are mainly nocturnal, but they are not picky about what they eat. Leopards can kill adult deer, but if this type of food is hard to find they will target much smaller prey, including rodents and even large insects. This adaptability helps them get through hungry times.

FIGHTING FOR LIGHT

In seasonal forestland plants and animals have to fit in with the calendar, and they breed at particular times of the year. But in tropical rain forests there are no real seasons, and life continues at the same hectic pace all year round. For rain forest plants the most urgent priority is to get enough light—a tricky task in a habitat where so many plants live side by side. The forest's tallest trees grab their share by towering over smaller ones. Called emergents, they can be as tall as 12-story buildings, and their crowns look like leafy islands floating on a deep-green sea.

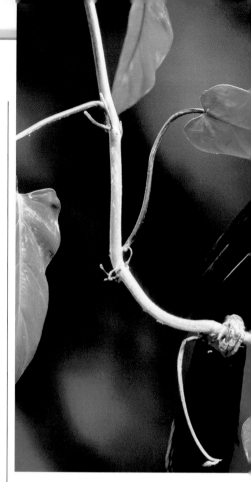

△ *Perched on a climbing plant, a fruit-eating toucan shows off its gigantic, brightly colored beak. The beak is filled with air spaces, so it is not as heavy or as cumbersome as it looks.*

Before an emergent can reach this gigantic size, it has to fight its way up from the gloomy depths of the forest floor. To do this many trees play a waiting game. They grow upward, but they stay thin, so they only need a small amount of energy to stay alive. Some never get past this stage, and they die before they reach a place in the sunlight. But others are luckier. If an old tree falls, light suddenly floods in from above, giving saplings the break they need. They rush to fill in the gap, and the winners stand a chance of becoming emergents themselves.

PRIVATE PERCHES

Some rain forest plants have a very different way of getting the daylight they need. Instead of growing up they spend their entire lives on

△ *This bromeliad uses brilliant red leaves instead of flowers to attract pollinating animals.*

branches and tree trunks high above the ground. These plants are called epiphytes, and they include thousands of types of orchids, as well as spiky-leaved bromeliads and ferns. Many epiphytes could easily fit into

a matchbox, but some are bigger than a garbage can and can weigh more than one fourth of a ton.

Unlike parasitic plants, epiphytes do not steal anything from their hosts. Instead they get water from the rain and nutrients from dust and fallen leaves. Some bromeliads have their own water tanks made out of a circle of leaves, while others soak up water through special scales that are as absorbent as cotton balls. Staghorn ferns from Australasia even make their own private compost heaps by trapping dead leaves that fall from above. Using this compost they can grow up to 6.6 ft. (2m) across.

DEADLY PASSENGERS

Epiphytes do not harm trees, although their combined weight can send branches crashing to the ground. But some perching plants have much more imposing ways of life. For rain forest trees the most dangerous is the strangler fig. This plant is a parasite, and it slowly

smothers its host to death.

A strangler fig starts life high above the ground from a seed that is lodged in a branch. When the seed germinates, it develops into a bush. The bush sprouts a handful of slender roots, and from here the trouble begins. These roots are as thin as a pencil, but they snake their way right down the tree's trunk until they touch the ground. Once they reach it the strangler starts growing much faster than its host. Its roots become thicker and stronger until they form a living straitjacket around the trunk. As the years go by the strangler's grip tightens, and the host tree is slowly choked and smothered to death.

After the host tree dies, its trunk often rots away completely, leaving the strangler standing on its own. Inside the strangler's trunk is a hollow space—a ghostly reminder of the tree that it killed.

PARTNERSHIPS IN THE FOREST

Strangler figs depend on birds because birds spread their seeds. They feed on the strangler's fruit, but the seeds pass through their bodies unharmed. When a bird lands on a branch, it often leaves droppings containing some strangler seeds.

△ *This strangler fig is starting to tighten its hold around its host. The strangler's roots merge together whenever they cross.*

In this convenient arrangement both the bird and the strangler win.

Partnerships like this are very common in tropical rain forests because so many different types of plants and animals live close together. Animals not only spread seeds—they also pollinate rain forest flowers. In temperate forests pollinating animals are almost always insects, but in the tropics very different animals perform this service as well. They include nectar-eating birds, such as hummingbirds and parrots, as well as hundreds of types of bats. Compared to insects, birds and bats are big and clumsy, so flowers that attract them have to be large and very tough. Bat-pollinated flowers are often creamy white, and they have a powerful musky smell after sunset that guides bats toward them in the dark.

Many pollinating animals visit a wide range of flowers, but some concentrate on one type. One of the most remarkable of these pollinators is a hawkmoth from Madagascar. Its tongue measures up to 12 in. (30cm) long, and it works like an extralarge drinking straw that can reach deep into orchid flowers.

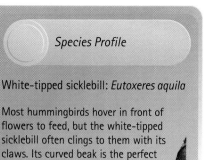

Once the moth has finished feeding, it rolls up its tongue and flies off to find its next meal.

A BUG HUNTER'S PARADISE

Scientists do not know exactly how many insects live in rain forests, but they include at least 5,000 types of crickets, 40,000 species of butterflies and moths (and their hungry

◁ *With their tapering wings and streamlined bodies, hawkmoths are designed to travel at fast speeds. They can fly long distances to find food.*

caterpillars), and over 100,000 types of beetles. Among them are some giants of the insect world. The goliath beetle from central Africa is the world's heaviest insect, weighing three times as much as a mouse. The harlequin longhorn beetle from South America has some of the longest antennae. Stretched out straight they would reach almost the entire way across this page.

It takes patience to track down these monsters, as they are mainly active after dark. But ants are much easier to find because most of them work during the day. At sunrise in the forests of Central and South America, leaf-cutter ants pour out of their subterranean nests and climb up into the trees. Walking out onto the thinnest twigs, they neatly snip off pieces of leaves and then carry them underground. They use the leaves to grow a fungus that provides them with their food. Leaf-cutter ants are amazingly industrious but do not work when it rains. At the first sign of a downpour they drop their loads, leaving a trail of leaf fragments leading to their nest.

THE NEST RAIDERS
Leaf-cutter ants are relatively harmless, but many tropical forest ants have powerful

bites or stingers.
Weaver ants live in bushes and trees, and although they are small they ferociously attack anything that comes within reach. These tiny ants make pouch-shaped homes out of leaves, sewing them together with sticky silk. Army and driver ants are even more dangerous. These nomadic insects live in roving swarms that can be up to 100,000 strong. They surge across the forest floor, overpowering anything that is too small or too slow to escape. As dusk falls the worker ants stop moving and link up their bodies to make a temporary camp on the forest floor. Called bivouacs, these camps can be as big as basketballs, with the queen ant hidden inside.

▽ These leaf-cutter ants are carrying pieces of leaves back to their nest. The ant getting a free ride is a "minima" worker—it will process the leaf once it is stored underground.

△ Many forest insects use bright colors to warn predators that they are dangerous, but this longhorn beetle is bluffing because it is actually harmless.

Few animals dare to eat army ants, although some birds flutter around their swarms. Called antbirds, they do this to pick off insects and other animals trying to get away. But some forest mammals specialize in breaking into ant and termite nests. They include the collared anteater, or tamandua, from South America, and scale-covered pangolins from Africa and Asia. They are all good climbers, and they have long, sticky tongues to lick up their food.

EIGHT-LEGGED HUNTERS
Some rain forest spiders protect themselves by looking like ants, even though they do not have stingers.

◁ Green tree pythons are born brown, red, or yellow. This young python has caught a mouse. Like all tree snakes, it has no difficulty swallowing upside down.

Species Profile

Goliath bird-eating spider:
Theraphosa leblondi

This gigantic spider from rain forests in Suriname and Guyana is the largest in the world. Females are heavier than males, and they can weigh 2.8 oz (80g)— over twelve times heavier than the forest's smallest birds. When these spiders breed, the female lays up to 1,000 eggs, storing them in a silk cocoon in her burrow.

lizards, as low temperatures make it difficult for them to move around. But in tropical forests conditions could hardly be better. It is always warm, and there are plenty of places to hide. Snakes and lizards are experts in the art of camouflage, and many of them are agile climbers. Tree pythons and boas lie in wait with their tails wrapped tightly around a branch. If a bird or monkey comes within range, the snake suddenly lunges forward with the front of its body, grabbing the prey in its jaws. In the forests of Central America the slender eyelash pit viper uses a similar technique, but it often lurks close to flowers. It waits for hummingbirds, snatching them out of the air as they feed.

Rain forest lizards do not have fangs or venom, so they need camouflage to hide from birds. Many of them are green, but Australian leaf-tailed geckos have an intricate pattern of gray and brown markings that makes them almost invisible when they rest on bark. To make their camouflage even more effective, their bodies are almost flat, so they do not cast any telltale shadows that could give them away.

LIFE ON THE FOREST FLOOR

Like the bird-eating spider, most forest floor animals hide away when the Sun is out. Butterflies are a big exception however. Although they usually live high up in the treetops, many of them flutter down to the ground at least once a day. They make these journeys to feed on salts and other substances that are essential to their diet. Butterflies find these in wet soil, in rotting fruit, and also in droppings left behind by animals. At good feeding sites hundreds

spend the day underground, emerging to hunt after dark. Although they are called bird-eating spiders, or tarantulas, these predators have a varied menu. They hunt by touch, feeling for their prey with hairy legs that measure up to 11 in. (28cm) from end to end. Once the spider has pinned down its victim, its poisonous fangs get to work. Birds often manage to escape, but insects, frogs, and other small animals are not as lucky. The spider usually feeds on the spot before returning to its burrow at dawn.

TREE-CLIMBING SNAKES

In cold parts of the world forests are not good places for snakes and

Rain forests are also home to giant orb-weaver spiders, which make webs up to 5 ft. (1.5m) across. But the largest webs are made by social spiders. These live in groups of several thousand animals, and they work together to spin enormous networks of silk up to 1,640 ft. (500m) long. Together they can catch much larger prey than if they lived on their own. But the rain forest's most famous spiders do not build webs at all. They

of them push and jostle as they try to get their fair share.

At the first sign of trouble butterflies quickly flutter into the air. But even in broad daylight tiny arrow poison frogs show no signs of fear. Small enough to fit into a thimble, these brilliantly colored amphibians hop over leaves and fallen logs, searching for small insects and worms. Arrow poison frogs can afford to be confident because their bodies contain some of the most powerful poisons in the animal world. Their gaudy colors warn other animals to stay far out of their way.

Arrow poison frogs are found only in Central and South America. At one time several types were used to make poison-tipped arrows, which is how they got their name.

TREETOP CHORUS

Compared to rain forest insects, few large animals manage to live entirely on leaves. This is because rain forest leaves are tough, and they often contain substances that make them taste unpleasant or difficult to digest. Insects have developed ways around these chemical defenses, but only a handful of mammals eat leaves all the time. Howler monkeys are some of the most successful. They live in tropical forests from Mexico to northern Argentina, and they are famous for their extremely loud calls. The calls are made by the males, which have a throat chamber that works like an amplifier built in just below the chin. Howlers live in small troops, and they use their calls to mark their feeding territories high up in the trees.

◁ *Threatened by a predator, a tamandua uses its prehensile tail like a ledge, allowing it to back up onto this termite nest and slash it with its front claws.*

▷ *This bug-eyed horned katydid lives in the Amazon rain forest. Katydids usually eat leaves and fruit, but their powerful jaws can deliver a painful bite.*

△ *A woolly spider monkey's tail works like an extra leg, leaving its hands free to collect food. This female is hanging from a branch with a baby clinging to her fur.*

Monkeys live throughout the tropics, but only New World monkeys—including howlers—have fully prehensile tails. These tails can wrap around branches, and they have a patch of bare skin on the underside that gives them

a good grip. Howler monkeys have heavy bodies, and they usually hang on with their hands and feet as well. But spider monkeys are more lightly built, and they often dangle from branches using their tails and nothing else.

TINY PRIMATES

Tropical forests are home to over half of the world's primates— the group of animals that includes apes, monkeys, and their relatives. Gorillas are the largest, while the smallest are mouse lemurs, which live in the forests of Madagascar. The rufous mouse lemur weighs around 1.4 oz (40g), which is roughly the same as a chicken's egg. These tiny creatures feed on fruit, nectar, and insects using their sharp hearing and eyesight to find food after dark. Madagascar is famous for its bizarre primates, but other parts

▽ *Male morpho butterflies can be as big as a human hand, with beautiful metallic-blue wings. These butterflies often glide through the forest around 10 feet above the ground, searching for their favorite food—rotting fruit.*

Species Profile

Tarsier: *Tarsius* species

Tarsiers are related to monkeys, but they behave more like tree frogs, using their strong back legs to jump from branch to branch. They can leap over 40 times their own length and move around almost entirely after dark. There are five species of tarsiers, and they all live in the forests of Southeast Asia.

of the world have theirs too. One of the most agile is the tarsier from the forests of Southeast Asia, which leaps on insects after dark. This pocket-sized primate hunts by sight, using enormous eyes that are bigger than its brain.

Despite the huge difference in their sizes, primates share many features. Most of them have nails instead of claws and fingers and toes that are good at gripping. Their eyes face forward, which helps them judge distances when they jump. Compared to other rain forest mammals, primates are often slow to reproduce. Tarsiers, for example, have only one baby at a time, and it takes almost six months before it is ready to be born.

FORESTS AND THE FUTURE

Sadly for primates— and for many other animals—tropical forests are disappearing fast. Already more than one third of the world's primates are threatened with extinction, together

> *There are over 100 types of poison arrow frogs. They usually feed on the ground, but they are also good climbers because their toes end in sticky pads. These strawberry poison arrow frogs from Costa Rica are only 1 in. (2.5cm) long.*

with hundreds of tropical forest birds—from parrots to toucans—and thousands of plants. Some of these species are rare because they are hunted or collected, but many are in trouble because they live in a shrinking world, where bulldozers and chainsaws move closer every day. Once the timber has been removed people move in, and the forest is replaced by farms.

Humans have cut down forests for thousands of years, and people depend on farmland for food. But tropical forests are being cleared at a record rate, destroying some of the richest wildlife habitats in the world. Endangered species—such as orangutans—can be helped by keeping them in reserves, but this rescue work is expensive, and it can only protect a tiny fraction of the forest species. Because tropical forests are so rich and complicated, we cannot save their wildlife without saving forests too.

RIVERS, LAKES, AND WETLANDS

FOR PLANTS, ANIMALS, AND MICROLIFE FRESHWATER IS ONE OF THE MOST POPULAR HABITATS ON EARTH. SOME SURVIVE IN THE TINIEST PUDDLES, BUT OTHERS TRAVEL LONG DISTANCES BETWEEN FRESHWATER AND THE SEA.

If all of the world's water was shrunk down so that it fit into a bucket, the amount contained in rivers, lakes, and wetlands would not even fill a thimble. But because the planet is so large, freshwater habitats can be immense. Russia's Lake Baikal is almost 1.2 mi. (2km) deep, while the Amazon River is over 4,030 mi. (6,500km) long. Every year it empties 50 billion tons of rainwater into the sea. Compared to seawater, freshwater is often full of nutrients, making it a good habitat for living things. But freshwater habitats can dry up in the summer or freeze over in the winter, and in rivers there is the risk of being swept away.

SMALL BEGINNINGS
Lakes and ponds are great places to study nature because they are home to an incredible variety of living things. These watery worlds contain many animals, but just as on land, life ultimately depends on plants. This is because plants make the food that animals need to survive. In freshwater the smallest "plants" are microscopic algae that drift near the surface of the water.

▽ *The glasslike surface of this South American river conceals a world that is brimming with life. This is the home of giant freshwater fish and also of the Amazonian river dolphin, or bouto.*

△ *North American bald cypresses are some of the few conifers that can grow in swamps.*

Although they are tiny, algae can reproduce at an amazing rate, sometimes turning the water bright green. These minute specks are devoured by microanimals, which provide food for larger hunters such as newly hatched fish. One common pond animal, called a hydra, gets the best of both worlds. Its body contains thousands of single-celled algae, which it shelters in return for food. But the hydra also has stinging tentacles, and it uses these to grab smaller animals passing by. Hydras can move but only slowly, so they have to be alert for predators. If anything threatening comes too close, they quickly pull in their tentacles until the danger has passed.

REEDS AND REED BEDS

Most water plants have roots, so they can anchor themselves to the bottom. Some stay underwater all of their lives, but most grow upward so that they can flower in the open air. One of the most successful is the common reed— an extratall grass that is probably the most widespread flowering plant in the world. Common reeds grow from the Arctic as far south as Australia, and they live in ponds and ditches, as well as in shallow lakes and lagoons. Where there is enough space, they form waterlogged reed beds that stretch as far as the eye can see.

▷ *Hydras reproduce by growing tiny buds that break off to start life on their own. This adult hydra has grown a two-day-old "baby" that is still attached to its side.*

△ *Reed beds can look deserted in the winter, but closely packed reed stems make good hiding places for moorhens and other birds.*

247

Species Profile

Giant water lily: *Victoria amazonica*

This South American water lily grows the largest floating leaves in the world. Each leaf can be up to 6.6 ft. (2m) wide and contains hundreds of air spaces that make it float. Its raised rim has a single notch where the rain drains away, and the bottom is reinforced by prickly struts. A large leaf can hold a child's weight—as long as he or she is lying down.

Reed beds are bad places to take a walk, but they make perfect hideouts for birds. Starlings and swallows use them as nighttime roosts, but other birds feed in them and use them as places to raise their young. Herons and bitterns nest on the ground, but the reed warbler stays high and dry. This skillful builder weaves a cup-shaped nest out of dead leaves, using reed stems as supports.

FLOATING ON THE SURFACE

Water lilies have a very different way of growing. Unlike reeds, their stems are floppy, and their leaves are designed to float. Water lilies can live in water several yards deep, and they grow upward from the bottom every spring. When their leaves reach the surface, they unroll and lay flat like plates. Some are only the size of a coin, but the largest leaves—grown by giant water lilies from South America—are as big as a paddling pool and have 6-in. (15-cm) -tall rims. Water lily leaves contain air cells—just like sheets of bubblewrap—and they have a waxy upper surface that makes rain roll off. These features mean that "lily pads" are practically unsinkable. They make ideal perches for dragonflies and also useful stepping stones for jacanas—small birds with oversize feet. Fish also use them as shields to hide behind

◁ *Watched by their nestlings, parent herons greet each other at their treetop nest. Many other wetland birds build their nests on the ground.*

△ *Water lilies are pollinated by insects and flower at different times. Some close up at sunset to keep insects "on board" overnight.*

from hungry birds. Water lily flowers attract many different insects, but beetles are their most frequent visitors. Some water lily flowers close up at sunset, trapping their visitors inside. During the night the insects become completely dusted with pollen, and they carry it off when the flower opens up the following day.

THE DRIFTERS

Some freshwater plants have cut adrift from the bottom and spend their lives afloat. The most common by far are duckweeds, which look like tiny green pills. Duckweeds are the world's smallest and simplest flowering plants. The tiniest species of all, from Australia, is no bigger than a grain of salt. Instead of leaves and stems, they have a rounded plant "body" and in most cases just a single trailing root. Stagnant ponds and shady ditches are ideal duckweed habitats. Here they cover the surface in floating lawns that can contain tens of thousands of duckweed plants. When the fall arrives the plants sink to avoid being frozen, and the duckweed disappears until the following year.

In warm parts of the world stagnant pools are often covered with floating ferns. Unlike land ferns these ferns are small and flat, and many of them have leaves that are covered in water-repellent "hairs." When it rains the water rolls off, so the fern does not sink. One type of water fern often lives in flooded paddy fields that are used to grow rice. It is a useful plant because it contains bacteria that help fertilize the soil.

△ *Covered with duckweed, a bullfrog looks out across a pond. In many parts of the world duckweed does not flower—it relies on animals to spread it from pond to pond.*

A much bigger plant, called water hyacinth, is even better at spreading. Water hyacinth originally came from slow-flowing waters in South America, but it was carried around the world by plant collectors because of its beautiful flowers. Unfortunately this attractive emigrant proved to be far too successful, and in some parts of the world it is now a serious pest. In Africa's Lake Victoria water hyacinth covers hundreds of square miles of shallow water, and it smothers wildlife and clogs up boats. Scientists are working on ways to control it, but they face a long struggle because it is so widespread.

The largest drifter of all is a plant called papyrus, which can be over 13 ft. (4m) tall. Papyrus comes from Africa, and the ancient Egyptians discovered how to flatten it to make paper over 4,000 years ago. Papyrus normally grows at the water's edge, but it sometimes breaks away in drifting islands many yards wide. In the Sudd—a swamp in the upper reaches of the Nile—some of these islands are inhabited by people,

◁ *With its amazingly long toes, a jacana uses water lily leaves as floating platforms. There are eight types of jacanas, and most live in warm parts of the world. This one is common in Southeast Asia and Australia.*

while others make useful pens for farm animals.

PART-TIMERS

Freshwater animals include permanent residents and part-timers. Some of the part-timers, such as otters, shuttle between the water and land every day. Others spend their early lives in the water and then leave it when they grow up. Most of these animals emerge on their own, but mayflies burst out in fluttering swarms, creating one of the most impressive spectacles in the freshwater world.

The best time to see these swarms is on calm summer evenings along

△ *The hippo is the largest and most dangerous freshwater mammal. Male hippos are unpredictable, and their huge tusks can bite 3-feet-wide holes in wooden boats.*

the banks of slow-flowing rivers. If conditions are right, immature mayflies crawl out of the water in their thousands before shedding their skins and soaring up into the air. These insects take up to four years to develop, but the adults do not have working mouthparts and live for only a single day. After mating the females scatter their eggs on the water in a final flight. Once this task is over all the adults die.

CHANGING DIETS

For most other freshwater insects adult life lasts much longer than this. Adult mosquitoes can survive for several weeks, while adult

damselflies and dragonflies last for several months. To live this long they need food, and the young eat very different things from the adults. Young damselflies and dragonflies feed on all types of water animals, and they snatch them up with a lethal weapon called a mask, which is like a set of telescopic jaws. The adults are also predatory, but they use their legs to snatch other flying insects in midair. But for mosquitoes growing up means a much bigger

▽ *Papyrus is one of the world's most useful water plants. In ancient Egypt it was used not only for making paper but also for mats, cloth, and even sails.*

change in diet. Young mosquitoes feed on microscopic organisms that they filter out of the water, and they can survive in the smallest imaginable habitats, including water that collects in abandoned tires. Once they become adults they switch to liquids—nectar for males and blood for females.

RETURNING TO THE WATER

Because freshwater habitats are often scattered, animals have to be in the right place at the right time to breed. Flying insects are well equipped to do this because they can easily move from place to place. Mosquitoes can find

Species Profile

Eurasian river otter: *Lutra lutra*

Sleek, limber, and agile, otters divide their time between land and water. Like other freshwater otters, this species has webbed feet, a streamlined body, and extremely thick fur. When it dives to catch fish, the surface of its coat gets wet, but its underfur stays dry. It breeds in riverbank dens and is a remarkably playful animal, sometimes sliding into the water just for fun.

△ *Mosquito larvae have to come up for air. Hanging beneath the surface, they breathe through a "snorkel" that has a water-repellent tip.*

water by sensing the humidity in the air, but many other insects—including dragonflies—find it by sight. Occasionally they make mistakes: diving beetles, for example, sometimes crash into greenhouses on moonlit nights because they mistake the shiny glass for the surface of a pond.

For frogs and toads the breeding season starts with a journey back to the same pond or lake

where they started life as tadpoles. In many species the males arrive first and begin a loud chorus of croaking that attracts the females to them. When the females arrive, the males compete with one another in a furious scramble for the chance to mate. Once mating is over they often abandon the water, leaving the tadpoles to grow up on their own.

Frogs and toads find their way by building up a memory map of their surroundings that guides them toward their goal. Because frogs and toads do not have good eyesight, this map works by smell. If a frog or toad is moved a few miles from its own home area, it will often discover a new place to breed. Amphibians seem to have good memories, because after three or four years many of them return to their original homes.

LONG-DISTANCE MIGRANTS
Amphibians are not the world's fastest movers, so their annual journeys are short. But rivers and lakes are also home to some of the greatest travelers in the animal kingdom. These are fish that divide their lives between freshwater and the open sea. Fish do this to get the best of two different worlds. For most of them freshwater is a safer place to breed, while the sea is a better place to find food. But strangely this rule does not always hold true, as some migratory fish do the reverse. The Atlantic salmon returns to freshwater to lay its eggs.

△ *Damselflies are graceful predators that flutter over pools and streams. They live all over the world—from the steamy tropics to Arctic tundra.*

Backswimmer: *Notonecta* species

Unlike most other water insects, backswimmers spend their lives upside down. They live in ponds and ditches, and they float just beneath the surface, waiting for other insects to crash land. When one does the backswimmer rows toward it, using its back legs as oars. With its sharp mouthparts, it then stabs upward from below. To breathe backswimmers collect a film of air around their bodies.

Adults make their first return journey at the age of three or four years, and they navigate by taste, finding their way back across the ocean to exactly the same river

△ *Slithering over the ground, a European eel makes its way toward a pond. Eels are covered in a slimy mucus that keeps them from drying out.*

where they grew up. The upriver journey is exhausting, but they eat nothing along the way. Once the fish have laid their eggs, some are so weak that they die, but most manage to return to the sea.

MYSTERIOUS TRAVELS

Atlantic salmon can migrate over 620 mi. (1,000km), but the European eel's migration is even longer. Unlike the salmon, this snakelike fish starts life in the open ocean in a part of the North Atlantic known as the Sargasso Sea. From here young eels travel northeast with the ocean currents until they arrive at the coast of Europe after a journey lasting over two years. They then make their way upstream to the rivers and wetlands where they slowly grow up. After a "childhood" lasting up to 30 years, the eels

▽ *For migrating salmon waterfalls are a major obstacle on the way to their breeding grounds. These muscle-packed fish can make vertical leaps of over 10 ft. (3m) at a time.*

△ *When frogs and toads breed, the male holds on to the female for several days. Males often have special pads on their thumbs to keep them from slipping off.*

With their elegant shape and pink plumage, flamingos are some of the world's most beautiful wetland birds. They can be up to 5 ft. (1.5m) tall, but despite their size they feed entirely on microscopic water plants and animals. To collect this food they use their strangely shaped beaks as sieves. Flamingos often feed in huge flocks, and they live in some of the toughest wetland habitats on Earth. In East Africa and South America they feed in barren, salt-encrusted lakes, where daytime temperatures can reach over 104°F (40°C).

△ *American alligators prey on anything that moves. Young ones eat small fish, crabs, and even snails, but the adults tackle much larger animals. They have even been known to attack cattle.*

become adults and begin breeding.

This is the time when eels move downriver on a one-way journey that takes them to their distant spawning grounds. These adult eels have silvery skin and large eyes, which suggests that they travel in deep water as they cross the ocean. But no one knows for certain how deep they swim or which route they take because amazingly not a single adult European eel has ever been caught at sea.

FRESHWATER WETLANDS
In rivers and lakes there is plenty of open water, making it easy to spot animals on the move.

▽ *The gavial is a large Asian crocodile with an amazingly long and slender snout. In the mid-1970s gavials almost became extinct, but a conservation program is now helping the species survive.*

But wetlands are a different matter. Here the water is often covered in plants, providing many places for wildlife to hide away. Marshes are one example of wetlands, but they also include dozens of other soggy habitats—from peat bogs in the Arctic to sticky tropical swamps.

Wetlands can be hostile places for humans because they are full of hazards—from poisonous snakes to treacherous mud. But for animals and plants these waterlogged worlds can be ideal places to live. One of the world's largest wetlands— Florida's Everglades—is home to over 250 species of birds, as well as the American alligator, one of the largest reptiles in the world. In southern Africa the Okavango Delta is even richer. This wetland is formed by a river that empties inland instead of flowing out to sea. Its inhabitants include hippos, elephants, and antelope, as well as some of the largest and noisiest frogs and toads in the world. It is also a favorite haunt of the black heron— the only bird that fishes under the shade of an umbrella made by its outstretched wings.

DROUGHT
In cool parts of the world wetlands stay wet all year round. But in the tropics some of them dry out for several months every year. As the water level begins to drop, plants die back and animals find

△ *Perched on an airboat, park rangers skim through Florida's Everglades. Wildlife here faces many problems, such as hurricanes, falling water levels, and expanding cities.*

themselves crowded into a smaller and smaller space. When life gets really difficult, birds can always fly away, but water animals need to find other ways of surviving.

In the Everglades alligators get around this problem by excavating private ponds, called "gator holes." While the rest of the ground dries up, gator holes stay full of water. These holes are scattered across the landscape, and they are not only used by alligators—fish, turtles, and frogs take refuge in them as well. In other parts of the world crocodiles and caimans often bury themselves in the mud. Like alligators they can survive without eating for several months, and often a pair of nostrils sticking out of the mud is the only sign that gives them away. Wetland fish are good at surviving

in shallow water, but when a drought really hits hard they take emergency action too. Catfish can crawl from pond to pond, while lungfish bury themselves in the mud and surround themselves in slimy cocoons. As long as they stay moist, they can stay alive by breathing air. Other fish are not as lucky. They die in their thousands, but they leave behind their eggs, which hatch when the rains return.

LOOKING AHEAD

Natural droughts are not the only challenge that freshwater plants and animals have to face. In many countries humans are using so much freshwater that wetlands are drying out permanently. Water pollution is another problem because humans have used rivers and lakes as a free way of getting rid of waste.

In Florida water that once flowed through the Everglades is now diverted to farmland and cities. As a result half of the state's wetlands have disappeared. This change has hit many of the Everglades' natural

inhabitants. In Europe many former wetland areas have been drained and used to grow crops. Today only a tiny fraction of Europe's original wetlands remain.

Water pollution harms river life, but it is especially damaging when it affects lakes. This is because lakes are dead ends—once polluting chemicals flow into them, they can stay there for years. During the 1970s pollution in the Great Lakes, especially in Lake Erie, became so bad that most of the fish disappeared. In Russia it threatens the unique wildlife of Lake Baikal, while in East Africa it threatens the flamingos that feed in the Rift Valley's salt lakes.

It is too late to bring back most of the wetlands that have disappeared, but because of antipollution laws many rivers in industrialized countries are now cleaner than they were one hundred years ago. But as the

▽ *A green anaconda is lifted from a swamp. This South American snake is the world's heaviest, weighing up to 550 lbs (250kg). It spends most of its life in or near water.*

Species Profile

Baikal seal: *Phoca sibirica*

Known in Russian as the *nerpa*, this seal is the only one that lives far from the sea. Its habitat is Lake Baikal in Siberia—the deepest lake in the world. During the winter, when the lake freezes over, Baikal seals survive by gnawing holes in the ice. Lake Baikal is home to at least 1,200 different animals, and three fourths of them are found nowhere else in the world.

world's population grows, more freshwater will be needed, and more waterborne waste will be produced. The battle to save freshwater habitats will be fought all around the world.

MOUNTAINS AND CAVES

LIFE IS TOUGH AT THE TOP—ESPECIALLY IF YOUR
HOME IS SWEPT BY ICY WINDS, BURIED BY SNOW,
OR SCORCHED BY THE GLARE OF THE AFTERNOON
SUN. BUT NATURE'S MOUNTAIN DWELLERS ARE
WELL ADAPTED TO THESE CONDITIONS, AND
THEY TAKE THEM IN THEIR STRIDE.

Mountains are an important habitat for wildlife because
they exist in every continent on Earth. But living in the
mountains is no easy matter. For every 3,280 ft. (1,000m)
that an animal climbs, the temperature drops by 41°F (5°C). To
make matters worse the air gets thinner, so it becomes harder to
breathe. Plants also face problems because the soil is thin, and
there is very little shelter. Caves are a very different habitat. Here
there is no weather, but there is also no light and very little food.

▽ *High up on the slopes of Mount Kenya,
giant lobelias are the tallest plants.
As the Sun sets their leaves fold
inward to keep out the cold.*

HIGH-ALTITUDE PLANTS
In 1887 a Hungarian explorer
named Samuel Teleki climbed
Mount Kenya in East Africa. As he
approached the summit, he traveled
through some of the most unusual
vegetation in the world.

On its lower slopes Mount Kenya is
covered by evergreen tropical forest,
which then gives way to bamboo.
At around 11,480 ft. (3,500m)
the bamboo is replaced by alpine
moorland, home to giant lobelias
and groundsels, enormous heathers,
and many other remarkable plants.
At almost 14,760 ft. (4,500m) this
strange landscape is replaced by
fields of ice and snow that lead
to the mountain's triple summit.
    Since Teleki's pioneering
expedition scientists have discovered
equally strange mountain plants in
other parts of the world. Mauna
Kea—an immense volcano in

△ *Unlike mountainsides, caves do not have any natural light, so plants cannot grow inside of them. Animals eat food from outside, or they eat one another.*

Hawaii—is the only habitat of the silversword, a spectacular plant that grows on lava fields close to the summit. In Venezuela flat-topped mountains, called *tepuis,* are like gardens floating in the clouds. Here the plants are small and stunted, but they include hundreds of species that are found nowhere else in the world.

DOUBLE PROTECTION

Mount Kenya and Mauna Kea owe their strange plant life to the fact that they are completely alone. These mountains are like ecological islands, and their plants have evolved in isolation with hardly any contact with the outside world. Mount Kenya lies exactly on the equator, so the sunshine there is fierce. Plants like the giant lobelia are protected by a layer of feltlike hair that stops the intense ultraviolet light from burning up their leaves. This covering also comes in handy at night, when temperatures can drop far below the freezing point on the upper slopes. Mauna Kea's silverswords have developed exactly the same adaptation, although they live on the other side of the planet.

In most other parts of the world mountains are linked together in ranges, so plants can spread from one mountain to another. Conifers are especially good at coping with sunshine and cold, which explains why they grow on mountains all over the globe. In the Rocky Mountains these extratough trees include some of the oldest living things in the world—bristlecone pines. For a bristlecone 1,000 years old is young, while 3,000 is only middle-aged.

△ *With its felt-covered leaves, the silversword plant is well protected from the Sun. After growing for around 20 years, it produces a giant flower head and then dies.*

Running from Canada to New Mexico, the Rocky Mountains rise up over 13,120 ft. (4,000m). With their jagged peaks and year-round snow, these mountains are home to the bighorn sheep—one of the animal world's greatest climbers. Bighorns can scale near-vertical slopes using their nonslip hooves.

SURVIVAL ABOVE THE TIMBERLINE

On high mountains trees stop growing at the point where frost kills their buds. This altitude is marked by the timberline—a ragged frontier that separates forested slopes from much tougher terrain. On tropical mountains like Mount Kenya the timberline is high up, but in colder places like Alaska it can be as little as 2,460 ft. (750m) above sea level.

Plants above the timberline have to face the worst possible weather,

△ *Like many mountain plants, moss campion has long roots so that it can grow on slopes of loose rock. When it dies, it helps create soil that other plants can use.*

△ *In the White Mountains of California bristlecone pines live for over 5,000 years. On the highest slopes they are twisted and gnarled by the mountain climate.*

and most of them survive by having tough stems, small leaves, and a cushionlike shape. This gives them maximum protection from the wind and helps keep them from drying out. During the winter they are often covered by snow. This actually helps them because it keeps them much warmer than they would be in the open air. These plants are known as alpines. Many of them— such as moss campion—start growing before the snow has fully thawed out. As soon as it starts to clear, their flowers burst open, giving them an early start in the race to produce their seeds.

STRANDED ON THE SLOPES

Spring is also the time when mountain insects begin to stir. Many of these animals spend the winter as eggs or chrysalides, which can be frozen solid for several months without being harmed. As the days

lengthen in the spring, they thaw out and start developing, and insects appear as if by magic, crawling or fluttering across the slopes. On mountains flying insects include midges, bees, and butterflies, all of which stay low to keep out of the wind. Butterflies usually avoid cold places, but apollos specialize in life high up. These butterflies fly slowly, and their bodies are covered in furry scales that help keep them warm.

Butterflies need plants, and they normally steer clear of ice and snow. But ice bugs, or grylloblattids, survive under rocks near the snow line and sometimes even higher up. These primitive insects do not have wings, and some of them do not have eyes. They feed on other animals— including insects that have been blown uphill by the wind, leaving them stranded in the cold. In the Rocky Mountains grasshoppers sometimes become stranded

△ *Apollo butterflies live on mountains in Asia, Europe, and North America. They make chrysalides that are hidden in low-growing plants, wrapped in silken webs.*

like this when they migrate. Grasshopper Glacier in Montana contains millions of dead grasshoppers. The ones deepest down are believed to be several hundred years old.

MOUNTAIN MAMMALS

Unlike insects, mammals are warm-blooded, so they can stay active no matter how cold it gets. But mammals need more oxygen than insects, a problem where the air is thin. Mountain species make up for this by having larger lungs, bigger hearts, and more oxygen-carrying cells in their blood. Vicuñas, from South America, spend their lives in mountain grassland up to 16,400 ft. (5,000m) high. At this altitude the air is so thin that engines have

△ *Despite its dainty appearance, the vicuña is one of the toughest animals on four hooves. It lives on the Altiplano— a high-altitude plateau in the central Andes.*

trouble starting, and planes need extralong runways to take off. But because of their special adaptations, vicuñas can run up steep slopes without even getting out of breath.

The snow leopard, a beautiful predator from central Asia, hunts far above the timberline, reaching an altitude of 18,040 ft. (5,500m). But the altitude record for large mammals belongs to the yak, a grazing animal related to farmyard cattle. Yaks live in the dry, windswept slopes of the Himalayas, and in the summer they roam as high up as 20,008 ft. (6,100m). In the Himalayas yaks are often kept as domesticated animals because they are useful for milk and for carrying loads. Wild yaks, on the other hand, have become very rare.

WINTER RETREAT

Snow leopards can usually find prey all year round, but for grazers winter is a difficult time. Vicuñas and yaks move to lower ground and so do ground-feeding birds such as grouse and ptarmigan. Food can be difficult to find even here, and the threat of starvation is never far away. To get around this problem many smaller mammals use a different way of surviving: they hide in underground burrows and hibernate until the winter has passed.

The champion hibernators are rodents, and some of them sleep for amazing periods of time. Marmots

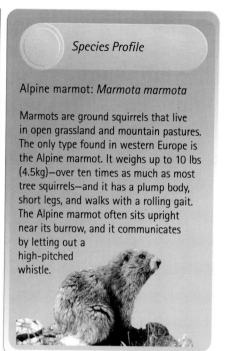

Species Profile

Alpine marmot: *Marmota marmota*

Marmots are ground squirrels that live in open grassland and mountain pastures. The only type found in western Europe is the Alpine marmot. It weighs up to 10 lbs (4.5kg)—over ten times as much as most tree squirrels—and it has a plump body, short legs, and walks with a rolling gait. The Alpine marmot often sits upright near its burrow, and it communicates by letting out a high-pitched whistle.

can hibernate for eight months of the year, while some ground squirrels manage even longer. Scientists studying one North American species, called the uinta ground squirrel, found that it was active for only 12 weeks a year. It sleeps through the entire winter and fall and most of the spring. During the summer ground squirrels feed almost nonstop because they need plenty of body fat to keep them alive during their long sleep.

▽ *A sprinting snow leopard shows off its beautiful coat. This graceful predator is endangered because it is hunted for its fur.*

△ *Gathering on a rocky ledge, feathered scavengers arrive for a meal. The bird in the center is a lammergeier—a specialist at making a meal out of bones.*

GIANT SCAVENGERS

Compared to mammals, birds have much less difficulty traveling over mountains. Geese have been seen flying over the highest peaks of the Himalayas, and radar echoes show that some birds fly even higher. In 1973 a plane hit a vulture over 7 mi. (11km) up—the highest altitude ever recorded for a bird. Birds can survive at this height because their lungs are extremely efficient at gathering oxygen, and their plumage keeps out the intense cold.

Many birds migrate over mountains, but some also use them as their homes. Vultures and birds of prey are tailor-made for this type of habitat, as they need open spaces to search for food. The world's largest vulture is the Andean condor, with a wingspan of almost 10 ft. (3m). It soars on strong updrafts along mountain ridges, staying airborne for hours at a time. The condor nests on remote ledges, returning to the same one all its life. These nesting sites become splashed with white droppings that are often easier to spot than the condors themselves.

In Africa, Asia, and southern Europe another mountain vulture has an extraordinary way of getting food. After it has stripped a carcass clean of meat, the lammergeier carries large bones into the air. It drops the bones onto rocks to break them open and then glides down to feed on the marrow inside.

BIRD MOUNTAINEERS

Mountain birds also include species that search for food on the ground.

▽ *The California condor is the rarest mountain vulture. In the 1980s only three wild birds were left. Because of a breeding program, there are now more than 170.*

Choughs probe mountain grassland for insects and worms, while wrens hop in and out of crevices looking for spiders living among the rocks. But in the Alps and the Himalayas the wallcreeper behaves much more like a true mountaineer. This small, gray bird has extra sharp claws, and its uses them like hooks to get a grip on rocks. Using its tail as a brace, it climbs up sheer walls and overhangs, inspecting the surface for any signs of food. Unlike a human mountaineer, however, the wallcreeper does not have to worry about falling off—it can stop climbing at any moment by fluttering into the air.

LIFE UNDERGROUND

Before humans learned how to build, they often used caves as shelters. In one cave in France footprints show that ice age humans reached at least 1.2 mi. (2km) underground. These people would have found their way using candles made of animal fat, although no one knows why they went this far. But animals have lived in caves for much longer than humans. Unlike us, they can navigate in total darkness, and one of the ways they do this is by using sound.

Bats use sound to hunt flying insects and to find their way to and from their homes. In one cave system near San Antonio, Texas, up to 50 million bats pour into the air every evening. After feasting on insects high up in the sky, they make their way back into the caves to feed their young. Amazingly the bats' echolocation system works even when such huge numbers are on the move. The bats do not only avoid hitting the cave's walls—they also avoid bumping into each other.

In northern South America, Trinidad, and Panama the oilbird performs a very similar feat. It feeds

△ *Most fruit bats roost up in trees, but these African fruit bats prefer rock crevices and caves. Every night they take off in a group, flying up to 15 mi. (25km) to find food.*

on oily fruit, but it nests on rocky ledges up to 1,640 ft. (500m) underground. Oilbirds have good eyesight, but once they enter a cave they rely on bursts of sound to find their way to their chicks.

Species Profile

Cave salamander: *Eurycea lucifuga*

Some cave-dwelling salamanders live deep inside of caves, but this North American species is usually found near cave mouths, where dim light filters in from the outside world. It feeds mainly on insects and is a good climber, sometimes hanging on with its prehensile tail. Its tadpoles grow up in subterranean streams and pools or sometimes in ones aboveground. Several other types of salamanders live in American caves—unlike this one, many of them are blind.

PERMANENT CAVE DWELLERS

Bats and oilbirds are part-time cave dwellers, but some animals spend their whole lives underground. For them darkness is a minor problem—a much more important one is finding food. Caves do not have any plant life, so no food is produced inside of them. Instead their full-time inhabitants depend on food that comes from the outside world.

The menu in caves is based on waste and dead remains. At the top of the list are bat droppings, which can build up into knee-deep layers over hundreds of years. This rich refuse is mined by primitive animals, called springtails, and by cave-dwelling millipedes and crickets. From time to time dead bats drop onto the heap—a welcome extra dish that is packed full of useful protein. While these animals feed, spiders and harvestmen prowl close by, waiting to pick off any

scavengers that come within reach.

In many caves flowing water brings in particles of food from the outside world. This food nourishes a completely different collection of animals, including cave fish, cave salamanders, and cave shrimps. Many of these animals have very small eyes and cannot see, but they are incredibly sensitive to movement and to any smell that might lead to a meal.

△ *Deep in a cave, an oilbird stares at the camera. Oilbirds can navigate using vision or echolocation no matter how dark it is.*

OCEANS

SEAWATER COVERS ALMOST THREE FOURTHS OF THE WORLD'S SURFACE AREA, BUT BECAUSE IT IS SO DEEP IT MAKES UP OVER 95 PERCENT OF ALL THE LIVING SPACE ON EARTH. OCEANS ARE WHERE LIFE FIRST APPEARED ALMOST FOUR BILLION YEARS AGO, AND THEY ARE STILL HOME TO MOST OF THE WORLD'S LIVING THINGS.

The oceans are so vast that they are like many habitats rolled into one. These habitats range from the sunlit shallows near tropical coasts to icy-cold sediment on the deep ocean floor. Oceans have their own mountains, valleys, and plains, and they even have their own deserts—huge spaces of almost empty water where a shortage of nutrients makes it difficult for living things to survive. Unlike life on land, ocean life does not have to face sudden changes in temperature or natural disasters, such as drought and fire. But living in the oceans is dangerous. No matter how carefully things protect themselves or how quickly they move, predators are always waiting to strike.

◁ *Giant spider crabs are the world's largest crustaceans, with leg spans over 11.5 ft. (3.5m). They are found in the North Pacific.*

LIFE AT THE SURFACE
If seawater was as transparent as air, the oceans would still be easy to see. The surface would look like a layer of mist floating high above the

◁ *Drifting close to the coast, a swarm of plankton looks like a blue-green stain. Plankton is normally invisible to the naked eye, but it can be detected by satellites orbiting above the oceans.*

plants by collecting the energy in sunlight. Drifting among the algae are single-celled protozoans and a whole galaxy of planktonic animals—from newly hatched fish to the larvae of lobsters and crabs. These animals are eaten by larger hunters, which are in turn swallowed by other predators. In plankton food is the most important thing in life, and everything—no matter how small—is on the menu of something else.

ATTACK FROM ABOVE

The busiest part of the plankton is closest to the surface, where there is maximum daylight for algae to use. This is also where most planktonic animals live because it is the best place for them to find food. But the ocean's surface is a hazardous place, especially for creatures that are big enough to be seen from the air. Planktonic animals are the oceans' equivalent of insects,

seabed. In some parts of the oceans the mist would be thin, but in others it would be more like fog on a winter's day.

This mysterious "mist" does exist, but water prevents us from seeing it. It is formed by plankton—a floating mixture that is brimming with small and microscopic living things. Its most numerous inhabitants are single-celled algae, which live like

and plenty of birds watch out for them, eager to get their share.

Terns splash headfirst into the water, and the same technique—dive-bombing larger prey—is used

△ *Jellyfish live in all of the world's oceans. These simple animals use stinging tentacles like fishing lines—most are harmless to humans, but a few can be deadly.*

▽ *Skimming over the waves, gulls keep a sharp eye open for food. Gulls usually stay close to the shore, but many other seabirds roam far out to sea, returning only to breed. For these birds land is a strange and dangerous place.*

Storm petrel: *Hydrobates* species

Storm petrels are some of the world's most common seabirds, roaming far out across the oceans. They feed mainly on shrimps, but they hardly ever settle on the water, despite spending most of their lives at sea. Storm petrels nest in burrows and crevices, but because they are clumsy on land they come ashore at night, when there is less risk of being attacked by gulls. There are 24 species of these birds, but at sea they are very difficult to tell apart.

by gannets and boobies. Albatross do their fishing from the air, snapping up food as they glide close to the surface of the waves. Because of this in-flight refueling, they can stay airborne for days at a time. But the world's smallest oceangoing birds, called storm petrels, feed in a very different way. They look as if they are walking on the water because they patter their feet on the surface. Although they can be smaller than blackbirds, they sometimes roam thousands of miles from land.

MAKING AN ESCAPE

When Christopher Columbus sailed to the Americas, he became the first person to cross the Sargasso Sea in the North Atlantic Ocean. Unlike all other seas, this one is an enormous

swirl of calm water famous for its drifts of floating weeds. In Columbus' time it developed a negative reputation as a place where ships could become tangled up and sink.

The Sargasso Sea is not really this dangerous, but it is one of the few areas of the open ocean where animals have somewhere to hide. One local inhabitant, called the sargassum fish, is almost perfectly camouflaged for life among the floating weeds. Around the size of a thumb, it lurks completely motionless until something edible wanders by. When this happens its mouth opens in less than one fiftieth

▽ *Lurking under a tangle of floating weeds, a sargassum fish is very difficult for other animals to spot. Its body has fleshy frills that look just like pieces of weeds.*

◁ *Atlantic spotted dolphins' beak-shaped jaws contain over 120 small but sharply pointed teeth. They are often plain when young—they develop spots as they age.*

leaps when enemies are on their tails. One of the most dangerous is the needlefish. Up to 5 ft. (1.5m) long and armed with spike-shaped jaws, it has been known to crash-land in boats, spearing people on board.

▽ *Needlefish have amazingly slender bodies with snouts that taper to a narrow point. All of their internal organs are stretched lengthwise to fit inside.*

of a second, sucking the unfortunate victim inside. Across other parts of the oceans there are no hiding places, and animals use different ways of concealing themselves. One common method is countershading—a two-tone color scheme that works like camouflage in open water. Countershaded fish have dark backs, which makes them blend in against the water when seen from above. Their undersides are much paler, so they blend in against the light when seen from below. The same color scheme can be seen in dolphins and also some of the largest whales.

SCHOOLS

In open water sticking together is another tactic for avoiding attack, as it is more difficult for a predator to pick out a single animal from a school. Over half of the world's fish live together in schools when they are young, and one fourth live together throughout their lives. In a school fish often move with amazing precision. They twist and turn as if they are following secret commands, and if attacked they can form a living tunnel so that predators swim right through the school. Schools can react like this because fish have built-in pressure sensors called lateral lines. Even without looking each fish can tell how its neighbors are moving, so it can behave in a similar way. In extreme circumstances open-water fish sometimes use other methods to make an escape. One of the most drastic is jumping right out of the water—a trick that can throw a predator off the trail. Flying fish can "jump" up to 984 ft. (300m) by gliding on their outstretched fins, and many other species make shorter

FILTER FEEDERS

Occasionally sticking together can backfire and lead fish into a trap. This is what happens when schools of fish are hunted by humpback whales. Humpbacks circle around a school and blow curtains of rising bubbles that surround the fish like a wall. Panicking, the fish form a tighter and tighter mass until the whales suddenly burst up from below, swallowing thousands of fish at a time.

Humpbacks have unusually varied feeding techniques, and most of their relatives—including the blue whale—hunt smaller prey. These whales, known as rorquals, have deep grooves along their throats. The grooves stretch when the whales open their mouths, allowing them to take in several tons of water at a time. A rorqual then closes its mouth, forcing the water

△ *Salps are some of the most common animals in the sea, but because they are transparent they often go unnoticed. These ones are connected together in a chain.*

Species Profile

Basket star: *Gorgonocephalus* species

With its highly branched, writhing arms, the basket star is one of the strangest inhabitants of the seabed, measuring up to 20 in. (50cm) across. It hides away during the day, but at night it creeps out and extends its arms to catch planktonic animals drifting past. The arms have tiny hooks that help trap food.

through the bristly baleen plates that hang from its upper jaw. As the water is pumped out of the whale's mouth, almost all of the plankton is left behind. This is the world's largest example of filter feeding— a highly efficient way of getting food that has made whales the largest mammals on Earth.

Whales are well-known animals, but many smaller and less familiar creatures filter their food from the sea. Some of the most numerous are animals called salps, which look like tiny transparent barrels open at both ends. Salps take in water through their front opening, and after filtering it they pump it out through the rear. This "exhaust" works like a tiny jet engine, pushing the salp

along. Salps' filters are extremely fine, allowing them to collect bacteria and other types of microscopic food. They are very successful, and in some parts of the world's oceans salps form invisible swarms hundreds of miles across.

OASES AND DESERTS

For centuries fishermen have known that ocean life is not evenly spread out. Some of the best fishing grounds are on continental shelves, where shallow water stretches out a long way from the coast. Here nets can reach the bottom, dragging up fish that live on or near the seabed. Continental shelves are important breeding grounds for fish, but many have been badly affected by fishing fleets. For example the Grand Banks off of Newfoundland once produced the biggest catches of cod in the world, but after decades of overfishing the large

◁ *Over the past 40 years fishing has had a growing impact on ocean life. Modern boats can fish in water over 3,280 ft. (1,000m) deep, using sonar to track schools.*

THE OCEAN DEPTHS

Between the surface of the oceans and the seafloor below, there is a lot of water and an almost unbelievable amount of space. Just 0.24 cu. mi. (1 km³) of ocean contains as much water as 500,000 Olympic swimming pools, but there are over 24 million cu. mi. (1 billion km³) of water in the oceans as a whole. Daylight quickly fades away with depth, and below around 820 ft. (250m) the oceans are always dark.

It is hard for any of us to imagine what this hidden world is really like. There is nothing to distinguish up from down and no solid surfaces at all. The water is under intense pressure, and its temperature is bone-chillingly cold. Sometimes there is a gentle current, but because everything is nudged along with it the water seems perfectly still. But here and there in this cavernous

schools of cod have disappeared. No one knows for certain if— or when—they will come back.

Other prime fishing grounds are found where currents flow up toward the surface, carrying nutrients from far below. These nutrients work like fertilizer for plankton, creating food for enormous schools of fish and squid. One of these upwelling zones is off the coast of northwest Africa, while an even richer one lies off of Peru. But there are some parts of the oceans where fish are few and far between. These are the oceans' great deserts, where the water contains so few nutrients that plankton find it difficult to grow. Most of them are in the tropics, far from the nearest coasts. Without plankton very little stirs in the water, and hardly any birds cross the sky. Aside from the polar ice caps, these watery deserts are some of the emptiest places on Earth.

▽ *Hurling its 30-ton body out of the water, a humpback whale "breaches" during the breeding season.*

△ *Most shark attacks on people happen near coasts. The great white shark has caused at least 300 human deaths, but it is rapidly becoming endangered itself.*

△ *Drop-down jaws and oversize teeth give the viperfish a fearsome appearance. Its fangs are so big that they protrude outside when its mouth is shut.*

one another. In the abyssal zone the water also reverberates with some strange sounds. Most of these eerie clicks and creakings are made by fish trying to find one another in the dark.

PERMANENT PARTNERS

In the vast emptiness of the abyssal zone, fish cannot afford to miss a meal. Because of their huge mouths and stomachs that can stretch out like balloons, many of them can eat fish as large as themselves. Once a fish has swallowed this much food, it does not need to make another catch for weeks. For marine biologists these deep-sea predators work like living collection devices. Some of the species found in the stomachs of these fish have never been found out in the open sea.

Finding a suitable partner can be even harder than finding food, so if a male and female do meet, they must not waste the opportunity to mate. Deep-sea anglerfish have developed a unique way of making sure this happens. The males are

much smaller than the females, and they are unable to hunt, so they cannot survive for long on their own. Instead each male seeks out a female and latches onto her with his jaws. The two fishes' bloodstreams join together, which means that the male is kept alive

blackness, there are signs of life.

In the oceans' depths—known as the abyssal zone—many animals use light to lure their prey. The bearded anglerfish has a luminous lure that dangles in front of its mouth and a light-up "beard" trailing beneath its jaws. It is a distant relative of the sargassum fish, and it has the same type of trap-door mouth that sucks its food on board. The viperfish also has a light-up lure, as well as light organs, or photophores, in a line along its sides. Some of these are constantly lit up, while others can flash on and off. If threatened, a few deep-sea fish can squirt out clouds of luminous fluids—a startling trick that may help them escape attack.

As well as to catch food, fish use these lights to attract mates. Males and females often have different patterns to help them identify

▷ *With her mate dangling beneath her, a female anglerfish hunts for prey. She feeds for two because the food that she eats also keeps the male alive.*

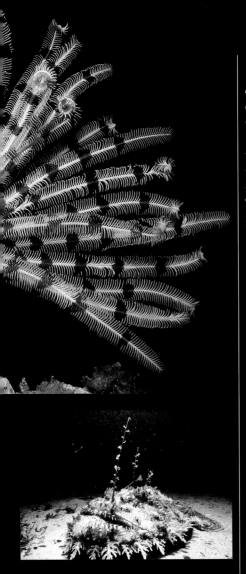

◁ Unlike other starfish, feather stars are good swimmers. This one has settled on a rock and is gripping it with its cirri, which work like tiny feet.

△ The goosefish uses the same hunting technique as deep-sea anglerfish, but it lies in wait on the seabed. Its camouflage hides a huge mouth—up to 12 in. (30cm) across.

by his mate. He stays permanently attached to his partner, fertilizing her eggs whenever she is ready to breed.

DEEP DIVERS

Many deep-sea fish start life in the plankton close to the water's surface and then sink down into the depths as they grow up. But

▷ Drifting near the surface, a sperm whale gets ready for its next dive. It can dive for over an hour, but it needs only five minutes to get its breath back at the surface.

the oceans also contain animals that travel down into the darkness and back again several times a day. These are the sea's deep divers, and all of them are mammals—animals that breathe air.

Using satellite transmitters, scientists have found that elephant seals can dive down at least 4,264 ft. (1,300m), and they can hold their breath for over an hour. They eat squid and deep-sea fish, although exactly how they find their prey is not known. Sperm whales dive even farther. These blunt-headed monsters eat fish and giant squid, and they can hunt at depths of 6,560 ft. (2,000m) or even 9,840 ft. (3,000m) if food is hard to find. Dives like this can last almost two hours—an amazing endurance test for an animal that needs to come to the surface to breathe.

Although experts know what the sperm whale eats, they are not at all sure how it dives or how it finds its prey. The spermaceti organ may provide some clues to answer these questions. This gigantic reservoir of waxy fluid fills most of the sperm

Species Profile

Vampire squid: *Vampyroteuthis* species

Despite its name this tiny deep-sea squid does not suck blood. Instead it catches small animals, using arms that are joined together by a web of skin. It can swim by rippling a pair of fins, but like many deep-sea animals it spends most of its time motionless, waiting for food to come within its reach. The vampire squid has an unusual way of defending itself: if it is attacked, it squirts out a cloud of luminous mucus while it makes its escape.

whale's head, and it contains passageways that can carry water or air. Some scientists think that it works like an adjustable ballast tank because spermaceti contracts and turns solid when it cools down. According to this theory, a sperm whale cools its spermaceti to make itself sink and then warms it up when it needs to rise. But not everyone is convinced. Some whale experts

Holding its arms out like a parachute, a day octopus swims over the seabed off of Hawaii. It feeds on shrimps and crabs and often surrounds its lair with their discarded remains. The day octopus can grow to be up to 3.3 ft (1m) long, but the world's largest species—the giant Pacific octopus—has an arm span of up to 26 ft. (8m) and can weigh over one fourth of a ton.

△ *Hydrothermal vents—or black smokers —are the strangest habitats on Earth. Here life is fueled by dissolved minerals that gush upward in clouds of superheated water.*

think that the spermaceti organ is actually a sound focusing device used by the whale to "see" its prey in the dark.

MYSTERIOUS GIANTS
No one has ever seen a sperm whale hunting, but scientists have found some signs of their prey. Sperm whales often have circular scars on their skin, and pincerlike beaks have been found in their stomachs.

These beaks are all that remains of giant squids because they are too tough to be digested. The circular scars are made by the squid's suckers as they make a desperate attempt to fight back.

Giant squid are shrouded in mystery because scientists have yet to find one that is still alive. Despite reports of boats being attacked by these animals, almost all of our knowledge of them comes from dead ones caught in nets or washed up on the shore. Atlantic giant squid can be 56 ft. (17m) long, and until recently they were thought to be the largest invertebrates in the world. But in 2003 a giant squid was found off Antarctica that belonged to a species that is even bigger. When fully grown this mega-invertebrate could be 82 ft. (25m) or even more.

LIFE IN THE DEPTHS
Until the mid-1800s biologists believed that the deep seabed was too hostile for living things. The cold, the darkness, and the extreme pressure made it seem very unlikely that anything could survive. But in 1871 a ship called *Challenger* collected animals from several miles down, proving that this was not true.

▷ *Glass sponges have fragile skeletons made of silica—the same material used to make glass. These seabed sponges are most common in the tropics.*

Almost one hundred years later in 1960 the two-man crew of the *Trieste*, a deep-sea submersible, reached the bottom of the Mariana Trench. Here at the oceans' deepest point—almost 7 mi. (11km) down— they found animal life.

△ *The bathyscaphe* Trieste *was the first submersible to reach the oceans' deepest point. The crew's quarters were underneath the vessel inside a steel sphere designed to withstand extreme pressure.*

In the oceans' greatest depths the lack of light means that algae cannot survive. Without them there is no homegrown food. Instead life is almost entirely fueled by dead remains that drift down from above. Occasionally a really huge meal makes its way down to the depths. The dead body of a whale, for example, is a gigantic banquet, and the scent of rotting flesh attracts scavenging animals. They include deep-sea crustaceans that resemble

◁ *Although it is covered in water, the seabed is just as rugged as dry land. This sonar picture shows the seabed off the coast of California. The shallow continental shelf, colored orange and yellow, ends in a sudden drop where deep water begins.*

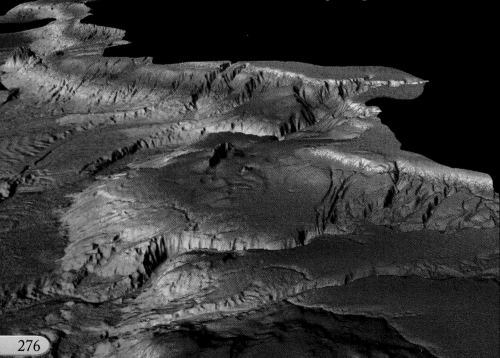

giant wood lice and the hagfish—an animal that looks more like a snake than a fish, with a mouth that does not have jaws. Together these animals pick the flesh from the carcass until nothing but bones is left.

SURVIVING ON SEDIMENT

Feasts like this are extremely rare, and most seabed animals live on a very different type of food.

▷ *Coiled up on the seabed, a hagfish takes a break between meals. Hagfish find their food by smell.*

They collect tiny particles of dead matter that drift down toward the seabed like snow. Most of these particles are the remains of plankton, including cases and tiny shells. They can be smaller than grains of salt, and it can take them weeks to complete their journey from the sunlit surface to the ocean floor.

Some deep-sea worms collect this food using fan-shaped tentacles, while brittle stars use their slender arms. These deep-water relatives of starfish can be incredibly common—in some places they cover the seabed in writhing masses many millions strong. Glass sponges use a different

technique—they pump water through their bodies, filtering out anything they can eat. When the sediment has finally settled, another group of animals takes over—one that bulldozes or burrows its way through it, extracting anything that can be used as food. Hidden away beneath miles of seawater, these scavengers and recyclers are the deepest animals on Earth.

HEAT IN THE DARK

The temperature on the deep seabed is only 39°F (4°C)—only a few degrees warmer than seawater around the poles. But in a few places underground water heated by volcanic rock pours up into the sea. Here the temperature of the water can be as high as 680°F (360°C), and only the crushing pressure of the ocean above keeps it from boiling away. These springs are known as hydrothermal vents. The first one was found in 1977. Since then many more have been discovered.

The water in hydrothermal vents is filled with dissolved minerals, which makes it look like black smoke. As the water gushes out the minerals are deposited, forming chimneys up to 33 ft. (10m) high. But the most remarkable

▷ *The seabed is an important habitat for worms. This species collects particles of food with its slender tentacles*

feature of vents is found on the rocks below, which teem with life. Giant tube worms grow in tangled clusters, while clams are attached to the seabed. Ghostly white crabs and lobsters clamber among them. These animals depend on bacteria that use minerals to get energy.

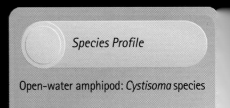

Species Profile

Open-water amphipod: *Cystisoma* species

Amphipods are shrimplike animals that live in many habitats, including beaches and the deep seabed. Measuring 6 in. (15cm) long, this species is one of the largest. It is unusual because it is a good swimmer, and it lives in the open sea. It has huge, upward-facing eyes, and it probably feeds on soft-bodied animals, such as salps, spotting them against the light shining down from above. When the open-water amphipod breeds, it carries its young until they are ready to take care of themselves.

If the Sun stopped shining tomorrow, most life on Earth would soon die, but vent life would carry on—exactly as it has for millions of years.

COASTS

IF THE WORLD'S COASTS COULD BE STRAIGHTENED OUT AND JOINED TOGETHER, THEY WOULD CIRCLE THE GLOBE MANY TIMES. COASTS ARE A VERY IMPORTANT HABITAT FOR WILDLIFE BECAUSE THEY BRING TOGETHER SPECIES THAT LIVE ON LAND AND ONES THAT SPEND MOST OR ALL OF THEIR TIME IN THE SEA.

Habitats are always changing, but on coasts nature really shows its power. In stormy weather waves smash against rocks and undermine cliffs, while powerful currents shift millions of tons of sand and mud. All of this energy turns the shore into a constantly moving battlefront—a place where buildings topple into the sea and ports silt up and become stranded inland. Coastal animals and plants have to cope with all of these changes without being smothered or swept away. They also have to fit in with something much more predictable—the twice-daily rise and fall of the tide.

WATER ON THE MOVE
Tides are caused by the Moon and the Sun as they move in relation to Earth. Their gravity tugs on seawater, making oceans bulge toward them as they travel across the sky. In the open sea these bulges are barely noticeable, but when they approach land the water piles up, creating a tide. The height of the tide depends on the shape of the coastline and also the

△ *Hawaii's northern coast is made up of volcanic lava, which is easily broken up by the sea. Strong waves and jagged rocks make it dangerous for boats to come ashore.*

amount of water on the move. If the coast is shaped like a funnel, the water is squeezed into a smaller and smaller space, leaving it nowhere else to go but up. One of the world's

biggest tidal funnels is the Bay of Fundy, a long inlet on the east coast of Canada. Here the highest tides reach 69 ft. (21m), and when the tide is coming in it can rise by an adult's height in as little as half an hour. But in landlocked seas such as the Mediterranean, there is hardly any tide at all. Tides can also travel up rivers—in the Amazon they reach over 248 mi. (400km) inland.

On coasts the tide is very important in deciding what lives where. Most coastal plants cannot survive in seawater, so they grow far enough up the shore to avoid the highest tides. Seaweeds are exactly the opposite because they need to be submerged. Some brown seaweeds can cope with several hours in the air, as their fronds are extratough. But red seaweeds are much more fragile, which explains why they live below the level of the lowest tides.

▽ *Limestone cliffs make good homes for plants and seabirds because they have many rocky ledges. These cliffs are in the Algarve in southern Portugal.*

△ *Starfish move over sunken rocks, looking for mussels and other mollusks. Their top speed is only around 6.6 ft. (2m) per hour.*

LIVING CLOCKS

For coastal animals the tide is like a timer that resets itself twice a day. As the tide rises and the shore is flooded, many of these animals begin feeding. Mussels open up their shells and start their onboard pumps, while barnacles beat their feathery legs. In their different ways both feed by trapping tiny particles of floating food.

△ *Mussels anchor themselves to rocks using extratough threads, but sometimes they get torn off during storms and thrown ashore.*

Limpets eat on the move, and for them the rising tide is the signal to get going. For three or four hours they crawl over the rocks, scraping up algae with their microscopic teeth. But as soon as the tide begins to fall, everything goes into reverse. Mussels and barnacles close their shells, while limpets make their way back home. They cannot afford to be late, as home is the only place where their shells fit exactly against the rock.

Many of these small animals can sense the tide's ebb and flow. But some also have a "clock" in their nervous system that tells them when to start and when to stop feeding. Scientists have tested this clock by collecting crabs and oysters and carrying them inland. Even when these animals are far away from their original homes, they stay in tune with the tides.

TIDAL LINE BIRDS

Coastal birds also fit in with the tides, but they work the other way around. For gulls and waders the busiest time is when the tide is falling, as the retreating water uncovers plenty of food. Gulls are the great scavengers of the seashore world, and they glide along the water's edge, looking out for live animals and dead remains. They are quarrelsome feeders, but they are also quick to spot any chance of a meal. If the weather turns bad or they run out of food, they often abandon the coast and head inland.

Compared to gulls, waders—also called shorebirds—are more picky about what they eat. Oystercatchers

△ *Many birds nest above the high-tide mark, but they have trouble finding a spot when the coastline is covered in houses and hotels.*

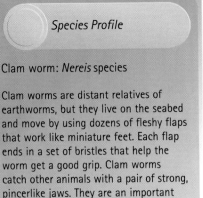

feed mainly on mussels and cockles and have chisel-shaped beaks that can smash open shells or pry them apart. Turnstones have much shorter beaks, and they feed by flipping over pieces of seaweed and snapping up small animals hiding underneath. The sanderling is one of the smallest waders but one of the fastest on its feet. It scoots along the surf like a windup toy, pecking up any

▽ *With their brightly colored beaks and noisy calls, oystercatchers are easy to recognize on muddy and rocky shores.*

△ *Peering out of its burrow, a mantis shrimp waits for victims to come within reach. Its barbed front legs can grab prey in four thousandths of a second—one of the fastest movements in the animal world.*

shrimps and sandhoppers that are stranded by the waves.

These three waders hunt by sight, but many others hunt by touch. One of the largest is the curlew—a long-legged bird with a curved beak over 6 in. (15cm) long. Curlews feed on muddy shores, and they specialize in finding buried animals that other shorebirds cannot reach. Their beaks are as slender as pencils and have sensitive tips that can feel animals that are hidden away. The tip can open while the rest of the beak stays shut, allowing a curlew to grip its food and pull it up out of the mud.

THE BURROWERS

Humans and wild animals have different ideas about what makes the perfect beach. For us the ideal beach has golden sand, no seaweed, and definitely no flies. But for wildlife, clean sand is not a good habitat because it is a sign that not much food comes in with the tide. Shingle is even worse. It can be uncomfortable for people to lie on, but for small animals it can be a killer. At high tide small stones are smashed together by the waves, crushing anything among them.

For many animals the ideal beach is one that has mud or sediment mixed in with the sand. Sediment contains particles of food, and because it is sticky it helps keep the sand in place. This type of gooey mixture is ideal for cockles

and burrowing shrimps, and incredible numbers of them can be hidden away. On muddy coasts, especially near river mouths, more than 5,000 shrimps can live in a piece of shoreline no bigger than a handkerchief. Together these animals are a huge store of food—one that attracts birds like a magnet.

SALT MARSHES AND SWAMPS

Life gets even stickier on really flat shores, where the tide travels a long way inland. Here land and sea meet in mudflats and salt marshes, far out of the reach of the waves.

△ *This muddy sand looks deserted, but thousands of animals are hidden beneath the surface, waiting for the tide to return.*

△ Lobsters feed on crabs and mollusks, but they also scavenge on dead remains. They have a very good sense of smell and are easily lured into lobster pots by pieces of dead fish.

When the tide comes in, the water winds its way through creeks and channels. When it goes out, it leaves behind a landscape of glistening mud.

For humans this type of habitat is tough going because the ground is treacherous, and the creeks are like a maze. But for plants that can cope with salt it is a perfect place to live. Most of these plants are low growing, and their leaves often have a crunchy feel. This crunchiness is produced by surplus salt, which the plants get rid of as they grow. Some salt-marsh plants even spread along roadsides, as road salt makes them feel right at home.

In the tropics salt marshes look completely different. Instead of being empty and open, they are covered in a tangle of trees. These trees are mangroves, and they are the only ones in the world that can survive in the zone between the tides. Many of them have stiltlike roots that anchor them in place. Some also have "breathing" roots that poke up like miniature snorkels from the mud.

Mangrove swamps are like tiny tropical forests, and they are home to many different types of animals—from monkeys and snakes to biting ants. But their most interesting inhabitants live farther down on the mud itself. They include hordes of tiny fiddler crabs and also mudskippers—finger-sized fish that use their pectoral fins to hop and climb and that survive out of the water by breathing air.

△ Perched above the sticky mud, mangrove trees spread out from the shore. They stop where the water at high tide is deep enough to reach their leaves.

ROCKY COASTS

Compared to sandy and muddy shores, the wildlife of rocky shores is easier to find. This is because animals have to live out in the open, unless there are crevices where they can hide. Sea urchins are armed with spines, but most other rock dwellers use hard shells or body cases to keep themselves out of trouble. A shell does several jobs at once—it protects the owner from the waves, and it keeps the animal from drying out at low tide. Even more

◁ Sea urchins use their brittle spines as a defense against attack. Hidden among the spines are small pincers that keep the urchin's surface clean.

Great scallop: *Pecten maximus*

This mollusk is one of the few that can swim by opening and shutting its shell. It normally rests on the seabed, but if it is touched by a starfish it activates an emergency escape system. The two halves of its shell snap shut, squirting out a jet of water and causing the scallop to jump in the opposite direction. Scallops sense danger with their eyes— they have over one hundred arranged around the edges of their shell.

importantly it keeps predators at bay.

Unfortunately for shell-owning animals, no shell is guaranteed to withstand a forceful attack. Oystercatchers can smash some shells open in seconds, but other predators go about opening them in much more stealthy ways. Starfish wrap themselves around mussels and clams, and then they use their tiny sucker-tipped feet to pry the two halves of the shell apart.

▽ *Most seabirds return to the same nesting site year after year. Gannets like steep, rocky islands, where there are no predatory mammals on the prowl.*

Once a paper-thin gap has opened up, the starfish slips its stomach through it and digests the soft body of the unlucky victim inside.

Lobsters can crack open shells with their claws, but shelled animals are also attacked by predators with shells themselves. One of the most common is the dog whelk, which often lives in mussel beds. It bores its way into its victims using drill-like mouthparts backed up by a shell-dissolving acid. It is a long job, but once the dog whelk starts work there is nothing that a mussel can do to escape.

△ *Terns' eggs are so well camouflaged that they are almost impossible to see when the parents are away from their nest.*

For thousands of years humans have also collected shellfish from rocky shores, and on some coastlines archaeologists have found mounds of empty shells that early humans left behind. These piles of ancient leftovers are known as shell middens. Some of them are many yards wide, and they are among the earliest and most unusual garbage dumps in the world.

This bird's-eye view shows the coast of Whitsunday Island off the northeast coast of Australia. Sandwiched between the mainland and the Great Barrier Reef, this tropical island is used as a nesting ground by turtles and by birds that breed along the shore. Every year between June and September the shallows are visited by humpback whales, which travel here from the Southern Ocean to give birth to their calves.

△ *Stretching its wings, an Atlantic puffin stands by its clifftop burrow. During the breeding season both males and females have brilliantly colored beaks and feet.*

CLIFFS AND ISLANDS

No matter how far they roam, seabirds have to come back to land to breed. Terns lay camouflaged eggs directly on the shingle or sand, and they fearlessly dive-bomb any animal—or human—that comes nearby. But at nesting time most seabirds steer clear of the hazardous

△ *Shearwaters dig their own burrows or take over ones that have been dug by rabbits. Where there are many shearwaters, the ground becomes riddled with holes.*

world of the open shore. Instead they breed on steep cliffs or on inaccessible islands, where they are much safer from attack.

At the height of the breeding season, these nesting sites become some of the busiest, noisiest, and smelliest wildlife shows on the planet. On Scotland's Bass Rock, for example, almost 100,000 gannets crowd onto a tiny island only a few hundred yards wide. On Babel Island, between Australia and New

△ *Seals use the coast as resting places, but they can also sleep in the sea. A sleeping seal floats like a bottle, with just its face and muzzle poking out of the water.*

Zealand, over two million slender-billed shearwaters arrive every year to raise their young. They reach the island after a migration that takes them around the entire Pacific Ocean—over 18,600 mi. (30,000km).

SEABIRD COLONIES

With so many birds nesting side by side, space is tight and tempers often blow. Gannets defend their nests fiercely, pecking at any neighbor who strays within reach. When an adult gannet comes back from a fishing trip, it has to locate its mate before it lands in order to avoid painful mistakes. It does this by making a landing call, which its

partner picks out from the noise created by the other birds. The bird on the ground is instantly on the alert and calls back to its mate to guide it toward the nest. Shearwaters nest in clifftop burrows, and they come and go after dark. But amazingly they also recognize their partners by sound. In the dead of night the air is filled with unearthly screeches and wails, as birds hidden underground call to ones flying overhead.

Some seabirds, such as pelicans and cormorants, are natural "landlubbers," and they stay near the coast all year round. Others are more adventurous and head out to sea as soon as their young are ready to follow. But shearwaters and puffins don't even wait that long. Once their chick has had enough food, the parents abandon it in its underground burrow. The chick waits until its feathers have grown, and then it heads out to sea alone.

Magnificent frigate bird:
Fregata magnificens

Soaring high above the sea, the magnificent frigate bird hardly ever lands on the water. Instead it steals food from other birds, chasing them until they drop their catch. The frigate bird goes into a sharp dive, intercepting the food before it hits the waves. There are five species of frigate birds—this one lives on the coasts of the American tropics. Male frigate birds inflate their bright-red throats to attract a mate.

BORN ON THE BEACH

Compared to most seabirds, seals are fully at home in the water and can stay in it for weeks at a time. But even seals have to come to land to breed. Like seabirds most of them are faithful to their breeding sites, and they return to the same piece of coastline year after year.

True seals are not very graceful out of the water, as they move by shuffling along on their undersides. They usually breed on flat coasts or on ice floes, where they find it easier to get around. But fur seals and sea lions are much more agile because they use their flippers like feet. They climb rocks to bask in the sunshine, and some of them can "gallop" almost as fast as a person can run.

Seals choose their breeding sites carefully, as they need to be in places where their young are safe from attack. Compared to birds, their young grow up incredibly quickly, nourished by some of the richest milk in the mammal world. Young gray seals, for example, often finish feeding on milk when they are only 16 days old. Their speedy growth is vital because it means that they can soon leave the land and move into the relative safety of the sea.

Unfortunately for seals many of their breeding sites can be reached by human hunters. In the early 1800s seals were hunted even more relentlessly than whales, and by the early 1900s many species were in serious danger of becoming extinct. This steep decline forced countries to bring in conservation measures, and since then some species have made spectacular recoveries. One of the biggest success stories is the Antarctic fur seal. In the 1930s there were only a few thousand left, but today there are several million.

MEADOWS UNDER THE SEA

Many flowering plants live along coasts, but hardly any manage to survive full-time in the sea.

△ *Sea grasses live in shallow waters close to the shore. Although they look like seaweeds, they are flowering plants with tough stems and strap-shaped leaves.*

▽ *Walrus use their sensitive whiskers to find clams and cockles on the seabed. They suck these animals out of their shells.*

△ *Dugongs and manatees eat up to 221 lbs (100kg) of sea grass a day. Between meals they spend their time resting at the surface.*

The rare exceptions are plants called eelgrasses or sea grasses, which form underwater "meadows" in many parts of the world. These meadows are invisible from the shore, but they look like large dark patches when seen from a boat or from the air. Sea grass usually grows in water at least 16 ft. (5m) deep, which means that

it is safely below the waves. But if it gets churned up by storms, banks of dead leaves are often washed ashore.

Sea grass meadows are an important habitat for many inshore animals. Fish shelter among the leaves, and turtles graze on them with their sharp-edged beaks. In the tropics barrel-shaped dugongs and manatees feed on leaves and also on sea grass roots. These large but harmless creatures look like seals, but they do not have to come to land to breed. They are the only marine mammals that feed entirely on plants—one reason why they used to be called "sea cows."

KELP FORESTS

Sea grasses grow by creeping sideways and spread out to form a mat. But in some parts of the world where the water is cool and the seabed is rocky, giant seaweeds grow up like trees. The largest seaweeds,

▽ *On the coast of southern California a lone heron stalks a sea grass meadow for food. At low tide the water is calm, making fish and crabs easier to spot.*

Species Profile

Leafy sea dragon: *Phycodurus eques*

This extraordinary fish lives among kelp-covered rocks off of southern Australia. It is a slow swimmer, but it is protected by amazing camouflage—the leafy flaps that sprout from its body make it look like a piece of drifting weed. Sea dragons are close relatives of sea horses. They feed on tiny animals, sucking them up with their tube-shaped mouths.

called kelps, are the fastest-growing living things in the seas. One North American species, bull kelp, can reach a length of 115 ft. (35m) in one year. But the record goes to the giant kelp—growing up to 213 ft. (65m) long, at top speed it can put on an extra 23 in. (60cm) every day.

These giant seaweeds create underwater forests that are filled with many types of life. On the rocky forest floor octopuses search for shrimps and crabs, while moray eels peer out of hidden lairs, waiting for prey. Above them fish and squid swim among the fronds, while sea otters dive down from the surface to collect abalones and clams. Sea otters are the only mammals besides apes and monkeys that use tools to reach their food. They hit abalones with stones to loosen them from rocks and smash open clam shells while floating on their backs.

More than 750 different types of animals live in the kelp forest itself, but over half a million individual animals may crowd together on the surface of a single kelp plant. These forests are the coast's farthest-flung outposts—beyond them lies the very different world of the open sea.

◁ *Sea otters spend almost all of their lives in the water, but their fur is so thick that it keeps them dry and warm. Young sea otter pups use their mothers as rafts—the mother floats on her back with the pups on top.*

CORAL REEFS

CORAL REEFS ARE BY FAR THE RICHEST WILDLIFE HABITATS IN THE SEAS. WITH THEIR COLORED CORALS, DEEP CREVICES, AND SHADOWY CAVES, THEY ARE HOME TO ONE THIRD OF THE WORLD'S FISH SPECIES—AND MANY OTHER ANIMALS AS WELL.

Just like forests on land, coral reefs are habitats that are created entirely by living things. They are built by coral polyps—soft-bodied animals that collect chalky minerals from the sea. Corals use these minerals to make cup-shaped skeletons that protect them and keep them in place. Coral skeletons are tough, and they survive long after their makers are dead. As they pile up they form rocklike outcrops and reefs. Today's reefs have taken thousands of years to develop. They are the largest objects ever built by living things, and many of them are clearly visible from space.

△ *A helicopter speeds over the Great Barrier Reef. This coral reef—the world's largest—runs parallel to the east coast of Australia for over 1,240 mi. (2,000km).*

HOW CORALS LIVE
Seen through a pair of goggles, a coral reef is like a fantastic and intricate landscape hidden just

This dazzling world is the work of coral polyps. Polyps are individual coral animals, and they spend their adult lives firmly attached in place. Each one has a short, hollow body topped by a ring of stinging tentacles that surrounds a tiny mouth. To feed, the polyp spreads its tentacles in the water to catch anything edible that comes its way. But reef-building polyps do not live just by catching food. They also use energy from sunlight through the millions of microscopic algae that live on each polyp. The algae make food by photosynthesis (see pages 84–85). In return for a share of the food, the polyp provides its guests with a home. Corals are not the only reef animals that harbor algae—giant clams, sea anemones, and flatworms do as well.

Most coral polyps feed at night, while their algae are busy during the day. It is a good arrangement, but it only works in places where the water is warm, clean, and clear. This is why

△ *Not all corals build reefs. These soft corals from the Red Sea grow in flexible colonies that bend as the sea washes past.*

most reefs are in the tropics in places where the water temperature never falls below 64°F (18°C). On muddy coasts reefs are very rare.

REEF SHAPES

In the days when ships were made out of wood, coral reefs were a major hazard. If a boat even just grazed a reef, its hull was likely to be ripped apart. This is one of the reasons why reefs were carefully charted and why scientists noticed that there are three

beneath the waves. Some of the corals spread out in delicate folds or sheets. Others look more like jagged antlers or the coiled, twisting surface of a brain. In the bright sunshine the entire reef overflows with color, and many of the fish that dart among the coral are so vivid that it is hard to believe they are real.

▽ *Sheltering among the tentacles of a sea anemone, a clown fish is well protected from danger. The tentacles have powerful stingers, but the fish does not set them off.*

△ *From the air an atoll's ring-shaped reef is easy to see. This atoll is near the Palau Islands in the western Pacific Ocean.*

main types of reefs. The first type, called a fringing reef, spreads out from the shore. Fringing reefs are the easiest to investigate because they are usually only a short swim away.

The second type, called a barrier reef, runs parallel to the coast, but it is often much farther out at sea. Australia's Great Barrier Reef is the most impressive example—actually several reefs in a row, it lies up to 155 mi. (250km) offshore.

The third type of reef is very different. Instead of being open-ended it is ring-shaped, and it surrounds a shallow lagoon. These reefs are called atolls, and they form on the slopes of ancient volcanoes that have subsided into the sea. Most of the world's atolls are in the Indian and Pacific oceans, and they include the thinnest, lowest, and most remote islands in the world. Some of them are vast: the world's largest atoll—Kwajalein in the Marshall Islands—would fit around the entire city of London, England, with plenty of room to spare.

CORAL SHAPES

Because coral polyps and their algae need food and light, they grow on the surface of the reef like a living skin. Some polyps live on their own, but most grow in clusters called colonies, which form many different shapes. Staghorn corals are the fastest growers—their spiky branches can add up to 6 in. (15cm) of new growth a year. This type of shape is good for collecting food and gathering light, but it has one disadvantage—the branches are easily broken by storms. As a result staghorn coral has to grow in the middle of the reef, where the water is shallow and fairly calm.

Finger-shaped corals are not as fragile, but brain corals are the toughest of all. These solid domes grow more slowly than other corals, but after two or three hundred years they can be bigger than a car. They live on the seaward edge of the reef and also in the middle of lagoons. Here ancient brain corals look like giant boulders rising up from the seabed sand.

HOW CORALS REPRODUCE

Coral colonies begin life when a single polyp sets up home on the surface of the reef. As the polyp grows it divides, producing many copies of itself. In turn these copies divide, creating a community of polyps that live separately but that are also joined together. If one polyp is touched, its neighbors "feel" it too. Polyps are close in more ways than one, as each colony is a genetic clone. This means that they are all exactly alike, like a giant set of identical twins.

On a few nights every year—usually on a full Moon—mature coral colonies spawn. Some shed

◁ *A giant clam's rubbery "lips" contain microscopic algae that soak up the energy in sunlight. These mollusks grow the world's heaviest shells—up to 663 lbs (300kg).*

△ *Staghorn corals grow quickly, shading out other corals with a tangle of spiky branches. The branches are sharp and break easily if they are stepped on at low tide.*

clouds of egg and sperm cells, while others give birth to developing eggs that have been fertilized before they are released. This burst of reproduction produces tiny coral larvae, called planulae, which drift in the open sea. After a few days or weeks each planula sinks to the surface of the reef and searches for somewhere to set up home. If it succeeds it turns into a polyp, and a completely new colony is formed.

△ *These spawning corals are releasing packets of egg and sperm cells into the sea. The packets break open as they approach the surface so that the egg cells can be fertilized.*

HIDING IN THE REEF

Compared to the open seabed, coral reefs are full of places to hide. This is one of the main reasons why so many animals use coral reefs as their home. Young fish swim close to the coral, ready to dart into nooks and crannies at the first sign of trouble. Mantis shrimps lurk in coral crevices, while octopuses hide in the reefs during the day and emerge to feed after dark. Holes in the reef are always in demand, so animals that "own" them have to be careful when returning home—just in case something else has moved in.

Some of the most aggressive reef predators venture into open waters but very rarely. Usually they remain in their lairs and lunge at passersby.

△ *Moray eels are shortsighted, but they can cause serious injuries to divers who venture too close to their lairs.*

These reef ambushers are moray eels—snakelike fish equipped with dozens of teeth and extremely powerful jaws. There are over 200 types of moray eels, and the largest of them is over 11.5 ft. (3.5m) long and is as thick as a human thigh. Morays are often vividly colored, with fleshy skin and glaring eyes. They hold their mouths open to

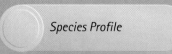
Brain coral: *Diplora* and other species

Named after its brainlike shape, this massively built coral reaches up to 6.6 ft. (2m) across and grows in an unusual way. Its polyps have separate mouths, but they share a double row of tentacles that winds its way over the surface of the colony. The tentacles open up at night to feed.

get oxygen, a habit that makes them look even more menacing.

SCRAPING THE SURFACE

Not all reef animals are this big or this dangerous. Coral reefs are also home to thousands of smaller animals that nip and nibble at plants and animals that carpet the coral surface. This food includes algae, sponges, sea anemones, and sea squirts, as well as bryozoans, or moss animals—tiny creatures that live in cases with tightly-fitting lids.

△ *Adult sea squirts have baglike bodies, and they live by filtering food from water. Their larvae are very different—they are shaped like small tadpoles and can swim.*

In the warm waters of the Red Sea corals soak up the energy
in sunshine. Corals get their amazing colors from chemical
pigments called carotenoids, which are often found in plants.
Pure carotenoids are normally orange, yellow, or red, but corals
can mix them with other substances to produce eye-catching blues,
purples, and violets. Many corals also fluoresce, which means that
they give off bright colors when seen under ultraviolet light.

△ *These two sea slugs are feeding on a reef off the island of Sulawesi in Indonesia. Each one has a pair of tentacles on its head and a tuft of feathery gills near its tail.*

Many of these animals are stuck in place, so they cannot get away.

Sea slugs specialize in this type of food, and they crawl slowly over the reef surface, scraping away at it with rows of microscopic teeth. Compared to mollusks that live on land, many sea slugs are brilliantly colored and very easy to spot. But regardless very few animals attack them, as sea slugs have an unusual and very effective system of self-defense— they steal sea anemones' stingers. When a sea slug eats a sea anemone, it digests most of the animal, but it leaves its stinging cells unharmed. The stinging cells then migrate through the sea slug's body and end up in its skin. Once in place they protect their new owner, just as if they were in their original home.

PARTNERS ON THE REEF

With so many species living side by side, it is not surprising that some join forces to improve their chances of survival. For small fish called gobies, teaming up is a way of finding a home. These fish often move into burrows dug by blind shrimps that live in coral sand. While the shrimp dutifully maintains the burrow, the goby acts as a lookout, alerting the shrimp if it spots danger approaching.

Clown fish have an even stranger partnership, as they live among the stinging tentacles of some of the world's biggest sea anemones. These tentacles can kill other fish on contact, but the clown fish darts among them without being harmed at all. It can do this because it is covered with a special coat of mucus—one that contains the same chemicals that anemones use to prevent their tentacles from stinging one another. This remarkable trick provides the clown fish with a perfect place to live, and it never wanders more than one inch or so from its home. For the fish the advantages are obvious, but for its host they are not as clear. The clown fish may work as a decoy, luring other animals toward the anemone, or it may keep the anemone clean. But some scientists suspect that it does not help the anemone at all.

The partnership between cleaners and their "clients" is much easier to

△ *Holding its mouth wide open, a spotted coral grouper lets a cleaner fish get to work. In coral reefs cleaning services are also provided by brightly colored shrimps.*

understand. Fish often become infested with parasites, but they cannot pick them off. Instead they have a cleaner fish or a cleaner shrimp to do this work for them. While the client fish patiently waits, the cleaner swims over the surface of its body, swallowing any parasites and also eating any damaged scales. Toward the end of the session the client fish often opens its mouth so that the cleaner can tidy up inside. Cleaners seem to be very important for reef fish. When scientists temporarily removed the cleaners from one section of reef, many of the client fish swam away.

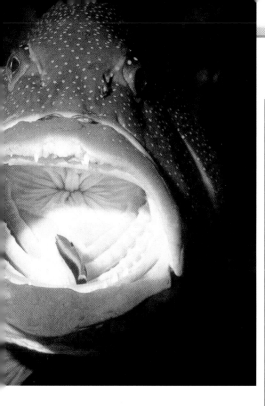

CRUNCHERS AND BORERS

Coral reefs are not only extremely colorful—they can be surprisingly noisy as well. Some of the noise is produced by parrotfish, which feed on algae and living coral—the reef's crunchiest food. Parrotfish bite off mouthfuls of coral polyps, using flat teeth that are joined together to form a beak. Once they have digested the soft parts of the coral, the remainder travels through their bodies and emerges as a shower of gritty sand. A parrotfish can eat more than one ton of coral a year, so if corals did not keep on growing, reefs would soon start shrinking.

Other tough-jawed animals also eat this difficult but plentiful food. One of the most notorious is the crown-of-thorns starfish, which lives in parts of the western Pacific Ocean.

Measuring up to 16 in. (40cm) across, the crown-of-thorns can have over 20 arms, each covered with poisonous spines. Crawling over the reef, it eats the soft parts of corals but leaves their hard parts behind. In recent years starfish plagues have swept over Australia's Great Barrier Reef, raising fears for the reef's survival. Today scientists believe that the plagues are not as much of a threat, as the starfish eventually die down, and the reef slowly recovers.

PEOPLE AND REEFS

Over the past 50 years there has been an explosion of interest in coral reefs. Millions of people visit them every year so that they can see their incredible wildlife firsthand. Internet sites give daily updates of diving conditions, as well as profiles of the animals that can be seen.

At the same time the world's reefs are in trouble. In some regions fish numbers have fallen by up to one half because they are caught by divers using spearguns or poisons. Reef sharks have been especially badly hit, as have sea cucumbers, because both are valued in the Far East as food. Scientists have found that if overfishing stops, reefs soon recover. But in poor regions few people fish for fun—instead they depend on it to make a living.

Reefs also face problems that are much harder to fix. On coasts deforestation and construction work create water pollution, which makes

Species Profile

Sea krait: *Laticauda colubrina*

Most snakes are good swimmers, but some species are especially adapted for life at sea. Sea kraits have paddle-shaped tails and nostrils that can be closed off when they dive. They live among the coral reefs and mangrove swamps of Southeast Asia, feeding on fish and other animals. Although sea kraits have small fangs, their venom is extremely strong—fortunately they rarely bite humans. Some sea snakes give birth to live young, so they can spend their whole lives at sea. But sea kraits lay eggs, so they have to come ashore to breed.

it harder for corals to grow. Coral is also damaged by boats, and it is sometimes collected to make building materials. But the greatest threat of all comes from global warming, which is raising sea temperatures worldwide. Corals need warmth, but too much warmth can kill them. Some stretches of reefs have already been affected, and scientists are anxiously waiting to see how others fare in years to come.

▽ *A gray reef shark searches for prey above the coral. Found in the Indian and Pacific oceans, this medium-sized shark has been known to attack divers, but it often only bites once before swimming away.*

TOWNS AND CITIES

WITH THEIR BUILDINGS, NOISE, AND BUSY TRAFFIC, TOWNS AND CITIES ARE VERY DIFFERENT FROM HABITATS IN THE WILDERNESS. DESPITE THIS THOUSANDS OF DIFFERENT PLANTS AND ANIMALS MANAGE TO USE BUILT-UP AREAS AS THEIR HOMES.

The world's first towns were built around 10,000 years ago, when people started farming and took up a settled way of life. Compared to today's cities, these towns were tiny and primitive, but they attracted wildlife right from the start. Weeds sprang up around the mud-brick houses, and birds nested in crevices in their walls. Today urban wildlife is still with us, but towns and cities are much bigger than they were before. Together they make up the fastest-growing wildlife habitat in the world.

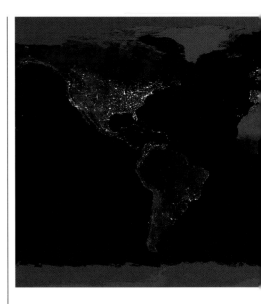

AT HOME WITH US
People have no difficulty telling the difference between towns and open country. But for animals there is no real difference at all. Instinct drives them to look for food and shelter, and wherever they find it that becomes their home. This is exactly what happened with the

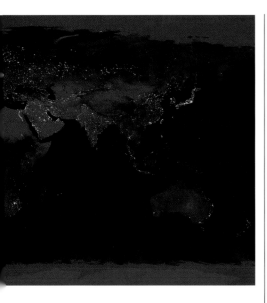

△ *Seen from space, the light from billions of buildings and streetlights floods into the sky. The far north, the Sahara, and Antarctica are some of the few completely dark areas.*

▽ *In cities like Hong Kong buildings seem to be everywhere, and open space is hard to find. But on the steep slopes behind the high-rises, wild plants and animals still survive.*

house sparrow, a small brown bird that originally lived in Africa. In the wild house sparrows nest in trees and feed mainly on seeds. But when humans started growing crops and building houses, house sparrows moved in. Towns gave them a safe haven from many of their enemies and a reliable supply of food.

Since those early days the house sparrow's spread has been incredible. It now lives throughout most of the world, except in the far north and parts of the tropics. Sparrows have been seen feeding on the 80th floor of the Empire State Building in New York City, and they are also a common sight in supermarkets, warehouses, subways, and multistory parking structures. One group of sparrows even lived and bred over 1,968 ft. (600m) deep in an English coal mine, where they fed on scraps that the miners gave them. With this adaptability it is no surprise that the house sparrow is such a success.

△ *The sparrow may not be the world's most colorful bird, but it is one of the most successful. This bird's black bib shows that it is a male.*

LIVING ON LEFTOVERS

For most urban animals the number one attraction of towns is food. Compared to wild animals, humans are amazingly wasteful eaters, and a lot of food is thrown away. In the days before organized garbage collection most of this waste ended up on the streets, where animals would be waiting to make it a meal. In Europe and Asia these

Black rat: *Rattus rattus*

An expert climber and jumper, the black rat is almost perfectly designed for life inside of buildings. Originally from Southeast Asia, it managed to stow away on sailing ships and spread to every continent except for Antarctica. Black rats eat stored food, and they carry some dangerous diseases. One of their main enemies—aside from cats and people— is the brown rat, a more aggressive species that is also found indoors.

scavengers included the black kite— a bird of prey with a 5-ft. (1.5-m) wingspan that would sometimes snatch food out of people's hands.

Today we generate even more waste, but because it is picked up it usually ends up out of town. Dumped in landfills it creates incredible feeding opportunities for any animals that can reach it. Some of the most successful of these scavengers are gulls. In many cities they wheel over garbage dumps in noisy flocks, waiting for a chance to feed. A gull's beak is the perfect tool for this type of work because it can tear apart plastic bags. Once a gull finds something edible, it swallows it as quickly as possible because its companions will not hesitate to steal its meal.

NIGHT PATROLS
Herring gulls sometimes breed in towns, but most of them live outside and fly in during the day. But towns and cities are also home to full-time scavengers that do their foraging at night. In North America one of the most successful is the raccoon. Raccoons are inquisitive animals, which gives them a head start in the search for food. Their nimble front paws are perfect for opening packages or for pulling off garbage can lids. Once the lid is off the raccoon rummages around inside, feeling for anything that it can eat.

◁ *Sifting through waste can be a dangerous way to find food. This white stork has become wrapped up in a plastic bag while feeding at a garbage dump in Spain. Without help its chances of survival are slim.*

Raccoons are quick learners. As well as raiding garbage cans, they can open doors and have been known to steal food from refrigerators. Before day breaks they hide under bridges or in hollow trees and stay there until night wakes them up again.

In parts of Europe and North America the red fox has a similar way of life. It is not as good at climbing as the raccoon, nor is it as agile with its paws. But red foxes make up for this by being quick and intelligent and by having a sharp nose for food. They often follow the same route every night, stopping off at fast-food restaurants and ripping open garbage bags. Urban foxes are not total scavengers, and they still have a hunting streak. They catch mice, birds, and small insects, but their most important prey is the humble earthworm—an animal they dig up in gardens and parks.

UNWELCOME VISITORS
Raccoons and foxes can be pests, but some types of urban wildlife can cause much more serious problems. At the top of the unwanted list are the black rat and the brown rat—two rodents that originally came from Asia but that have spread around the world.

△ *Backyards, city parks, and campsites are good feeding grounds for raccoons, one of the most adaptable mammals in North America.*

Rats can cause serious damage in buildings because they gnaw through anything in their way, and they also spoil stored food. But the greatest danger comes from the diseases they carry, which include the much-feared bubonic plague. Rats can catch the plague, and they pass it on indirectly when rat fleas jump onto humans instead.

During the 1300s an outbreak of the plague—known as the Black Death—moved west from Asia and killed one fourth of Europe's entire population. In the country villages were abandoned, and deserted farmland quickly turned into wilderness. In towns and cities matters were even worse. Here rats, fleas, and people were crowded together in insanitary conditions, creating a perfect setting for the disease. In London, England, around four fifths of the city's inhabitants perished, while in Italy some cities locked their gates for weeks and refused to let outsiders enter. When the

horrific epidemic finally died down, Europe's population took almost three hundred years to recover.

The plague returned to Europe in the 1660s, and a further outbreak began in the 1850s, sweeping around the world and claiming at least 100 million lives. Even today it continues to flare up, but fortunately it is not the threat that it once was. The disease can be treated with antibiotics, and it can be prevented by keeping rats—and their fleas—firmly under control.

URBAN PLANTS

Compared to animals, wild plants have a tougher time in built-up areas because living space is hard to find. The moment even the smallest piece of ground is cleared, dandelions and other fast-spreading plants move in. Another way to tackle the space shortage is to stay small. Pearlworts can flower when they are only 0.8 in. (2cm) high, so they can spend their entire lives tucked away in gaps in the sidewalk.

◁ *Herring gulls nest on building rooftops, furiously attacking anyone who comes too close to their chicks.*

△ *Hawkweeds and dandelions have deep taproots that help them survive many of the problems of city life. If they are driven over or cut down, they soon grow back.*

Plants cannot grow through solid brick or concrete, but they are amazingly good at widening any cracks and crevices that they find. As they grow, their roots and stems get thicker, steadily increasing the pressure until the hardest materials start to break up or split apart. When buildings are abandoned, plants soon spring up around them, and their roots start undermining foundations and walls. One of the most spectacular examples of a plant takeover is in Angkor in northwest Cambodia. Here an entire city was smothered by jungle after being abandoned around 600 years ago. Over hundreds of years tree roots probed deep into walls, prying apart stone blocks weighing many tons.

Even without soil some plants still get a foothold, as long as there is water to keep them alive. Ragweed seeds have feathery parachutes, and they are often blown up onto roofs, where they settle in gutters and cracks. If they find a corner with dust and dead leaves, they have an

From its nesting site high up on a window ledge, a peregrine falcon looks out over the skyline of New York City. The peregrine has one of the widest ranges of any land bird. Most live on rocky coasts and mountainsides, but some manage to survive among tall buildings in the world's busiest cities. Peregrines dive-bomb other birds in midair, and the city pigeon is one of their favorite foods.

△ *Lichens can grow on bare concrete, but old stonework is an even better habitat because it has a rougher surface.*

even better chance of survival. These rooftop weeds are usually small, but high-rise plants also include scrubs and even trees. One of the most successful is the butterfly bush, or buddleia, which originally comes from China. Its roots penetrate crumbling mortar in walls and rooftops, prying the bricks apart.

FLATLAND
Roofs are difficult places to set up home, but bare walls and sidewalks are the toughest minihabitats of all.

After a shower of rain it can be cool and damp, but after a few hours of sunshine it is boiling hot and completely dry. If a plant starts growing in surroundings like these, it soon shrivels up and dies.

Mosses and lichens are much better at clinging to life in these surroundings. Unlike plants, many of them can survive without water for days or weeks at a time. When it is dry they shrivel up and turn crisp, but as soon as it rains they soak up moisture and start working again. Mosses usually need a thin layer of dust, but lichens can live on bare concrete and bricks. Many lichens are concrete-colored themselves, so the only way to see them is to get up really close.

These lichens make up the first rung in an unusual urban food chain. They are grazed by tiny animals called springtails, and these in turn are eaten by bright-red spider mites, which look like hyperactive furry dots. The mites are sometimes caught by spiders—top predators in this world without soil.

△ *The butterfly bush thrives on walls and alongside railroad tracks, as well as in backyards. Butterflies find its honeylike smell irresistible.*

GREEN OASES
In a landscape filled with buildings and roads green spaces are magnets for city wildlife. Parks often have collections of semitame animals, but they attract many unofficial visitors as well. Squirrels live in the trees, coots set up their homes on lakes, and city pigeons keep a sharp eye open for leftover food. Most of these animals are no different from their country-dwelling relatives, but city pigeons have a more complicated past. Their wild ancestors were birds called rock doves, which were first tamed more than 5,000 years ago. Over time hundreds of different breeds were

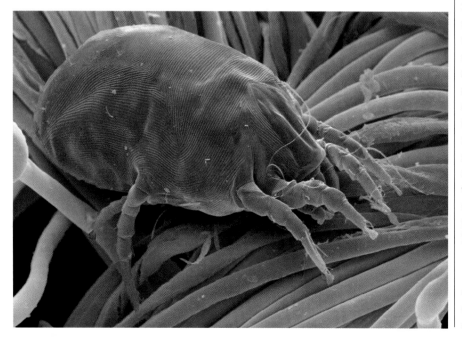

◁ *Magnified more than 2,500 times, a house dust mite looks like some form of alien life. These microscopic relatives of spiders are common in almost every home.*

▷ *As soon as they can fly, city pigeons learn their next important lesson—where there are people there may be food. These pigeons are waiting in the hope of a meal.*

raised, but at the same time tame pigeons often "went missing" and started life on their own. Because these pigeons were used to people, they often headed for towns, creating the flocks that flap around urban areas today.

City pigeons are not everyone's favorite animals because they pester people for food and splatter droppings wherever they perch. But most urban birds are less pushy and more welcome. All over the world cities have their local favorites, including blackbirds in Europe, cardinals and chickadees in North America, and cockatoos in Australia. Parks are good places to see them, but so are backyards because they often have a wide variety of plants in them.

A lot of plants means plenty of insects and seeds. The big drawback is that backyards also have cats, which kill millions of adult birds and nestlings every year.

Backyards are also good places to see butterflies because many species use them as places to stop and refuel. In the spring and summer most city butterflies are only pausing along the way before they head on to places where they can breed. But as the days shorten in the fall, finding somewhere to hibernate becomes their top priority. Butterflies can hibernate successfully in garages and sheds, but heated houses are too warm for a successful winter's sleep. If they fly indoors, the best thing to do is to gently pick them up and put them back outside.

WILDLIFE INDOORS

Many urban animals come indoors accidentally, but some spend their entire lives inside buildings. These household animals are usually small or microscopic, and most of them are good at surviving in warm surroundings with little or no water. Some of them eat stored food or fallen crumbs, but the house dust mite lives in household dust and feasts on dead remains, including flakes of human skin, insect scales, and the bodies of other mites.

One of the strangest indoor animals is the silverfish—a creature with six short legs and a silvery, scale-covered body measuring around 0.4 in. (1cm) long. At one time scientists classified it as a primitive insect, but it is so different from the average insect that they have changed their minds. The silverfish's favorite habitat is in the dark corners of kitchen cupboards and drawers, where it feeds on anything starchy or sweet, including bread crumbs, flour, grains of sugar, paper, and even some types of glue. Silverfish have small appetites, so they rarely cause much harm.

The same cannot be said for the clothes moth, which is one of the few types of moths that can spend its whole life indoors. The dusty-colored males are good fliers and are easy to spot as they flutter around in rooms. Female clothes moths spend much less time in the air and shuffle around instead.

Species Profile

Silverfish: *Lepisma saccharina*

This insectlike animal gets its name from its silvery scales and tapering body. It feeds on starchy substances, although it can go for up to three months between meals and never needs water. It finds food mainly by taste and touch. Unlike most insects, silverfish never have wings, and they periodically shed their skin even when they are fully grown. They scatter their eggs where they feed.

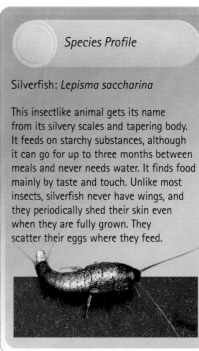

◁ A column of pharaoh ants carries food back to its nest. These ants originally came from South America, but they are now common in heated buildings around the world.

Once the females have mated, they lay their eggs on anything containing wool, and around ten days later their caterpillars hatch and begin feeding. They can ruin woolen clothes and blankets, but fortunately they cannot digest cotton or synthetic fabrics, so they leave these alone. Before humans started living indoors, clothes moths led a useful life as scavengers in the wild. Most still do, and they perform a valuable job by breaking down wool and fur after animals have died.

INDOOR SCAVENGERS

Cockroaches were some of the world's first insects, and for the past 300 million years they have lived on forest floors. But like clothes moths, they also thrive in houses and other buildings. Cockroaches like rooms that are warm and humid, which is why they spend most of their time in kitchens. They feed on almost anything containing organic matter—from bread to shoe polish and soap—and although they do not spread dangerous diseases, they taint anything that they touch with an unpleasant "roachy" smell. Female cockroaches carry their eggs in portable cases, and they can breed at a frightening rate. Each one can produce up to 150 young, so a small outbreak of cockroaches can soon turn into a major infestation.

Ants usually nest outdoors and come inside only when they are foraging for food. But one of the smallest species, called the pharaoh ant, often lives indoors full-time. Unlike most ants, this species makes dozens of nests that are hidden in out-of-the-way places, including the insides of walls and floors. From here the workers fan out in search of food, often using electricity wires or telephone lines as trails. They are only 0.08 in. (2mm) long, so they can squeeze through the smallest crevices. As a result hardly anything is out of their reach. Pharaoh ants

△ A housefly lands on a slice of bread to feed. Because of humans, houseflies are probably the world's most widespread insects.

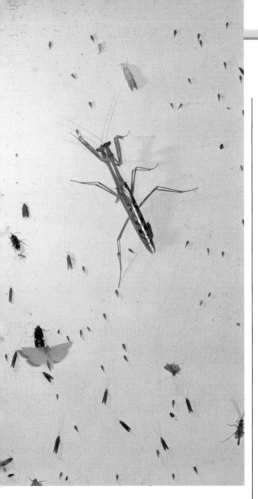

△ *This lightbulb has attracted many moths, plus two moth-eating predators—a gecko and a praying mantis. Mantises sometimes eat young geckos, but this one is large enough to be safe from danger.*

can be a serious problem in hospitals because they carry bacteria, and their hidden nests are difficult to destroy.

INDOOR PREDATORS

In the summer houseflies and mosquitoes can also be indoor pests. But nature lends a hand in controlling them, as houses are full of predators that catch flying insects. The most important of these hunters are spiders. A typical house is home to hundreds—some actively stalk their prey, but most spin webs and patiently wait for it to come their way.

▷ *Cockroaches are extremely good at sensing vibrations. The slightest movement sends them rushing for cover.*

The slender daddy longlegs spider builds messy webs that hang from ceilings and rafters. Sitting in its web, the spider is easy for humans to see. But insects are not as good at recognizing the spider or its web, and they often get tangled up in its haphazard threads. The house spider has a different hunting technique— it makes a hammock-shaped web in a secluded corner and hides in a tunnel that reaches into a crack or crevice in the wall. If an insect lands in the web, the spider rushes out, overpowers it, and carries it back to the lair. Male house spiders often leave their webs at night to search for females. During these excursions they occasionally fall into bathtubs or unexpectedly sprint across floors. Despite their large size and hairy legs, they are actually harmless and are useful at keeping troublesome insects under control.

For spiders one disadvantage of indoor life is that their webs are often cleaned away by humans. When this happens, a spider simply waits until the coast is clear and then spins a new one in its place.

HUNTING UPSIDE DOWN

Warm parts of the world are the place to see geckos—the largest wild animals that catch their prey indoors. Geckos are unusual lizards with sticky toe pads covered in microscopic hairs. Using these

a gecko can climb up walls and across ceilings, and it can even run upside down. In the wild geckos usually hunt after dark, but indoor geckos quickly learn that bright lights are good places to catch food. When dusk falls and lights are turned on, they emerge from their hiding places and gather around to feed. Their hunting technique is simple—they stay completely still and then dart forward when an insect comes in to land. With their croaky calls and helpful eating habits, these acrobatic lizards make welcome house guests.

GLOSSARY

The following pages explain most of the technical terms that are used in this book.
When a definition includes words in **bold**, it means that these words have entries of their own.

Abdomen
The rear part of an animal's body containing the organs that are used for digesting food, getting rid of waste, and reproducing.

Adaptation
A feature produced by **evolution** that helps a living thing survive. Adaptations include physical features and also different types of behavior.

Alga (plural: **algae**)
Simple, plantlike **organisms** that grow by collecting the energy in sunlight. Most algae live in water. Many are microscopic, but seaweeds, which are the largest algae, can be many feet long.

Amoeba
A single-celled creature that moves by changing shape.

Annual plant
A plant that germinates, flowers, and dies within a single growing season.

Antenna (plural: **antennae**)
A long, slender feeler on an animal's head that is used to obtain information by touching or smelling. Antennae are always in pairs.

Arthropods
A huge and highly successful group of **invertebrate** animals that have a hard body case, or **exoskeleton**, and legs that bend at flexible joints. Living arthropods include insects, spiders, scorpions, and crustaceans, as well as centipedes and millipedes.

Bacterium (plural: **bacteria**)
A **microorganism** with a single **cell**. Bacteria are the smallest, simplest, and oldest living things on Earth.

Baleen
The fibrous substance that large whales use to filter food from the water. It hangs down from a whale's upper jaw.

Biennial plant
A plant that lives for two years. During the first year it germinates and grows. During the second it flowers, makes seeds, and then dies.

Biosphere
All of the areas of the world where living things are found.

Blubber
A layer of fat that helps some sea animals keep warm. Whales, penguins, seals, and polar bears all have blubber.

Boreal forest
The great coniferous forest that grows in the far north, close to the Arctic Circle.

Broad-leaved tree
A tree that usually has broad, flat leaves. Unlike **conifers**, broad-leaved trees are flowering plants.

Browser
A plant-eating animal that feeds on the leaves and shoots of trees and bushes.

Cambium
A layer of **cells** just beneath the surface of a plant's roots and stems. The cells divide to make the plant grow.

Camouflage
A pattern or color scheme that helps something blend in with its surroundings. Animals use camouflage to ambush their **prey** or to avoid being eaten.

Canine teeth
Long, pointed teeth that meat-eating mammals have at the front of their mouths.

Carnivore
Any animal that lives by eating others. The word carnivore is also used for a specific group of mammals that includes cats, dogs, and bears. These mammals have specialized meat-eating teeth.

Carpel
One of the female parts of a flower. Carpels contain female **cells**, called ova, which develop into seeds once they have been pollinated.

Cell
A microscopic unit of living matter. Cells are surrounded by membranes, and they contain all of the equipment needed to stay alive and reproduce. Some living things, such as **bacteria**, have only one cell, while others have many millions, specialized to carry out different tasks.

Cellulose
A substance that plants make as a building material.

Chaparral
A type of scrubland found in southern California and on some slopes of the Rockies.

Chlorophyll
The green substance that plants use to collect energy from sunlight so that they can carry out **photosynthesis**.

Chloroplast
A microscopic green structure inside a plant's leaf that contains **chlorophyll**. Chloroplasts carry out **photosynthesis**, which enables plants to grow.

Chromosome
A threadlike chemical package that contains a length of **DNA**. In plants and animals chromosomes often have a shape like an X.

Chrysalis
A hard case that protects a caterpillar while it turns into a butterfly or a moth.

Cocoon
A silk case spun by an insect or a spider to protect itself or its **eggs**.

Cold-blooded
Describes an animal whose body stays at the same temperature as its surroundings. Cold-blooded creatures make up most of the animal kingdom.

Colony
A group of individual animals, plants, or **microbes** that lives together as a single unit. Many colonies look like single living things.

Compound eye
An eye that is divided up into many separate compartments that work

together to produce an image. Crustaceans and insects have compound eyes.

Conifer
A tree that grows its seeds in cones. Unlike **broad-leaved trees**, conifers do not have flowers, and they often keep their leaves all year round.

Continental drift
The gradual movement of continents across Earth's surface. Continental drift is driven by heat from deep within Earth, which keeps the crust on the move.

Convergent evolution
The evolution of similar features in **species** that share a similar way of life. Convergent evolution can make unrelated species difficult to tell apart.

Courtship
The behavior that an animal uses to attract a mate. Male animals use courtship to show that they are fit and healthy.

Cyanobacteria
Bacteria that live in the same way as plants by collecting the energy in sunlight. Cyanobacteria are also known as blue-green **algae**.

Deciduous tree
A tree that loses all of its leaves for part of the year. Many **broad-leaved trees** are deciduous, but not all of them—in rain forests broad-leaved trees keep their leaves all year round.

Decomposer
Any living thing that feeds on dead remains.

Diatom
A type of microscopic **alga**. Diatoms have transparent protective cases that are often made out of silica.

Digestion
The breaking down of food so that it can be absorbed and used. Animals digest their food after they have swallowed it, but many **microbes** digest food on the spot.

Distribution
All of the places in the world where an individual **species** is found.

DNA (deoxyribonucleic acid)
The substance found in living **cells** that makes up **genes**. DNA contains all of the chemical instructions needed to assemble a living thing and to make it work.

Echolocation
A way of sensing objects that works by using high-pitched bursts of sound that bounce back as echoes. Animals that use echolocation include bats, whales, and dolphins.

Ecosystem
A **habitat**, together with all of the living things that use it as their home.

Egg
A fertilized **cell** that can develop into a new living thing. Eggs are the largest cells in the animal world.

Embryo
A plant or animal at a very early stage of development.

Endemic species
A **species** that is found in one place and nowhere else.

Ephemeral plant
A plant that grows, flowers, and dies in a short time. Most ephemeral plants live in deserts and other dry places.

Epiphyte
A plant that grows on trees and other plants.

Evolution
A very slow process of change that enables living things to adapt to the world around them. During evolution new **species** develop, and existing ones eventually become extinct.

Exoskeleton
A skeleton that supports an animal's body from the outside rather than the inside. Exoskeletons are a common feature in **invertebrates—arthropods** have exoskeletons made out of separate plates, while many mollusks have shells.

Extinction
The permanent disappearance of a **species**. Extinction happens in nature, but it can also be caused by human activities.

Fertilization
The process that enables a male and a female **cell** to join together, forming a single **egg**.

Filter feeder
An animal that gets its food by filtering it from the water. Filter feeders include animals in **plankton** and also the world's largest whales.

Floret
A small flower in a **flower head**.

Flower head
A collection of flowers growing on a single stem.

Food chain
A food pathway that connects several different **species**. When one species eats another, food and energy move along the chain.

Fossil
The preserved remains of living things. Some fossils are formed by remains themselves, while others are signs that living things leave behind such as burrows or footprints.

Fynbos
A type of scrubland found in southern Africa.

Gene
A chemical instruction that is carried by **DNA**.

Gill
A body part that animals use to collect oxygen from the water. Gills sometimes stick out from an animal's body, but in fish they are usually hidden away inside.

Grazer
A plant-eating animal that feeds mainly on grass.

Grub
A young insect that has very short legs or no legs at all. See **larva**.

Habitat
The surroundings that an individual **species** needs to survive. Most species live in only one habitat, but some can survive in several.

Herbivore
An animal that eats plants.

Hibernation
A deep winter sleep. Animals hibernate so that they can survive during a time of year when food is difficult to find.

Host
Any living thing that a **parasite** uses as its home and its food.

Hyphae
A network of feeding threads produced by a fungus.

Incubation
Sitting on **eggs** to keep them warm, so they can develop.

Instinct
Any type of behavior that is inherited instead of having to be learned.

Invertebrate
Any animal that does not have a backbone.

Larva (plural: **larvae**)
A young animal that looks completely different from its parents and that changes shape as it grows up.

Lichen
A plantlike **organism** formed by fungi and **algae** living together in a close partnership.

Life cycle
All of the steps in the life of a living thing—from the moment it begins life to the time when it produces young.

Metabolism
All the chemical processes that take place inside of a living thing. Some of these processes release energy, while others use it up.

Metamorphosis
A major change in body shape as an animal grows up.

Microbe
See **microorganism**.

Microorganism
Any living thing that is too small to be seen with the naked eye. Microorganisms include **bacteria**, as well as many other forms of life. For several billion years they were the only living things on Earth. Microorganisms are also known as microbes.

Migration
A long journey that animals make to breed or find food. Most animals migrate along set routes and are guided by **instinct**.

Mimic
An animal that imitates something else—usually to avoid being eaten. Many mimics imitate leaves, twigs, or pebbles, but some imitate poisonous animals.

Molecules
A group of atoms that are linked together. Some molecules have only a few atoms, but molecules made by living things—such as **DNA** and **cellulose**—can have many millions.

Natural selection
The driving force behind **evolution**. Natural selection works by favoring those living things that leave the most young.

Nectar
A sweet, sugary liquid produced by many flowers. Plants make nectar to attract animals. In return for nectar, animal visitors spread the plants' **pollen**.

Nocturnal
Describes an animal that is active mainly or entirely after dark.

Nucleus
The control center of a **cell**, containing the cell's **genes**.

Nutrient
Any substance that a living thing needs in order to stay alive.

Organism
Any living thing.

Parasite
A living thing that feeds on or inside of something else while it is still alive. Unlike a **predator**, a parasite is usually smaller than the thing it attacks. Parasites often have a complicated **life cycle**.

Perennial plant
A plant that lives for a number of years instead of just one or two. Trees and scrubs are all perennials.

Petal
A flap in a flower that often helps attract animal pollinators. In some flowers petals are separate, but in others they are joined together to form funnels or tubes.

Photosynthesis
A process that works by collecting energy from sunlight and using it to build up carbon-containing chemicals. Plants, **algae**, and some **bacteria** use photosynthesis to grow.

Phytoplankton
The plantlike part of **plankton** made up of **organisms** that need sunlight to grow.

Plankton
Small or microscopic living things that drift near the surface of lakes and oceans. Plankton includes **algae** and also a wide range of tiny animals that eat algae or eat one another.

Pollen
The dustlike substance that flowers use to produce seeds. Pollen contains a plant's male **cells**.

Pollination
The movement of **pollen** grains from flower to flower so that seeds can be formed. Pollen is usually carried by animals or by the wind.

Polyp
An animal that has a tube-shaped body with a ring of **tentacles** around its mouth. Corals and sea anemones are examples of polyps.

Predator
Any animal that lives by hunting others. Predators are usually larger than their **prey**—unless they hunt in packs—and they are always less common.

Prehensile
Describes something, such as a trunk or a tail, that can wrap around things to hold on to them or to pick them up.

Prey
An animal that a **predator** hunts as food.

Protists
Single-celled **organisms** that are larger and more complicated than **bacteria**. They include **protozoans** and **algae**.

Protozoan
An animal-like **organism** that is made up of only one **cell**. Protozoans live mainly in the water or in damp **habitats** such as the soil. Some are **parasites** of animals or plants.

Pupa (plural: **pupae**)
A resting stage in the **life cycle** of an insect. Inside the pupa the young insect's body is broken down, and an adult one is assembled in its place.

Ruminant
A plant-eating mammal that has hooves and a four-chambered stomach. Deer, antelope, and cattle are all ruminants.

Seasonal forest
A type of tropical forest that grows in places with both a wet season and a dry season. It is also known as monsoon forest.

Sepal
An outer flap that protects a flower bud. Unlike **petals**, sepals are normally green,

but in some flowers they are large and brightly colored.

Species
A single type of living thing. The members of a species can all breed with each other, but they do not normally breed with anything else.

Spiracle
A small opening that lets air into an insect's body.

Spore
A microscopic package of **cells** that is used in reproduction. Most fungi and **algae** reproduce using spores.

Stamen
One of the male parts of a flower. Stamens produce **pollen**, which travels from plant to plant so that seeds can be formed.

Stoma (plural: **stomata**)
A microscopic pore on the surface of a leaf. Stomata let gases flow into and out of leaves so that plants can carry out **photosynthesis**.

Stromatolite
Rocklike mounds produced by **cyanobacteria** growing in shallow water. Fossilized stromatolites are among the oldest signs of life on Earth.

Symbiosis
A partnership that involves two different **species**. By teaming up each partner often has a better chance of survival. Both partners may be animals, or one may be an animal and one a plant.

Taiga
A Russian word for the **boreal forest**.

Tentacles
Long, fleshy "feelers" that some animals use to catch their food.

Territory
A space that is claimed by an animal so that it can breed. With most types of animals, territories are claimed and defended by males.

Thorax
The middle part of an animal's body. In insects, legs and wings are attached to it.

Toxin
A poison made inside of the body of a living thing.

Tundra
A cold, treeless **habitat** found in the far north and sometimes near the summits of high mountains.

Transpiration
The movement of water from a plant's roots, along its stem, and out of its leaves. When water reaches the leaves, it evaporates through pores called **stomata**.

Vertebrate
An animal that has a backbone. Vertebrates include fish, amphibians, reptiles, birds, and mammals.

Virus
A chemical particle that reproduces by infecting living **cells**.

Warm-blooded
Describes an animal whose body stays at a steady, warm temperature. Warm-blooded animals are well insulated, and they can stay active even in cold conditions.

WEB SITES

waynesword.palomar.edu/wayne.htm
One of the best plant sites on the web, containing over 2,000 photos of interesting and unusual plants from all over the world, plus a huge collection of plant myths, legends, facts, and figures.

www.bbc.co.uk/nature/wildfacts
Find out about hundreds of different animals—from aardvarks to whales—at this wildlife site run by BBC TV's natural history unit.

www.eia-international.org
The Environmental Investigation Agency (EIA) is an international organization that was established in 1984 to investigate and expose environmental crimes—from illegal logging to animal smuggling.

www.euronet.nl/users/janpar/virtual/ocean.html
Find out about microscopic life at sea by visiting this "virtual ocean" page.

www.microscopy-uk.org.uk/mag/wimsmall/smal1.html
Claiming to be the "smallest page on the web," this fascinating site is an introduction to the microscopic organisms you can find in a freshwater pond.

www.mbayaq.org
The Monterey Bay Aquarium's web site includes the award-winning "E-quarium"—an introduction to undersea life.

www.mnh.si.edu/museum/VirtualTour/index.html
The Smithsonian National Museum of Natural History (NMNH) is one of the largest museums. This web page opens the door to its collections with a range of virtual tours.

www.nhm.ac.uk/interactive/kids/index.html
Find out more about the natural world by visiting London, England's Natural History Museum. This regularly updated site includes webcam pictures of animals on the move.

www.sandiegozoo.org
The San Diego Zoo is famous for its work with endangered animals. Its web site features news about animals in captivity and in the wilderness, updates about the status of threatened species, as well as offering a range of virtual tours.

www.unep-wcmc.org
The World Conservation Monitoring Centre, part of the United Nations, publishes "Red Lists" of threatened and endangered species from all over the world. Check out Red List species by visiting this web site.

INDEX

Page numbers in **bold** refer to main sections.

ACKNOWLEDGMENTS

The publishers would like to thank the following for permission to reproduce their material. Every care has been taken to trace copyright holders. However, if there have been unintentional omissions or failure to trace copyright holders, we apologize and will, if informed, endeavor to make corrections in any future edition.

Key: b = bottom, c = center, l = left, r = right, t = top

FLPA—Frank Lane Picture Agency NGIC—National Geographic Image Collection OSF—Oxford Scientific Films
Naturepl—Nature Picture Library NHPA—Natural History Picture Agency SPL—Science Photo Library

Cover Tim Flach/Getty Images, London; **back cover cr** Adrian Warren/Ardea, London, **back cover br** Jacques Jangoux/Science Photo Library, London; **page 1** SPL; **3** NGIC; **4c** SPL; **4bl** Corbis; **5tr** Corbis; **5cl** Corbis; **5b** Corbis; **6** NGIC; **8–9** Getty/Imagebank; **10–11t** SPL; **10cr** SPL; **10–11b** Getty; **11c** SPL; **12c** Getty/Stone; **13b** Getty/Imagebank; **14t** Getty/Imagebank; **14bl** SPL; **15tr** SPL; **15c** SPL; **15bl** SPL; **16cr** Corbis; **16rbc** Getty/Stone; **16br** Corbis; **17tc** SPL; **17cr** SPL; **17rbc** Corbis; **17br** SPL; **18–19c** SPL; **18rbc** SPL; **18rb** Getty/Stone; **19rc** Ardea; **19rbc** Corbis; **19rb** SPL; **20–1** Corbis; **20br** Corbis; **21tl** OSF; **21br** NHPA; **22tl** Getty/Stone; **22tr** Getty/Imagebank; **22cb** Getty/Taxi; **23tc** OSF; **23cr** Getty/Imagebank; **23b** NHPA; **24–5t** Corbis; **24c** Naturepl; **24bl** Corbis; **25tr** Naturepl; **26tl** NGIC; **26–7b** Ardea; **27tr** Corbis; **27br** Corbis; **28–9** Steve Bloom; **28tl** Naturepl; **28tcl** Naturepl; **28tcr** Naturepl; **28tr** Naturepl; **29b** Getty/Stone; **30cl** Corbis; **30–1** Getty/Imagebank; **31tr** Corbis; **31cr** Corbis; **32–3** Corbis; **32tr** Corbis; **33t** SPL; **33br** Corbis; **38tl** Naturepl; **38bc** Naturepl; **39tl** Corbis; **39cr** FLPA; **39b** Corbis; **40tr** SPL; **40–1** NHPA; **41br** NHPA; **42bl** Getty/Stone; **42br** Getty/Imagebank; **43t** Corbis; **43br** SPL; **44tr** Getty/Stone; **44cr** Corbis; **44b** Corbis; **45tr** Corbis; **45cl** NHPA; **46tl** Corbis; **46bc** Corbis; **46–7** Corbis; **47tc** Naturepl; **47br** Ardea; **48cl** Getty/Imagebank; **48bl** Naturepl; **48tcr** Corbis; **49cl** SPL; **46tl** NHPA; **49tc** Naturepl; **49crt** Naturepl; **49crb** Naturepl; **50tl** Ardea; **50cr** SPL; **50bl** Naturepl; **51tl** Corbis; **51cr** David Brufford/Harvard University Herbaria; **52tr** Still Pictures; **52cl** Naturepl; **52cr** NHPA; **52bl** Corbis; **53tr** Getty News; **53bl** Corbis; **54tl** Getty/Stone; **54bl** Corbis; **54br** Naturepl; **54–5t** Corbis; **55c** Steve Bloom; **55b** Naturepl; **56–7** SPL; **58cl** SPL; **58–9c** SPL; **58br** SPL; **59t** NGIC; **59cr** NGIC; **60** FLPA/Minden Collection; **61** SPL; **62–3t** SPL; **62bl** SPL; **63br** SPL; **64l** SPL; **64cr** SPL; **64bl** SPL; **65tr** SPL; **65c** SPL; **65bl** SPL; **66–7** Corbis; **68–9t** SPL; **68bcr** SPL; **69tr** SPL; **69bc** OSF; **69br** OSF; **70tl** SPL; **70bl** SPL; **70–1b** SPL; **71tr** SPL; **71bc** Getty/Imagebank; **72tl** Corbis; **72–3c** Corbis; **72bc** Corbis; **73tl** SPL; **73cr** SPL; **73bc** SPL; **74cl** SPL; **74cr** OSF; **75tl** OSF; **75cr** SPL; **76tr** Corbis; **76bl** SPL; **77tc** SPL; **77cl** Nature Photographers; **77br** Nature Photographers; **78tl** Corbis; **78cr** Corbis; **78–9b** Premaphotos; **79tl** Nature Photographers; **79cr** SPL; **80tr** SPL; **80c** Corbis; **81tl** SPL; **81tr** Corbis; **81br** Premaphotos; **82l** Corbis; **82cr** OSF; **83tl** Premaphotos; **83cr** OSF; **83b** Corbis; **84tl** Getty/Imagebank; **84b** Redcover; **85tr** SPL; **86 inset** Getty/Stone; **86cl** SPL; **86cr** OSF; **86–7t** Corbis; **87tr** OSF; **87b** Corbis; **88–9** Corbis; **90cl** SPL; **90cb** SPL; **90–1c** SPL; **91tr** Corbis; **91br** SPL; **92tl** SPL; **92cr** Corbis; **93tl** Corbis; **93b** SPL; **94bl** SPL; **94–5** SPL; **95t** SPL; **96tl** Corbis; **96bl** Corbis; **97tr** OSF; **97cl** Steve Shattuck, CSIRO, Australia; **97b** Corbis; **98l** SPL; **98br** Corbis; **99tl** SPL; **99br** SPL; **100cl** Corbis; **100bl** Corbis; **100br** SPL; **100–1** OSF; **101t** OSF; **101cr** OSF; **102tl** SPL; **102–3** Still Pictures; **103t** Woodfall Images; **104tl** Corbis; **104cr** Getty/Imagebank; **104b** OSF; **105tl** OSF; **105c** OSF; **106tr** Corbis; **106cl** Corbis; **106br** OSF; **107bl** Corbis; **107r** Naturepl; **108tl** Corbis; **108br** Getty/Imagebank; **109tl** Corbis; **109cr** OSF; **109b** OSF; **110–1** NGIC; **112tr** NHPA; **112lb** OSF; **112–3** Corbis; **113tr** SPL; **113cl** OSF; **113br** OSF; **114t** OSF; **114b** Robert Brons; **114–5** SPL; **115c** Corbis; **116tr** OSF; **116tc** SPL; **116bl** SPL; **117cr** Corbis; **117cl** Premaphotos; **117br** SPL; **118tr** SPL; **118cl** Ardea; **118–9b** SPL; **119tc** SPL; **119br** OSF; **120l** Corbis; **120–1** NHPA; **121tl** Corbis; **121tr** NHPA; **121b** Corbis; **122–3** NHPA; **122cr** NHPA; **122bl** NHPA; **123tl** Corbis; **124tl** Naturepl; **124lc** Corbis; **125tl** Corbis; **125** NHPA; **126tr** Corbis; **126cl** NHPA; **126b** SPL; **127tl** Corbis; **127tr** NASA; **128tl** Corbis; **128b** Getty/Taxi; **129tl** Naturepl; **129cl** Corbis; **129b** Steve Bloom; **130t** NGIC; **130cl** OSF; **130br** Corbis; **131t** Steve Bloom; **132tl** NHPA; **132cl** Corbis; **132b** Corbis; **133tl** Corbis; **133cr** Corbis; **133b** Corbis; **134tl** Corbis; **134b** Premaphotos; **135tl** Jens Christian Shou; **135tr** Corbis; **135cl** OSF; **135br** Corbis; **136l** NHPA; **136br** NGIC; **137cr** OSF; **137cl** OSF; **137br** OSF; **138cl** OSF; **138br** Corbis; **138–9** Premaphotos; **139tr** Steve Bloom; **139cr** Getty/Taxi; **140tl** Corbis; **140c** OSF; **140b** Naturepl; **141tl** Corbis; **141c** NHPA; **141br** NHPA; **142cl** OSF; **142–3t** OSF; **142–3b** OSF; **143cr** Naturepl; **143bl** Naturepl; **143bc** Naturepl; **143br** Naturepl; **144tr** Corbis; **144b** Naturepl; **145tr** Getty/Stone; **145cl** OSF; **145cr** Naturepl; **145b** Naturepl; **146–7** Steve Bloom; **148tl** Naturepl; **148bl** Naturepl; **148br** Naturepl; **149tr** Corbis; **150tr** Naturepl; **150b** Corbis; **151c** Naturepl; **151br** Naturepl; **152tl** Getty/Taxi; **152tc** Naturepl; **152–3** NGIC; **153br** Steve Bloom; **154l** Naturepl; **155tl** SPL; **155tc** SPL; **155cr** Naturepl; **155bl** OSF; **156tr** Naturepl; **156cl** Steve Bloom; **157** Naturepl; **158bl** Corbis; **158tl** Corbis; **158br** Naturepl; **159tl** Naturepl; **159tr** NHPA; **161–2** Corbis; **164–5** SPL; **164c** FLPA; **164–5b** Steve Bloom; **165t** Ardea; **165c** NHPA; **166t** FLPA; **166cr** Ardea; **166–7b** Corbis; **167** SPL; **167cr** Still Pictures; **168t** NHPA; **168bl** Corbis; **168–9** Corbis; **169** Ardea; **170tl** Corbis; **170c** FLPA; **170c** Corbis; **170–1** Corbis; **171tl** Corbis; **171br** NHPA; **172–3** Polar Institute, Norway; **173 inset** Greenpeace; **174tl** SPL; **174–5** Brian & Cherry Alexander; **175tr** Corbis; **176tl** Still Pictures; **176–7** Naturepl; **176b** Ardea; **177cr** Naturepl; **177b** Corbis; **178–9** NHPA; **180tr** Steve Bloom; **180–1** Naturepl; **180bl** Corbis; **181bl** NHPA; **182–3t** NGIC; **182–3b** Naturepl; **183cr** NGIC; **183b** NGIC; **184br** Naturepl; **184tl** Corbis; **183–4** NGIC; **185t** Corbis; **185 inset** Naturepl; **186tl** Ardea; **186b** Corbis; **187t** Ardea; **187b** Corbis; **188–9** Corbis; **190tl** NHPA; **190–1** Naturepl; **191br** Corbis; **192–3t** Ardea; **192–3b** NHPA; **193tr** Naturepl; **193c** Ardea; **193cr** Ardea; **194l** Corbis; **194b** Getty/Taxi; **195t** NGIC; **195b** Corbis; **196tl** SPL; **196cr** OSF; **196–7t** Corbis; **197b** NGIC; **197cr** Corbis; **198–9** Getty/Imagebank; **200cl** NHPA; **200tr** OSF; **200–1** Corbis; **201tr** Corbis; **202cl** Corbis; **202tr** Corbis; **202–3** OSF; **203t** NHPA; **204–5t** Corbis; **204–5b** NHPA; **205r** Derek Hall; **206** Corbis; **207t** SPL; **207bl** FLPA; **207cr** NHPA; **208–9** Corbis; **210t** Corbis; **210bl** Naturepl; **210br** Naturepl; **211tc** Naturepl; **211cl** Naturepl; **211br** Corbis; **212–3t** Ardea; **212–3b** Corbis; **213cr** Corbis; **214tl** Ardea; **214–5b** Naturepl; **215tl** NHPA; **215cr** Corbis; **216tl** Naturepl; **216b** NHPA; **217tl** Naturepl; **217tr** Naturepl; **217b** NHPA; **218tr** Corbis; **219** Ardea; **219b** Corbis; **220l** Naturepl; **220b** Ardea; **221t** Corbis; **221cl** Ardea; **221b** NHPA; **222–3** Corbis; **224–5t** Corbis; **224–5b** Corbis; **225r** Naturepl; **226–7** Steve Bloom; **228tl** FLPA; **228b** NGIC; **228–9t** Corbis; **229r** NHPA; **229b** Ardea; **230t** Corbis; **230br** Ardea; **230br** Ardea; **231t** Corbis; **231b** Corbis; **232t** NHPA; **232l** NHPA; **232br** Still Pictures; **233tr** Corbis; **233b** Still Pictures; **234–5t** Corbis; **234–5b** Ardea; **235tr** Corbis; **236–7** Corbis; **238–9t** NHPA; **238b** Corbis; **239tr** Still Pictures; **239bl** Naturepl; **240tl** Woodfall Images; **240tr** Corbis; **240bl** Naturepl; **240–1b** Corbis; **241tr** Naturepl; **242tl** NHPA; **242c** NHPA; **243tl** NGIC; **243br** NGIC; **244tl** NHPA; **244bl** NHPA; **244tr** Naturepl; **245r** NHPA; **246–7t** Corbis; **246–7b** Getty/Stone; **247tr** SPL; **247cr** NHPA; **248cl** Ardea; **248b** Corbis; **248–9t** Naturepl; **249tr** Corbis; **249b** Corbis; **250–1** Corbis; **250t** Steve Bloom; **251t** Corbis; **252tl** NHPA; **252tr** Corbis; **252bl** Corbis; **252br** Corbis; **253tl** NHPA; **253b** Corbis; **254–5** Getty/Imagebank; **256tl** NGIC; **256b** Corbis; **256–7t** Corbis; **257** OSF; **257b** NHPA; **258–9t** Corbis; **258–9b** Corbis; **259r** Corbis; **260–1** Getty/Imagebank; **262tl** Still Pictures; **262bl** Corbis; **262cr** Corbis; **263cl** Getty/Imagebank; **263cr** FLPA; **263b** Getty/Stone; **264tl** Corbis; **264b** Corbis; **265t** Corbis; **265bl** OSF; **265br** NHPA; **266c** Corbis; **266–7t** Corbis; **266–7b** NHPA; **267r** Ardea; **268tl** NHPA; **268cr** Naturepl; **269tl** NHPA; **269cr** Corbis; **270bl** SPL; **270cr** Corbis; **271t** Corbis; **272tl** NGIC; **272b** Naturepl; **272–3t** Corbis; **273cl** Corbis; **273b** Ardea; **274–5** Getty/Taxi; **276tl** SPL; **276cr** Corbis; **276bl** SPL; **277tl** Ardea; **277c** Corbis; **277cr** Naturepl; **277br** Naturepl; **278–9t** Corbis; **278–9b** Getty/Stone; **279tr** Corbis; **280tl** NHPA; **280tr** Corbis; **280c** Corbis; **280–1b** Corbis; **281tl** NHPA; **281r** Corbis; **282tl** Corbis; **282cr** Edward Parker; **282bl** Corbis; **282tl** NHPA; **283tr** NHPA; **283b** Corbis; **284–5** Ardea; **286tl** NHPA; **286cr** Corbis; **286bl** NHPA; **287tl** NHPA; **287b** NGIC; **287b** NGIC; **288tl** NHPA; **288cr** Naturepl; **288–9b** Corbis; **289t** Corbis; **290–1t** Corbis; **290–1b** Corbis; **291tr** Corbis; **292tl** Corbis; **292bl** Corbis; **292–3t** Corbis; **293tr** Corbis; **293c** Corbis; **293bl** NHPA; **293br** NHPA; **294–5** Getty/Taxi; **296tl** NHPA; **296–7t** NHPA; **296–7b** Naturepl; **297tr** Corbis; **298–9t** SPL; **298–9b** Corbis; **299tr** Corbis; **300bl** Still Pictures; **300–1t** Corbis; **301tr** Getty/Stone; **301b** NHPA; **302–3** Naturepl; **304tl** SPL; **304bl** SPL; **304–5t** Corbis; **305t** Corbis; **305b** NHPA; **306l** NHPA; **306–7t** NHPA; **306br** NHPA; **307tr** NHPA; **307b** NHPA